CASE PROBLEMS IN FINANCIAL MANAGEMENT

WILLIAM H. MARSH
University of South Carolina at Aiken

HARRY R. KUNIANSKY
Augusta College

PRENTICE HALL, Englewood Cliffs, New Jersey 07632

LIBRARY OF CONGRESS
Library of Congress Cataloging-in-Publication Data

Marsh, William H.
    Case problems in financial management / William H. Marsh, Harry R.
Kuniansky.
       p.   cm.
    ISBN 0-13-118944-1
    1. Cash management--Problems, exercises, etc.   I. Kuniansky,
Harry Richard.   II. Title.
HG4028.C45M227 1988
658.1'5'076--dc19   88-23265
                                                              CIP

Editorial/production supervision and
   interior design: Linda Behrens
Cover design: Baldino Studio
Manufacturing buyer: Margaret Rizzi

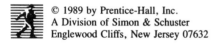 © 1989 by Prentice-Hall, Inc.
A Division of Simon & Schuster
Englewood Cliffs, New Jersey 07632

Printed in the United States of America
10 9 8 7 6 5 4 3 2 1

ISBN 0-13-118944-1

Prentice-Hall International (UK) Limited, *London*
Prentice-Hall of Australia Pty. Limited, *Sydney*
Prentice-Hall Canada Inc., *Toronto*
Prentice-Hall Hispanoamericana, S.A., *Mexico*
Prentice-Hall of India Private Limited, *New Delhi*
Prentice-Hall of Japan, Inc., *Tokyo*
Simon & Schuster Asia Pte. Ltd., *Singapore*
Editora Prentice-Hall do Brasil, Ltda., *Rio de Janeiro*

CONTENTS

PART IV

CAPITAL STRUCTURE, COST OF CAPITAL, VALUATION, AND DIVIDEND POLICY

PART V

LONG-TERM FINANCING

PART VI

SELECTED TOPICS IN FINANCIAL MANAGEMENT

APPENDICES

PREFACE

Financial management, one of the more challenging areas in business administration, requires knowledge of accounting, economics, and quantitative methods before the student begins studying the subject. To gain a working knowledge of financial principles, the basic course must include such topics as financial analysis and planning, working capital management, capital budgeting, capital structure, cost of capital, valuation, dividend policy, long-term financing, mergers, and reorganization. Multinational finance concepts are integrated into this structure.

In teaching the basic finance course, the instructor presents explanatory material and examples. Students are then assigned problems to determine if they understand the fundamental concepts. At this point, the student usually feels that a real-world viewpoint is lacking, since frequently neither the examples nor the problems allow for alternative solutions, which are usually generated by varying the assumptions or asking "what if" questions.

The case method is designed to bridge the gap between the real world and the structured world of examples and problems that appear in textbooks. In a real situation, the relationships are generally quite complex, and the variables interact in ways that are difficult to forecast. The case must, by necessity, be simpler than actual experience, while still giving the student a feel for the complexities of the real world.

The original business case, the Harvard-type case, was totally unstructured. Since one of its major purposes was to demonstrate to the student that problem identification was no easy matter, no questions were included at the end. A significant portion of the student's preparation time was spent simply defining the problem. As the case method spread to a larger audience, many students felt lost in attempting to use this approach. The major complaint arose from working long hours with little results.

The case problems in this book are designed to combine the advantages of the unstructured case with the focus achieved by providing structured problems. This is accomplished by furnishing general company data, while supplying enough information to focus the discussion toward a specific finance topic. The student is thus forced to separate the useful from the extraneous, make assumptions, and, in some cases, generate forecasts of missing data. At the same time, enough information is available to make decisions using standard techniques of financial management.

Level and Method of Use

This casebook is intended for use in basic finance courses at both the undergraduate and graduate levels, as well as in the advanced undergraduate course in managerial finance. When used in the basic course, the instructor generally leads the discussion, and the emphasis is on answering the directed questions found at the end of each case. When used in the advanced undergraduate course or at the graduate level, presentations are normally made by student teams.

The method of using student presenters leads to greater participation by classmates, as well as a higher general level of creativity. The directed questions are useful in this process, but should not form the only basis for discussion. Students are encouraged to generate new ideas and approaches to the decision process.

Students appreciate efforts by the instructor to reduce the amount of "busy work" in the preparation of cases. Such consideration often leads to greater levels of productivity. The directed questions are useful in this regard. Additional motivation is provided by 15 selected industry ratios included as the last exhibit in each case.

The use of personal computers may also increase productivity. To this end, directed questions that require a response using Lotus 1–2–3 have been included in some cases. Instructors may choose to omit these questions without interfering with the solution process.

Instructors who choose to adopt this casebook and are interested in using the optional computer questions may obtain a copy of a *Resource Disk*. This diskette contains the Lotus 1–2–3 models for the computer-oriented questions.

An instructor's manual is also available to adopters of this casebook. This manual contains answers to the directed questions, including the Lotus 1–2–3 output. As a further aid, it keys the cases to specific chapters of popular finance texts. Although this reference does not provide all the answers, it will demonstrate the methodology involved in each case.

William H. Marsh
Harry R. Kuniansky

ACKNOWLEDGMENTS

A large number of people were involved either directly or indirectly in the production of this casebook. We would like to acknowledge the tireless effort of our graduate assistant, Theresa Seader, in editing and improving the manuscript. We also wish to give special recognition to our colleague, F. X. McGahee, for writing the Lotus 1–2–3 models for the computer-oriented questions. We are pleased to recognize Martha Farmer and William House, deans at Augusta College and the University of South Carolina at Aiken, respectively, for providing support for our work. In addition, our undergraduate and graduate finance students should receive appreciation for working the cases and making suggestions for improvement. Finally, special thanks are due to Scott Barr, Linda Behrens, and the staff of Prentice Hall who are responsible for the development and production of this book.

CASE PROBLEMS
IN FINANCIAL
MANAGEMENT

PART I

FINANCIAL ANALYSIS AND PLANNING

Industrial Plastics, Inc.
RATIO ANALYSIS

Industrial Plastics was a producer of plastic products for a wide range of industrial uses. Products included such diverse items as plastic trays used in large manufacturing plants, windshields for golf carts, and housings for computer terminals. All the firm's output was custom produced.

The production process involved vacuum forming in combination with hand fabrication. Vacuum forming required the use of a machine that sold for approximately $60,000. Ten of these machines formed the core of the firm's productive capacity. The manufacture of most products began on the vacuum forming machines. Products were then transferred to the fabrication department where operations such as routing, scraping, and beveling were performed.

The firm marketed its products through the use of manufacturers' representatives. Their territories covered an area within a 300- to 400-mile radius of the company headquarters in Memphis, Tennessee. The selection and training of representatives was the responsibility of the sales manager, Mr. Neville Harris.

Industrial Plastics manufactured only special-order products; therefore, they held no finished goods inventory. All goods were shipped as soon as they were completed. The orders for the custom-produced products were secured through a bidding process. This required the sales representatives to be knowledgeable of what products Industrial Plastics was capable of producing. Representatives also had to have the ability to convince customers of the superiority of plastic over other materials. It was found that a sales representative with these qualities usually had an outstanding sales performance.

The company was founded in 1953 by two brothers, Karl and Beryl Blyden. Each invested $25,000. In addition, they borrowed $40,000 from the Cotton City National Bank of Memphis.

When they started the business, the use of plastics was fairly new, so the brothers spent a significant amount of time convincing customers that the material was competitive with wood and metal. The firm experienced steady growth, and by 1973 annual sales were $3,000,000. About that time, the company began to advertise through industry magazines and trade shows. By

1977, sales had doubled to $6,000,000. However, by 1978, Industrial Plastics was beginning to suffer a significant decline in sales. Consequently, the company was forced to rethink its position in the industrial market.

In analyzing the situation, the brothers concluded that their strength was in products that required both vacuum forming and fabrication. They wanted to have a reputation as a quality producer, capable of making sophisticated plastic products. They decided not to compete with firms that vacuum formed only, since these firms competed primarily on the basis of price, and the company was not a low-cost producer in the industry. These factors led to the development of their marketing strategy.

Sales growth renewed in 1979. By 1983, the firm had annual sales of approximately $10,000,000. This growth was financed by the internal generation of funds, plus short- and long-term debt from the Cotton National Bank and the Volunteer Insurance Company. The latter had financed a building completed in 1981.

The firm's banking relationship with the Cotton City National Bank had been satisfactory. Mr. Jason Hargrove, vice-president of the bank, met each year at the beginning of March with the Blydens and Mr. Thomas Arcadi, the controller of Industrial Plastics. At that meeting the firm's short-term requirements for the following year were discussed. In preparation for the annual meeting, Mr. Arcadi gathered a number of exhibits (Exhibits 1.1, 1.2, and 1.3) that facilitated ratio analysis of the firm's current financial position.

EXHIBIT 1.1

Industrial Plastics, Inc.

Balance Sheets for the Year Ending February 28, Except for 1988, Which Is February 29 (In Thousands)

	1985	1986	1987	1988
Assets:				
Cash and Marketable Securities	$ 174	$ 436	$ 300	$ 456
Accounts Receivable, Net Inventory	1,460	1,591	2,202	1,883
Raw Materials	1,120	1,107	1,667	1,559
Work-in-Process	189	204	394	301
Prepaid Expenses	46	63	93	70
Total Current Assets	$2,989	$3,401	$4,656	$4,269
Land and Building	1,752	1,760	1,783	1,804
Machinery and Equipment	1,225	1,200	1,315	1,479
Office Furniture and Equipment	147	139	160	170
Automobile and Truck	176	206	198	232
Less: Accumulated Depreciation	(957)	(1,287)	(1,639)	(2,046)
Total Fixed Assets	$2,343	$2,018	$1,817	$1,639
Other Assets	84	62	76	80
Total Assets	$5,416	$5,481	$6,549	$5,988

EXHIBIT 1.1 (Continued)

	1985	1986	1987	1988
Liabilities and Stockholders' Equity:				
Accounts Payable	$1,239	$1,223	$1,496	$1,385
Accrued Taxes	101	166	202	214
Current Maturities of Long-Term Debt	97	98	100	100
Demand Note Payable, Bank	200	0	400	200
Total Current Liabilities	$1,637	$1,487	$2,198	$1,899
Long-Term Debt				
Institution Notes Payable				
Less: Due in One Year	115	82	146	115
Volunteer Insurance Loan	1,280	1,216	1,152	1,088
Total Long-Term Debt	$1,395	$1,298	$1,298	$1,203
Stockholders' Equity				
Capital Stock Common, $5 Par				
Authorized 50,000 Shares				
Outstanding 28,000 Shares	140	140	140	140
Paid-in Capital	326	326	326	326
Retained Earnings	1,918	2,230	2,587	2,593
Total Stockholders' Equity	$2,384	$2,696	$3,053	$3,059
Total Liabilities and Stockholders' Equity	$5,416	$5,481	$6,549	$6,161

EXHIBIT 1.2

Industrial Plastics, Inc.

*Income Statement and Selected Data for the Periods Ending
February 28, Except for 1988, Which Is February 29*
(In Thousands)

	1985	1986	1987	1988
Gross Sales	$11,442	$12,006	$13,886	$13,280
Returns and Allowances	17	39	88	102
Net Sales	$11,425	$11,967	$13,798	$13,178
Cost of Goods Sold	8,298	8,490	9,693	9,626
Gross Profit	$ 3,127	$ 3,477	$ 4,105	$ 3,552
Operating Expenses				
Selling	1,008	1,179	1,247	1,388
General and Administrative	1,224	1,307	1,406	1,504
Total Operating Expenses	$ 2,232	$ 2,486	$ 2,653	$ 2,892
Operating Income	895	991	1,452	660
Interest Expense	144	141	157	184
Income Before Taxes	$ 751	$ 850	$ 1,295	$ 476
Federal and State Income Taxes	300	340	518	190
Net Income	$ 451	$ 510	$ 777	$ 286
Depreciation Expense	$ 320	$ 340	$ 364	$ 410

EXHIBIT 1.3

Industrial Plastics, Inc.

*Selected Ratios for the Plastics Manufacturing Industry for
the Following Calendar Periods*

	1984	1985	1986	1987
Liquidity:				
1. Current Ratio	1.5	1.6	1.5	1.6
2. Acid Test	0.8	0.9	0.8	0.9
3. Current Assets/Total Assets (%)	59.4	57.5	57.2	57.3
Activity:				
4. Receivables Turnover	7.9	8.2	8.0	7.8
5. Cost of Goods Sold/Inventory	7.2	7.6	7.4	7.6
6. Net Sales/Net Working Capital	11.8	11.0	12.0	12.0
7. Net Sales/Total Assets	2.1	2.1	2.0	2.0
Leverage:				
8. Total Debt/Total Assets (%)	61.5	61.0	61.8	61.6
9. Debt/Net Worth	1.7	1.6	1.6	1.7
10. EBIT/Interest	3.7	2.4	2.4	2.1
Profitability:				
11. COGS/Net Sales (%)	74.2	74.5	74.5	74.0
12. Operating Profit/Net Sales (%)	6.1	5.0	5.4	4.4
13. Profit Before Taxes/Net Sales (%)	4.6	3.5	3.7	2.8
14. Profit Before Taxes/Total Assets (%)	9.5	6.7	7.2	5.4
15. Profit Before Taxes/Net Worth (%)	12.9	5.0	7.4	2.1

QUESTIONS

1. Calculate the firm's liquidity, activity, leverage, and profitability ratios for the years 1985–1988.

2. Using ratio analysis, examine Industrial Plastics on both an historical and an industry-wide basis.

3. Prepare a report listing the strengths and weaknesses of Industrial Plastics from the point of view of Mr. Arcadi.

4. Discuss the limitations of financial ratio analysis. What other types of information would improve the analysis of Industrial Plastics?

5. Calculate the 15 selected industry ratios for the years 1985–1988 using Lotus 1-2-3.

Palton's
RATIO ANALYSIS

Dorothy Wilson, vice-president of the Northern New England Bank, Portland, Maine, was reviewing the credit file of Palton's, pursuant to a meeting with Lonnie Eastly, vice-president and controller of the firm. The meeting was an annual occurrence usually held about a month after Palton's year-end close, January 31. Traditionally, the meeting was held to review the firm's financial position and to establish the basis for Palton's financial needs in the coming year. However, this year's meeting was overshadowed by Palton's uncertain financial picture, characterized by their fiscal 1988 financial statements. (See Exhibits 2.1 and 2.2.)

Palton's was a full-line department store, the largest in northern New England. Its trade area encompassed all of Maine and that portion of New Hampshire north of Concord. The metropolitan area of Portland, however, accounted for about two-thirds of the firm's sales volume. Until late 1984 Palton's only location was in downtown Portland, but in that year two new stores were opened in newly built shopping malls in suburban Portland.

Portland's present management team had been in place since 1979 when Mr. Arnold Palton retired from the presidency. He was the last in a line of Paltons, holding the presidency since 1902. Mr. Jack Geldman, formerly vice-president of merchandising for a large department store in Hartford, Connecticut, became president. Mr. Eastly became vice-president and controller. The new team did not make any major changes until early 1983, when Mr. Geldman became convinced that Palton's would have to change its merchandising image. It had become stodgy and conservative. Independent marketing surveys revealed that the young, upwardly mobile shoppers (those 25 to 40 years old) were still shopping at Palton's, but that a significant percentage of their purchases were for nonfashion goods. In addition, the surveys disclosed that a greater number of shoppers chose not to go downtown to the firm's only store.

By mid-1983, Mr. Geldman became convinced that a new marketing strategy must be adopted and that at least two stores would have to be built in shopping malls. The length of the recession temporarily stopped the building plans, but the new marketing strategy was begun and fully implemented by late 1984. With the improvement in the economy, a more aggressive marketing strategy, and the building of two new stores, sales and profits increased markedly in fiscal 1986.

Dorothy Wilson had serviced Palton's since the Geldman management team had come to power. She found them reasonably competent, although she worried about the tendency of Mr. Geldman to reserve all major operating decisions for himself. She had the highest regard for Mr. Eastly as a financial executive, but she wished he would exert more influence on the operating decisions of the president.

Ms. Wilson prepared for the meeting in a careful meticulous manner. She began her preparation after receiving the certified financial statements from Palton's outside accountants, Myndan and Smithe. She planned to calculate the pertinent financial ratios, and she assembled industrywide ratios (see Exhibit 2.3). In addition she gathered information about the current status of the department store industry. She talked with her peers at Northern New England as well as contacts at correspondent banks in Boston and New York. She was in touch with a securities analyst for a large national firm, who provided her with valuable insights as to the future prospects for the industry.

EXHIBIT 2.1

Palton's

Balance Sheets as of Year Ending January 31 (In Thousands)

	1985	1986	1987	1988
Assets:				
Cash	$ 350	$ 407	$ 521	$ 94
Accounts Receivable	11,333	12,801	13,725	13,737
Merchandise Inventory	10,969	11,318	11,605	12,136
Prepaid Expenses	412	447	449	416
Total Current Assets	$23,064	$24,973	$26,300	$26,383
Land	1,883	1,883	1,908	1,908
Building, Net	6,404	6,236	7,808	7,640
Equipment, Net	7,137	7,148	7,356	7,388
Total Fixed Assets	$15,424	$15,267	$17,072	$16,936
Other Assets	508	386	377	286
Total Assets	$38,996	$40,626	$43,749	$43,605

EXHIBIT 2.1 (Continued)

	1985	1986	1987	1988
Liabilities and Stockholders' Equity:				
Accounts Payable	$10,766	$10,345	$10,522	$11,693
Accruals	227	383	405	396
Notes Payable	0	500	1,555	1,300
Current Maturities of Long-Term Debt	500	500	500	500
Taxes Payable	800	934	1,023	360
Total Current Liabilities	$12,293	$12,662	$14,005	$14,249
Long-Term Debt	7,600	7,100	6,600	6,100
Total Liabilities	$19,893	$19,762	$20,605	$20,349
Stockholders' Equity				
Common Stock, $10 Par	2,950	2,950	2,950	2,950
Retained Earnings	16,153	17,914	20,194	20,306
Total Stockholders' Equity	$19,103	$20,864	$23,144	$23,256
Total Liabilities and Stockholders' Equity	$38,996	$40,626	$43,749	$43,605

EXHIBIT 2.2

Palton's

Income Statements for the Years Ending January 31
(In Thousands)

	1985	1986	1987	1988
Net Sales Including Leased Departments	$76,958	$79,943	$86,667	$82,276
Cost of Goods Sold	54,000	56,444	60,667	58,970
Gross Profit	$22,958	$23,499	$26,000	$23,306
Selling and Administrative Expenses	10,774	11,704	12,009	12,405
Other Expenses	5,959	5,632	5,683	5,822
Operating Profits	$ 6,225	$ 6,163	$ 8,308	$ 5,079
Interest Expense	1,155	971	1,160	1,304
Net Profit Before Taxes	$ 5,070	$ 5,192	$ 7,148	$ 3,775
Federal and State Income Taxes	2,028	2,076	2,859	1,510
Net Profit After Taxes	$ 3,042	$ 3,116	$ 4,289	$ 2,265
Depreciation Expense	$ 680	$ 688	$ 846	$ 852

EXHIBIT 2.3

Palton's

*Selected Ratios for Department Stores for the Following
Calendar Periods*

	1985	1986	1987	1988
Liquidity:				
1. Current Ratio	2.3	2.2	2.3	2.3
2. Acid Test	0.8	0.9	0.8	1.0
3. Current Assets/Total Assets (%)	74.4	72.1	70.8	70.4
Activity:				
4. Receivables Turnover	12.4	12.2	9.5	8.7
5. Cost of Goods Sold/Inventory	3.3	3.6	3.6	3.5
6. Net Sales/Net Working Capital	5.6	5.9	5.4	5.6
7. Net Sales/Total Assets	2.2	2.1	2.1	2.1
Leverage:				
8. Total Debt/Total Assets (%)	54.6	54.6	50.9	53.7
9. Debt/Net Worth	1.2	1.2	1.2	1.3
10. EBIT/Interest	2.6	2.3	2.0	2.0
Profitability:				
11. COGS/Net Sales (%)	65.9	65.4	64.2	64.4
12. Operating Profit/Net Sales (%)	2.9	3.1	3.4	3.4
13. Profit Before Taxes/Net Sales (%)	2.6	2.2	3.1	2.7
14. Profit Before Taxes/Total Assets (%)	3.1	4.3	5.2	5.0
15. Profit Before Taxes/Net Worth (%)	12.9	10.9	12.7	11.9

QUESTIONS

1. Calculate the key financial ratios for Palton's for 1985–1988.

2. What do those ratios tells Ms. Wilson about the financial condition of Palton's?

3. Prepare a report detailing the financial problems of Palton's from the viewpoint of Mr. Eastly. Use both information presented in the case and information from outside sources concerning the department store industry.

4. Devise a financial plan that would improve Palton's working capital position and would be satisfactory to the bank.

5. Calculate the 15 selected industry ratios for the years 1985–1988 using Lotus 1-2-3.

The Midvale Company
STATEMENT OF FINANCIAL
POSITION

The Midvale Company, located in Tacoma, Washington, manufactured various types of equipment used in the forest products industry. The firm began operations in 1937 and experienced steady, long-term growth. There were, however, wide swings in earnings that were closely correlated with the cyclical housing market. A prolonged slump in construction activity in most world markets had a severe impact on sales of construction as well as forestry equipment that made up Midvale's main product line. In 1982, production schedules were reduced for the first time in the history of the company. In addition to operating at lower rates, the company's equipment factory was shut down for four weeks in January and again for two weeks in May to prevent additional buildup of inventories.

The company added several new products to its line during the years 1983–1985 with the hope of increasing equipment sales. These included a tree harvester to broaden the company's equipment line in both size and the number of tasks that could be performed. One of the new harvesters had a six-wheel undercarriage, rather than tracks, to provide it with improved mobility and versatility. This equipment proved to be particularly useful to forest products companies in the harvesting of planted trees, and sales were better than anticipated.

Other new product lines added were a narrow-gauge bulldozer and a custom skidder. The bulldozer was designed for logging-road construction or for other jobs in which important considerations are constricted operating width and the ability to transport the equipment without obtaining wide-load permits. The custom skidder had a unique design that could be easily modified for a variety of applications of fertilizer and herbicides.

These new products brought the company into promising specialty markets and demonstrated the company's commitment to respond to the specific needs of the end user. Because of these new products, Midvale had slowly increased its sales, and profits were expected to continue to increase in the foreseeable future as forest products companies replaced their outdated equipment with the more efficient equipment Midvale had to offer. However, this was not the case in 1988 as production and delivery problems plagued the firm during the year.

Mr. Ralph Arbruzzi, controller of the firm for the last 10 years, was responsible for all of Midvale's accounting information, including the balance sheet, income statement, and statement of sources and uses. Mr. Arbruzzi hired Mr. Glenn Hopstein, a recent accounting graduate of Washington State University. Mr. Hopstein's first assignment was to prepare the statement of sources and uses for the year ending December 31, 1988. The balance sheet and income statements for 1987 and 1988 were available as shown in Exhibit 3.1 and Exhibit 3.2. Mr. Hopstein realized that the two statements would provide only a starting point for the sources and uses statements, so he began to gather other pertinent information.

From year-end reports, Mr. Hopstein discovered that the firm had written off $4,000,000 of fully depreciated equipment in 1988. He also learned that the firm had repurchased 200,000 shares of its common stock at $30 per share. That was the first stock repurchase in the firm's history. Dividends for 1988 were $11,000,000, equaling the 1987 payout. Mr. Hopstein decided to prepare the statement of sources and uses from both the working capital and cash approaches.

Selected ratios for farm machinery and equipment manufacturers are presented in Exhibit 3.3.

EXHIBIT 3.1

The Midvale Company

Balance Sheets as of December 31 (In Millions)

	1987	1988
Assets:		
Cash	$ 15	$ 18
Marketable Securities	6	0
Accounts Receivable	84	91
Less: Allowance for Bad Debts	(3)	(4)
Inventory	101	105
Prepaid Expenses	1	1
Total Current Assets	$204	$211
Land	20	20
Building and Equipment	165	200
Less: Accumulated Depreciation	(50)	(68)
Total Fixed Assets	$135	$152
Other Assets		
Investment in Eidex Company	9	14
Total Assets	$348	$377

EXHIBIT 3.1 (Continued)

	1987	1988
Liabilities and Stockholders' Equity:		
Accounts Payable	$ 46	$ 54
Demand Notes Payable	35	20
Accruals	2	6
Total Current Liabilities	$ 83	$ 80
Long-Term Debt		
8% Bonds Due 1988	50	0
13% Bonds Due 2010	0	90
Total Long-Term Debt	$ 50	$ 90
Stockholders' Equity		
Common Stock, $25 Par	60	60
Retained Earnings	155	153
Less: Treasury Stock	(0)	(6)
Total Stockholders' Equity	$215	$207
Total Liabilities and Stockholders' Equity	$348	$377

EXHIBIT 3.2

The Midvale Company

Income Statements for the Years Ending December 31
(In Millions)

	1987	1988
Net Sales	$348	$386
Cost of Goods Sold	226	277
Gross Profit	$122	$109
Operating Expenses		
Selling	35	38
General and Administrative	45	48
Total Operating Expenses	$ 80	$ 86
Operating Income	42	23
Interest Expense	5	9
Net Income Before Taxes	$ 37	$ 14
Federal and State Income Taxes	14	5
Net Income	$ 23	$ 9

EXHIBIT 3.3

The Midvale Company

Selected Ratios for Farm Machinery and Equipment Manufacturers for the Following Calendar Periods

	1985	1986	1987	1988
Liquidity:				
1. Current Ratio	1.8	1.7	1.9	1.8
2. Acid Test	0.6	0.7	0.8	0.6
3. Current Assets/Total Assets (%)	73.1	74.2	74.3	71.5
Activity:				
4. Receivables Turnover	9.0	8.4	8.1	8.7
5. Cost of Goods Sold/Inventory	3.0	2.9	2.8	2.6
6. Net Sales/Net Working Capital	6.1	6.1	5.3	4.9
7. Net Sales/Total Assets	1.8	1.7	1.7	1.5
Leverage:				
8. Total Debt/Total Assets (%)	58.0	61.0	57.6	59.7
9. Debt/Net Worth	1.5	1.7	1.4	1.8
10. EBIT/Interest	2.7	1.7	1.8	1.2
Profitability:				
11. COGS/Net Sales (%)	73.6	72.7	70.5	70.8
12. Operating Profit/Net Sales (%)	6.2	5.3	5.4	2.5
13. Profit Before Taxes/Net Sales (%)	4.7	2.4	2.2	(0.6)
14. Profit Before Taxes/Total Assets (%)	8.6	3.7	5.0	0.8
15. Profit Before Taxes/Net Worth (%)	22.8	10.5	12.9	2.7

QUESTIONS

1. Prepare a statement of sources and uses using the working capital approach from the point of view of Mr. Hopstein.
2. Prepare a statement of sources and uses using the cash approach from the point of view of Mr. Hopstein.
3. Analyze the information provided by the statements prepared in the previous questions.

Case 4

Delsing Company
CASH BUDGET

Delsing Company was a manufacturer of creative toys and games. Since its founding in Omaha, Nebraska, by Henry Delsing in 1970, the firm had specialized in the design and production of challenging games for children ages 4 to 14. A balance sheet and an income statement are included as Exhibit 4.1 and Exhibit 4.2.

The company was known for introducing toys and games based on ideas not fully tested in the industry. Henry Delsing believed that this type of risk taking would lead to highly profitable operations as well as an exciting environment in which to work. Although Delsing Company was highly successful, the firm had experienced cash flow problems due to rapid growth during the period 1976–1986. Sales had grown at an annual rate of 20 percent but had declined to 15 percent the last two years. During the same 10-year period, earnings had increased at an annual rate of 14 percent. In addition to cash problems caused by growth, the company had seasonal cash requirements due to demand generated at Christmas. Since toys and games were attractive gift items, one-third of Delsing's output was purchased during October and November.

With such a large need for funds, Mr. Delsing wanted to keep investment in cash to a minimum. Therefore, he believed it was essential to spend adequate time in preparing the information needed for a cash forecast.

Delores Cantino, the controller at Delsing, was responsible for the preparation of the firm's financial statements and for all internal managerial reports. Among the more important documents was the cash budget.

Ms. Cantino received the sales forecast from the sales manager, Brigette Hallston, during the first five days of April. The forecast reflected a conservative estimate of sales growth of less than 15 percent. Increased competition from two large game producers had begun to have a negative effect on the growth rate of the firm. The two competitors were marketing creative games through large discount houses, forcing Delsing to meet the price competition. Sales for fiscal 1988, all sold on credit, were targeted at $33,000,0000. The sales data are included as Exhibit 4.3. Selected ratios for manufacturers of children's games and toys are given in Exhibit 4.4.

Ms. Cantino had conducted a study to determine an appropriate sales collection pattern. Based on the study, she concluded that 10 percent of accounts were collected in the month of sale, 50 percent in the month following the sale, and 40 percent two months following the sale. Ms. Cantino decided to apply bad debts, averaging about 1.0 percent of sales, against all sales as is shown in Exhibit 4.3. For convenience, she decided to apply the bad-debt estimate in the second month following the sale. For example, the bad debts from the $2,000,000 March 1987 estimated sales would be charged in May.

Costs of goods sold was projected at 65 percent of sales. This included raw materials, direct labor, and overhead costs. Raw materials, estimated at 45 percent of cost of goods sold, would be paid in the month following the purchase. Although sales were expected to grow, management believed it could operate with the same level of raw material inventory. Direct labor cost was assumed to be 25 percent, and overhead cost, 30 percent of cost of goods sold. Both would be paid in the month in which they were incurred. Depreciation, amounting to about 20 percent of overhead costs, was classified as a manufacturing expense.

Operating expenses, including that portion of selling expenses not represented by commission, were paid in the month they were incurred. Sales expenses, which were represented by commission, were remitted in the month following the sale, at a rate of 8 percent of sales.

Ms. Cantino believed yearly operating expenses would be spread evenly over fiscal 1988: selling expenses not represented by commissions, $960,000; office costs, $2,000,000; office salaries, $640,000; supplies, postage, and telephone, $180,000; insurance, $340,000; and other, $200,000. The company planned to make principal payments of $350,000 on the mortgage of $1,400,000 at the end of September and March. Interest payments would not be made at the same time as the principal payments. Interest on short-term debt during the next fiscal year was difficult to calculate since it depended on the amount borrowed. For simplification, Ms. Cantino included the short-term interest cost as part of the other expenses. The notes payable outstanding matured in August and was scheduled to be paid at that time.

From information obtained from the capital budgeting committee, the controller determined that $160,000 of new capital equipment would be purchased and paid for in July. In addition, a deposit of $55,000 would be made in March 1988 on capital equipment expected to be delivered during May 1988. Income tax remittances were scheduled for July, October, January, and April. The July payment covered the total amount of income taxes that had been accrued to that time. Ms. Cantino estimated fiscal 1989 income taxes to be $1,500,000. The firm planned to maintain a minimum cash balance of $300,000; any amount over $300,000 would be applied against cumulative borrowing for fiscal 1988. Delsing expected, beginning in May, to pay quarterly dividends of $4.50 per share on the outstanding common shares, with no shares expected to be bought or sold during the fiscal year.

EXHIBIT 4.1

Delsing Company

Balance Sheet as of March 31, 1987 (In Thousands)

Assets:	
Cash	$ 300
Accounts Receivable, Net	2,600
Inventory	1,816
Prepaids	55
Total Current Assets	$4,771
Fixed Assets, Net	1,494
Other Assets	14
Total Assets	$6,279
Liabilities and Stockholders' Equity:	
Accounts Payable	$ 570
Accrued Income Taxes	332
Accrued Sales Commissions	160
Note Payable	400
Total Current Liabilities	$1,462
Mortgage, 14%	1,400
Stockholders' Equity	
Common Stock, $20 Par	840
Retained Earnings	2,577
Total Stockholders' Equity	$3,417
Total Liabilities and Stockholders' Equity	$6,279

EXHIBIT 4.2

Delsing Company

Income Statement for the Year Ending March 31, 1987
(In Thousands)

Net Sales	$28,874
Cost of Goods Sold	18,842
Gross Profit	$10,032
Operating Expenses	
Selling	3,568
Office Costs	2,093
Officer Salaries	727
Supplies, Postage, Telephone	162
Insurance	364
Other	156
Total Operating Expenses	$ 7,070
Net Operating Expenses	2,962
Interest Expense	230
Net Profit Before Taxes	$ 2,732
Federal and State Income Taxes	1,093
Net Profit	$ 1,639

EXHIBIT 4.3

Delsing Company

Actual Sales for the Last Three Months of Fiscal 1987 and
Projected Sales for Fiscal 1988 (In Thousands)

January (fiscal 1987)	$1,600
February	2,000
March	2,000
April (fiscal 1988)	2,000
May	2,400
June	2,400
July	2,000
August	2,000
September	3,000
October	6,200
November	4,800
December	2,400
January	1,800
February	2,000
March	2,000

EXHIBIT 4.4

Delsing Company

*Selected Ratios for Children's Games and Toys Manufacturers
for the Following Calendar Periods*

	1983	1984	1985	1986
Liquidity:				
1. Current Ratio	1.9	1.8	2.0	1.9
2. Acid Test	0.8	0.9	0.9	0.9
3. Current Assets/Total Assets (%)	77.6	74.7	74.9	74.9
Activity:				
4. Receivables Turnover	7.2	6.6	7.4	6.9
5. Cost of Goods Sold/Inventory	3.3	4.0	4.2	3.7
6. Net Sales/Net Working Capital	6.7	6.2	5.4	6.0
7. Net Sales/Total Assets	2.0	1.9	2.0	1.9
Leverage:				
8. Total Debt/Total Assets (%)	56.8	56.4	52.5	59.5
9. Debt/Net Worth	1.4	1.4	1.1	1.6
10. EBIT/Interest	2.6	2.9	2.4	1.8
Profitability:				
11. COGS/Net Sales (%)	69.2	69.0	65.2	65.3
12. Operating Profit/Net Sales (%)	6.2	5.9	8.4	4.8
13. Profit Before Taxes/Net Sales (%)	3.8	3.7	5.6	1.8
14. Profit Before Taxes/Total Assets (%)	8.6	9.7	9.5	6.5
15. Profit Before Taxes/Net Worth (%)	21.4	23.3	18.0	14.8

QUESTIONS

1. Prepare a monthly cash budget for fiscal 1988 (April 1, 1987–March 31, 1988).
2. What significant information was revealed in the cash budget?
3. What were the crucial assumptions in preparing the cash budget?
4. How realistic are the assumptions made by Ms. Cantino? Would you make any changes in her assumptions?
5. Prepare a monthly cash budget for fiscal 1988 using Lotus 1-2-3.

Jack Martin, Inc.
PRO FORMA STATEMENTS

Jack Martin, Inc. produced and marketed a wide range of products, including roofing, insulation, wallboard, flooring, pipe, and gypsum. The firm's sales were distributed as follows: industrial construction, 45 percent; commercial construction, 35 percent; and residential construction, 20 percent. Since construction sales were closely tied to the movements of interest rates, the company had experienced significant swings in sales and income during the last several years. Earnings in 1981 and 1982 were both negative at $3,000,000 and $1,500,000, respectively. By 1984, earnings had risen to $6,200,000. A balance sheet and income statement are included as Exhibit 5.1 and Exhibit 5.2.

The company was founded by Jack Martin in 1952 at Charlotte, North Carolina. For the previous five years, Mr. Martin had traveled the Carolinas selling building products. The numerous contacts he developed were the basis for the early sales of the new company, but the building boom in the region during the 1950s and 1960s was the primary reason for its growth. By 1970 sales had grown to $40,000,000. The economic downturn during 1973 and 1974 was particularly devastating, causing a decline in sales to $35,000,000 by 1975. Since management had not previously experienced a sales decline, the necessary adjustments were not made. Sales did not return to the 1970 level until 1983.

Evan Harlett, controller of the firm since 1980, was an accounting graduate from the University of North Carolina at Charlotte. He believed strongly in the preparation of pro forma financial statements. He knew they had improved planning by allowing top management to observe the financial effect of changing assumptions on the operation of the firm. To prepare the statements, he needed predictions from several executives for the following year. Since the fiscal year ended July 31, he began collecting his estimates in June for the pro forma statements of fiscal 1988 (August 1, 1987–July 31, 1988).

Mr. Harlett first looked at the sales estimate for fiscal 1988 provided by the marketing manager. He adjusted this figure downward because of expected increases in interest rates that would inhibit construction gains in the following year. After discussion with other executives in the firm, he reduced the $66,000,000 amount to $62,000,000. He then determined working capital items by assuming the following historical relationships with sales: accounts receivable, 16 percent; finished goods and work in process, 6 percent; raw materials purchases, 4 percent; and prepaid expenses, 1 percent. The minimum cash balance was set at $625,000. It was also company policy to keep accounts payable at two times raw materials purchases. Mr. Harlett estimated accrued income taxes at one-fourth of the tax liability for the year. Other assets and accrued expenses were expected to grow at a 10 percent rate.

No land acquisition or building expansion was expected, but capital budgeting plans included $675,000 for state-of-the-art machinery and $300,000 for furniture and fixtures. A total of $250,000 of fully depreciated machinery and equipment would be scrapped. Total depreciation charges in fiscal 1988 amounted to $2,220,000. Mr. Harlett knew the annual $1,250,000 principal payment on the firm's long-term debt was due in November 1987. Since JMI had no plans to issue or repurchase any preferred or common stock, Mr. Harlett normally prepared the pro forma balance sheet so that notes payable was the balancing account.

Certain operating efficiencies were probable during the next year. Cost of goods sold was estimated to be 81 percent of sales, while selling, administrative, and general expenses were 3.3 percent, 3.8 percent, and 3.0 percent of sales, respectively. Other expenses were forecasted at $50,000. Mr. Harlett realized that interest expense was difficult to project due to the volatility of short-term borrowings, but he felt that $1,928,000 was a reasonable figure with which to work. Corporate federal and state taxes were estimated at 40 percent of taxable earnings. Common dividends would equal 55 percent of net income after taxes with preferred dividends paid on the outstanding shares.

Selected ratios for the building construction industry appear in Exhibit 5.3.

EXHIBIT 5.1

Jack Martin, Inc.

Balance Sheet as of July 31, 1987 (In Thousands)

Assets:	
Cash	$ 643
Accounts Receivable	8,706
Inventory	
Finished Goods and Work-in-Process	3,675
Raw Materials	2,422
Prepaid Expenses	621
Total Current Assets	$16,067
Fixed Assets	
Land	$ 1,350
Buildings	10,720
Machinery and Equipment	29,996
Furniture and Fixtures	1,487
Less: Allowance for Depreciation	(20,377)
Other Assets	110
Total Fixed Assets	$23,286
Total Assets	$39,353
Liabilities and Stockholders' Equity:	
Accounts Payable	$ 4,546
Accrued Expenses	50
Accrued Income Taxes	380
Current Maturity of Long-Term Debt	1,250
Total Current Liabilities	$ 6,226
Long-Term Debt, 13%	11,250
Stockholders' Equity	
Preferred Stock, $100 Par, 13%, Cumulative	7,000
Common Stock, $5 Par	1,000
Retained Earnings	13,877
Total Stockholders' Equity	$21,877
Total Liabilities and Stockholders' Equity	$39,353

EXHIBIT 5.2

Jack Martin, Inc.

Income Statement for the Year Ending July 31, 1987
(In Thousands)

Net Sales	$54,955
Cost of Goods Sold	44,788
Gross Profit	$10,167
Operating Expenses	
Selling	1,750
Administrative	2,094
General	1,681
Other	54
Total Operating Expenses	5,579
Net Operating Income	$ 4,588
Interest Expense	1,622
Net Income Before Taxes	$ 2,966
Federal and State Income Taxes	1,126
Net Income After Taxes	$ 1,840

EXHIBIT 5.3

Jack Martin, Inc.

Selected Ratios for the Building Construction Industry for the
Following Calendar Periods

	1983	1984	1985	1986
Liquidity:				
1. Current Ratio	2.63	2.51	2.60	2.67
2. Acid Test	1.20	1.27	1.29	1.36
3. Current Assets/Total Assets (%)	39.84	40.62	41.77	42.03
Activity:				
4. Receivables Turnover	6.00	6.20	6.41	6.40
5. Cost of Goods Sold/Inventory	7.00	6.84	7.03	6.94
6. Net Sales/Net Working Capital	5.63	5.67	5.89	5.92
7. Net Sales/Total Assets	1.50	1.48	1.48	1.43
Leverage:				
8. Total Debt/Total Assets (%)	40.82	39.61	40.54	41.36
9. Debt/Net Worth	78.83	80.64	79.87	78.80
10. EBIT/Interest	2.63	2.59	2.58	2.79
Profitability:				
11. COGS/Net Sales (%)	80.64	80.82	81.14	81.65
12. Operating Profit/Net Sales (%)	8.27	8.04	8.36	8.44
13. Profit Before Taxes/Net Sales (%)	5.82	5.80	5.79	5.65
14. Profit Before Taxes/Total Assets (%)	7.86	8.02	8.00	7.91
15. Profit Before Taxes/Net Worth (%)	15.13	15.47	14.86	14.66

QUESTIONS

1. Prepare a pro forma income statement and balance sheet for fiscal 1988.
2. What are the key assumptions in preparing these statements? How reasonable are these assumptions?
3. Assume that accounts receivable is being estimated by the linear equation $Y = \$1,550,000 + 0.126X$ (Y = accounts receivable and X = forecasted sales). Calculate accounts receivable for fiscal 1988. Explain the reasons for the difference in this calculation and the percent of sales calculation used in the pro forma balance sheet.
4. Prepare a pro forma income statement and balance sheet for fiscal 1988 using Lotus 1-2-3.

Langhorne Industries, Inc.
CASH BUDGET AND PRO
FORMA STATEMENTS

Langhorne Industries, Inc. was a producer and distributor of decorative orna-ments for both business and the home. The firm, headquartered in Kansas City, Missouri, was begun in 1950 by George and Emily Langhorne, brother and sister. In the earliest organization, Emily Langhorne was charged with production responsibilities, and George Langhorne with distribution. From its beginning and until 1970, the firm sold only in Missouri, Oklahoma, and Kansas. Sales in 1974 were slightly in excess of $2,000,000. An income statement and a balance sheet are included as Exhibit 6.1 and Exhibit 6.2.

During 1975 both of the Langhornes retired, and George's daughter, Suellen Langhorne Harvin, became president. Ms. Harvin was a 1965 marketing graduate of the University of Missouri. In 1972 she earned her MBA from the University of Missouri at Kansas City. Since that time she had been given increasingly responsible positions. Her last job before joining Langhorne was that of vice-president of marketing for a large retail firm in Kansas City, Missouri.

As president of the firm, Ms. Harvin initiated a vigorous campaign to increase sales. She believed that geographical expansion into the total Midwest-ern market would be relatively easy; she was right. By 1982, the firm was selling in all Midwestern states and Texas. Sales had climbed to over $16,000,000.

Ms. Harvin also decided to broaden the firm's product line. The move caused sales to increase to over $20,000,000 by 1987. Hidden in this figure was a declining profit picture. By 1986, net profits after taxes had decreased to less than one-half of 1 percent of sales, far below the industry average.

Ms. Harvin knew she needed to take steps to improve profit margins by establishing a system of financial controls. To begin this process, she hired Leland Kruppka as vice-president of accounting and finance. Mr. Kruppka was a CPA and had previously worked for almost 10 years as controller for a building materials firm. One of his first tasks was to prepare a fairly simple cash budget for fiscal 1987.

Mr. Kruppka wanted a complete cash budget, a pro forma income state-ment, and a year-end pro forma balance sheet for fiscal 1988 (October 1,

1987–September 30, 1988). He believed that preparation of these statements was necessary to determine the firm's cash needs and surplus cash for the coming year. He knew that preparation of the cash budget and the pro forma statements would help companywide planning by allowing the firm to establish priorities. Mr. Kruppka also felt that the budget was helpful in dealing with the company's major bank, Mizzou National Bank of Kansas City.

Until 1982 Mizzou National was the only bank Langhorne Industries used. At that time, the company established a relationship with the Second Bank of Missouri. Mizzou National, however, still handled 90 percent of the firm's loan requests and kept about 80 percent of its deposits. Horatio Carborni, a vice-president at Mizzou, had serviced the account for the last six years. He was therefore well acquainted with the financial and operational aspects of the firm. Langhorne Industries had lines of credit with the two banks that allowed them to cover their short-term needs. Both banks required the loans to be reduced to zero for at least one month during the year. Langhorne's policy was to be short-term debt free for two months, usually during August and September.

Mr. Kruppka realized that an accurate sales forecast was crucial for the cash flow statement to provide a reasonable picture of its funds flow. To accomplish this goal, he first gathered information on the economy by consulting a number of government publications as well as newsletters from Kansas and Missouri banks. The consensus forecast was for a modest growth rate of between 2 and 3 percent, with consumer confidence declining as the year progressed. There was no threat of recession, however. Mr. Kruppka concluded that Langhorne would need to advertise and promote heavily to meet sales projections for the new year.

Consultation with the vice-president for sales, Dorothy Sands, produced a net sales forecast of $22,000,000 for fiscal 1988. All sales were on credit. The monthly sales forecast shown in Exhibit 6.3 was developed by applying the firm's historical monthly pattern to the yearly sales figure. Normally, the firm sold 40 percent of its output between June and September. This was due primarily to Christmas buying, though the effect had lessened during the last three years. The remainder of the output was sold fairly evenly throughout the rest of the year, with the first quarter of the fiscal year a bit lower than the other quarters.

To determine the firm's collection pattern, Mr. Kruppka prepared an analysis of the firm's collection experience. He discovered that on the average, the collection period was 60 days. Although the terms were net 45 days, he knew the firm did not plan to enforce that standard, so the 60-day average would hold. Noncollectible sales were approximately 1 percent of net sales. As far as bad debts were concerned, it was company policy to write off 1 percent of sales as bad debts at the end of the year. It was assumed that cash collections equaled 99 percent of sales at the forecasted time of collection.

Using historical data, Mr. Kruppka and Jarred Leberg, the production manager, estimated the cost of goods sold to be 75 percent of sales. Exhibit 6.3 also details forecasts of raw materials purchases, as well as direct labor and overhead expenditures. With terms for raw materials at net 30 days, the company was committed to meeting the terms of sale. Direct labor and overhead were to be paid in the period incurred. In light of a planned increase in capital expenditures, Mr. Kruppka determined that yearly depreciation would amount to $600,000, spread evenly throughout the year. All depreciation costs were charged to the manufacturing operation.

Ms. Harvin and Mr. Kruppka frequently consulted with each other regarding the purchase of new capital equipment. Both agreed that the firm must continue to acquire new equipment to improve the company's efficiency. Expected improvements would play an important part in increasing sagging profit margins. Accordingly, the firm placed an order for $540,000 of new production machinery to be delivered in January 1988. Langhorne planned to pay the seller one-half of the amount in January and the remainder in equal installments during April and July. The machinery vendor agreed to charge interest during the period from January through July. In addition, Mr. Kruppka expected to spend $5,000 per month for small recurring capital needs.

In estimating capital requirements, Mr. Kruppka took a conservative stance. He felt it was unwise to operate with an extremely low cash balance since the bank would tend to regard this as poor planning. Mr. Kruppka knew that in fiscal 1987, Langhorne's cash balance had been too low during the months from June through September. During those months, cash balances were subject to greater volatility. With that in mind, the controller decided that monthly cash balances should be at least one-tenth of total projected cash outlays for raw materials, direct labor and overhead, and operating expenses. Although prepaid expenses had shown a steady reduction in fiscal 1987, Mr. Kruppka believed this asset, along with other assets, would remain at the year-end figure.

The estimation of operating expenses, which included the approximate interest on short-term bank debt, had been proven unreliable in the past. Previously, all operating expenses had been assumed to be fixed. Upon analysis, Mr. Kruppka discovered a definite variable element and concluded that fixed monthly operating expenses should be budgeted at $300,000 plus 4 percent of projected net sales. For fiscal 1988, an additional operating expense of $180,000, to be paid quarterly beginning in November, was budgeted for advertising and promotional expense. The 4 percent variable cost included 1 percent for bad-debt expense. Although this formula would make the calculation more difficult, Mr. Kruppka knew it would significantly reduce the budget variance experienced by the company.

On September 30, 1984, Langhorne borrowed $4,000,000 for five years at 15 percent interest. The loan specified repayment in 10 equal installments on March 31 and September 30 of each year. Mr. Kruppka estimated that prepaids and accruals would maintain the same balances.

Federal and state income tax payments presented a difficult problem in terms of cash flow forecasting. Even though the firm's earnings were uneven during the year, Langhorne paid income tax based on its estimated earnings for the entire year. On October 31, 1987, the firm paid its remaining income taxes payable from fiscal 1987. On January 31, April 30, and July 31, the firm paid one-fourth of the estimated tax on the projected year's income (fiscal 1988). Income tax liability was estimated at 40 percent of net income before taxes.

Mr. Kruppka did not anticipate purchases for land and buildings or changes in other assets during the next year. He also did not foresee the sale or repurchase of common stock. No dividends were planned for fiscal 1988.

Mr. Kruppka needed to have the cash budget completed by the end of September. To speed up the process, he decided to round off figures to the nearest thousand dollars. He also concluded that excess cash balances each month should be applied to short-term notes payable.

Selected ratios for the ornament industry are presented in Exhibit 6.4.

EXHIBIT 6.1

Langhorne Industries, Inc.

Balance Sheet as of September 30 (In Thousands)

	1986	1987
Assets:		
Cash	$ 250	$ 197
Accounts Receivable, Net	3,960	4,356
Inventory	1,651	1,590
Prepaid Expenses	348	302
Total Current Assets	$6,209	$6,445
Fixed Assets		
Land	50	100
Buildings	950	1,200
Machinery and Equipment	3,692	3,775
Less: Accumulated Depreciation	(1,441)	(1,981)
Total Fixed Assets	$3,251	$3,094
Other Assets	260	147
Total Assets	$9,720	$9,686

EXHIBIT 6.1 (Continued)

	1986	1987
Liabilities and Stockholders' Equity:		
Accounts Payable	$ 550	$ 750
Accruals, Including Interest Payable	145	230
Notes Payable to Banks	1,420	1,477
Current Maturities, Long-Term Debt	800	800
Income Taxes Payable	10	86
Total Current Liabilities	$2,925	$3,343
Long-Term Liabilities	1,600	800
Total Liabilities	$4,525	$4,143
Stockholders' Equity		
Common Stock	213	213
Paid-in Capital	1,143	1,143
Retained Earnings	3,839	4,187
Total Stockholders' Equity	$5,195	$5,543
Total Liabilities and Stockhold-		
ers' Equity	$9,720	$9,686

EXHIBIT 6.2

Langhorne Industries, Inc.

Income Statements for the Years Ending September 30
(In Thousands)

	1986	1987
Net Sales	$20,476	$20,925[1]
Cost of Goods Sold	15,451	15,648
Gross Profit	$ 5,025	$ 5,277
Operating Expenses	4,435	4,339
Operating Profit	$ 590	$ 938
Interest	480	360
Net Income Before Taxes	$ 110	$ 578
Federal and State Income Taxes	22	230
Net Income After Taxes	$ 88	$ 348
Depreciation Expense	$ 500	$ 540

[1] Includes estimated income figure for September.

EXHIBIT 6.3

Langhorne Industries, Inc.

*Projections of Monthly Sales, Raw Materials Purchases, and
Direct Labor and Overhead for August and September 1987
and for Fiscal 1988 (October 1, 1987–September 30, 1988)*
(In Thousands)

	Sales	Raw Materials Purchases	Direct Labor Overhead[1]
August	$2,400	$900	$900
September	2,000	750	750
October	1,800	675	675
November	1,400	525	525
December	1,400	525	525
January	1,400	525	525
February	1,600	600	600
March	1,800	675	675
April	1,800	675	675
May	2,000	750	750
June	2,000	750	750
July	2,200	825	825
August	2,600	975	975
September	2,000	750	750

[1] Includes depreciation.

EXHIBIT 6.4

Langhorne Industries, Inc.

*Selected Ratios for the Ornaments Industry for the Following
Calendar Periods*

	1983	*1984*	*1985*	*1986*
Liquidity:				
1. Current Ratio	2.06	2.04	2.70	1.97
2. Acid Test	1.39	1.38	1.31	1.20
3. Current Assets/Total Assets (%)	64.97	65.21	63.08	62.67
Activity:				
4. Receivables Turnover	5.34	5.44	5.52	5.41
5. Cost of Goods Sold/Inventory	9.47	9.21	9.39	9.56
6. Net Sales/Net Working Capital	6.77	6.42	6.16	6.27
7. Net Sales/Total Assets	2.02	2.02	2.00	1.98
Leverage:				
8. Total Debt/Total Assets (%)	44.36	43.21	45.06	44.78
9. Debt/Net Worth	0.83	0.80	0.81	0.84
10. EBIT/Interest	3.16	3.29	2.87	3.04
Profitability:				
11. COGS/Net Sales (%)	75.36	76.02	75.87	75.47
12. Operating Profit/Net Sales (%)	5.21	4.98	4.96	5.11
13. Profit Before Taxes/Net Sales (%)	3.06	3.09	2.99	3.04
14. Profit Before Taxes/Total Assets (%)	6.12	6.34	6.43	6.29
15. Profit Before Taxes/Net Worth (%)	12.87	13.42	14.04	13.77

QUESTIONS

1. Prepare a pro forma income statement for fiscal 1988.
2. Prepare a monthly cash budget for fiscal 1988.
3. Prepare a pro forma balance sheet as of September 30, 1988.
4. Reconcile the income statement, cash budget, and balance sheet to ensure that the calculations are correct.
5. What were the key assumptions made by Mr. Kruppka in preparing the cash budget and the pro forma statements? Comment on the reasonableness of these assumptions.
6. Interpret the cash budget and the pro forma statements.
7. Prepare a pro forma income statement for fiscal 1988 using Lotus 1-2-3.
8. Prepare a monthly cash budget for fiscal 1988 using Lotus 1-2-3.
9. Prepare a pro forma balance sheet as of September 30, 1988, using Lotus 1-2-3.

Rempson, Inc.
OPERATING LEVERAGE

Rempson, Inc. was founded by George E. Rempson in 1968 in Santa Fe, New Mexico, his boyhood home. Mr. Rempson held both undergraduate and graduate degrees from the California Institute of Technology. Shortly after he completed school in 1963, he found a job near the campus as a technical consultant for a medium-sized computer company.

George Rempson dreamed of starting his own company but realized he did not have the necessary capital. By 1968 he had managed to save 60 percent of the required amount. The other 40 percent was supplied by his brother, Harvey, although he had no plans to take an active part in the business.

Rempson manufactured microwave relay links, amplifiers, and other similar equipment. These products were produced to extremely close tolerances and were used in a varying range of adverse operating conditions, such as wide temperature variances and high internal pressures. Company products tended to have a relatively short life cycle. Technological improvements came with amazing rapidity and with a minimum of advance warning. The customers of Rempson were among the elite of the industrial world. Client engineers were employed to solicit the prospective buyer because competition was so intense.

More than 80 percent of sales came from products built to order. Each contract was negotiated to meet the needs of the customer. Rempson was responsible for all phases of design, for cost determination, for installation to the specifications, and ultimately for the product's performance. The company product warranty covered a period of two years against defects in design and installation and was thus subject to loss whenever a serious error was made. This was true even though there were cost protection features in the contract. Generally, there were also cancelation provisions that allowed customers to cancel the contract upon payment of a percentage of production costs. Originally all contracts were on a fixed-fee basis, but the highly variable rate of inflation in the late 1970s forced the company to adopt a cost-plus or a cost-escalation contract.

Company sales grew from $1,200,000 in 1972 to $7,800,000 in 1982. During the next five years, sales doubled, and this growth placed pressure on the firm to expand its facilities. Balance sheets and operating income data for 1982 and 1987 are included as Exhibit 7.1 and Exhibit 7.2.

George Rempson, president, in conjunction with Jill Arkody, vice-president for sales, and Lucius Hintow, vice-president for production, decided to explore the cost of purchasing land and constructing a new building. Len Danstein, the controller, was asked to provide the information on which to base the decision.

The cost of a structure to house corporate and production personnel for the next 20 years was projected to be about $30,000,000. Depreciation charges on the new building amounted to $1,200,000 per year. Additional equipment purchaes would add another $300,000 to yearly depreciation costs. Mr. Danstein believed the new building, due to its layout and energy saving features, would reduce variable costs 2 cents per dollar of sales. He also felt increased efficiency from the new equipment would reduce variable costs 3 cents per dollar of sales. Mr. Danstein further estimated that fixed manufacturing costs would rise to about $1,290,000 per year, and fixed selling and administrative charges would increase by $180,000 in 1988.

Even though the president and two vice-presidents generally agreed with the cost estimates of Mr. Danstein, there was still strong disagreement on whether or not to proceed with the expansion plans. Mr. Hinton believed the risk was too great to undertake at the time. He pointed out that sales were subject to wide variation due to the bidding process. Since the company's sales were even riskier than the market, Mr. Hinton wondered about the effect on Rempson should there be a significant decline. Ms. Arkody felt that the firm must expand. She reasoned that any delay would cause the company to trail its competitors technologically, and she knew that would be fatal in this business. She was confident in going ahead with the plant expansion since she was sure that fixed costs would be covered. Mr. Rempson was undecided, but he thought it was important to arrive at a decision quickly so that the group could turn its energies to other more pressing problems. All three agreed that the financing of the expansion would not significantly affect approval of the plan.

Selected ratios for current carrying wire devices manufacturers appear in Exhibit 7.3.

EXHIBIT 7.1

Rempson, Inc.

Balance Sheets as of December 31 (In Thousands)

	1982	1987
Assets:		
Cash and Marketable Securities	$ 1,934	$ 2,078
Accounts Receivable, Net	4,316	8,172
Inventory	5,037	9,431
Prepaids	469	302
Total Current Assets	$11,756	$19,983
Fixed Assets, Net	4,206	11,043
Other Assets	678	1,094
Total Assets	$16,640	$32,120
Liabilities and Stockholders' Equity:		
Accounts Payable	$ 2,382	$ 5,884
Notes Payable	1,380	3,192
Accruals	1,605	3,316
Current Maturities of Long-Term Debt	330	700
Total Current Liabilities	$ 5,697	$13,092
Long-Term Debt	2,876	7,040
Stockholders' Equity		
Common Stock, $25 Par	875	1,005
Paid-in Capital	1,465	1,985
Retained Earnings	5,727	8,998
Total Stockholders' Equity	$ 8,067	$11,988
Total Liabilities and Stockholders' Equity	$16,640	$32,120

EXHIBIT 7.2

Rempson, Inc.

Operating Income Data for the Years Ending
December 31 (In Thousands)

	1982	1987
Sales	$7,800	$15,600
Less: Variable Costs		
Raw Materials	2,496	4,680
Direct Labor	1,404	2,184
Manufacturing Overhead	858	1,716
Selling	468	780
Total Variable Costs	$5,226	$ 9,360
Contribution Margin	2,574	6,240
Less: Fixed Costs		
Manufacturing	465	1,128
Selling and Administrative	810	1,800
Depreciation	675	1,440
Total Fixed Costs	$1,950	$ 4,368
Net Profit Before Taxes	624	1,872
Federal and State Income Taxes	250	742
Net Profit After Taxes	$ 374	$ 1,130

EXHIBIT 7.3

Rempson, Inc.

Selected Ratios for Current Carrying Wire Devices
Manufacturers for the Following Calendar Periods

	1984	1985	1986
Liquidity:			
1. Current Ratio	2.4	1.8	2.1
2. Acid Test	1.3	1.0	1.1
3. Current Assets/Total Assets (%)	67.6	68.5	67.2
Activity:			
4. Receivables Turnover	6.8	7.4	7.5
5. Cost of Goods Sold/Inventory	3.8	4.6	4.5
6. Net Sales/Net Working Capital	5.5	6.5	5.9
7. Net Sales/Total Assets	1.9	2.0	1.9

EXHIBIT 7.3 (Continued)			
	1984	*1985*	*1986*
Leverage:			
8. Total Debt/Total Assets (%)	44.6	54.8	53.8
9. Debt/Net Worth	0.8	1.0	1.1
10. EBIT/Interest	11.3	3.6	3.2
Profitability:			
11. COGS/Net Sales (%)	65.0	72.3	70.8
12. Operating Profit/Net Sales (%)	11.1	8.1	5.9
13. Profit Before Taxes/Net Sales (%)	9.3	7.1	5.1
14. Profit Before Taxes/Total Assets (%)	19.8	13.2	9.6
15. Profit Before Taxes/Net Worth (%)	34.5	28.3	19.3

QUESTIONS

1. Calculate the break-even point for 1982 and 1987 in thousands of dollars. Point out any significant differences between the two years with respect to cost behavior.

2. Calculate the break-even point for 1988 in thousands of dollars using the cost-volume relationships established in 1985. Assume no sales changes in 1988 if the firm adopts the expansion plan.

3. Calculate the degree of operating leverage assuming 1987 sales, a 25 percent increase in 1987 sales, and a 25 percent decrease in 1987 sales:
   (a) Under present operations.
   (b) Under the expansion plan.

4. Calculate the cash break-even point assuming the 1987 sales level and no other noncash charges except depreciation:
   (a) Under present operations.
   (b) Under the expansion plan.

5. Calculate the sales level at which net profit before taxes under present operations is equal to net profit before taxes under the expansion plan.

6. Which plan should Rempson select? Give both quantitative and nonquantitative reasons in your answer.

Computal
FINANCIAL AND
COMBINED LEVERAGE

Computal, founded in Santa Rosa, California, in 1971, manufactured and sold multipurpose computer systems, as well as related products and services, such as peripherals, software, training, and maintenance. The company marketed its computer systems directly to the end user and to original equipment manufacturers or to distributors for subsequent resale. Since customers normally bought computers in large quantities, Computal's ability to provide a high level of quality at a competitive price greatly influenced the purchasing decision. A balance sheet and an income statement are included as Exhibit 8.1 and Exhibit 8.2.

Computal was structured into two divisions, computer products and information systems. The computer products division manufactured and sold to two groups: customers who included the computer in products for resale and customers who used the computer directly for scientific and industrial purposes. The original equipment manufacturer incorporated computers into specialized systems in computer-control devices, medical and hospital electronics, factory automation, and process control. Scientific and industrial users employed computer equipment to measure or control physical parameters and to perform calculations.

The information systems division developed and marketed computer systems for scientific and commercial applications. A large percentage of the time, customers purchased the computer systems directly from the company. Management felt that reliable performance, total solution to problems, and comprehensive, but competitively priced, service were the keys to customer satisfaction. Major growth areas in this market included management of large data bases, office automation, computer-assisted design and manufacturing, and distributed data processing.

Computal was required to make large investments in technology, in equipment, and in human resources to stay competitive with respect to price, reliability, and delivery. This required that funds be spent for more automated equipment as well as for training of employees in dealing with customers. To finance these investments, Harold Worthington, vice-president for finance, was required to develop a plan.

It was Mr. Worthington's policy to contact the division managers at the beginning of each January to get their funds requirements for the coming year. For fiscal 1988, Computal decided to increase the size and scope significantly of the information systems division. Conversations with Jackson Dilts, the general manager of that division, revealed that $65,000,000 was needed to meet expansion requirements. In addition, the computer products division required $43,000,000. The total of $108,000,000 represented a sizable increase over 1987.

Mr. Worthington estimated that internal sources would provide approximately $33,000,000. That left $75,000,000 to be financed from outside sources. He was pondering which of two financial plans to recommend to the board of directors. The first plan involved the issuance of long-term bonds; the second, the sale of common stock.

Mr. Worthington had contacted several investment banking firms concerning the prospective terms of both the stock and bond issues. Since long-term interest rates had declined, it was estimated that the firm could borrow at a 12 percent interest rate. The bonds would mature in 20 years. A sinking fund payment of $5,000,000 would begin the sixth year and continue until maturity. The consensus among the investment bankers was that the firm could market common stock at $80 per share. The firm's stock was widely held; no invester held more than 4 percent. Even though the stock plan would increase the number of shares by more than 23 percent, loss of control was not expected to be a consideration.

Mr. Worthington believed that sales for fiscal 1988 would be approximately $620,000,000. Variable costs were expected to remain at 51 percent of sales; fixed operating costs were forecasted at $220,000,000. Mr. Worthington was satisfied that the marginal rate for federal and state income taxes would be in the 40 percent range.

Selected ratios for electronic computing equipment manufacturers are presented in Exhibit 8.3.

EXHIBIT 8.1

Computal

Balance Sheet as of March 31 (In Thousands)

	1986	1987
Assets:		
Cash and Temporary Cash Investments	$ 13,582	$ 50,112
Marketable Securities	43,956	44,323
Net Receivables	128,698	134,125
Inventories	196,122	199,011
Other Current Assets	5,316	5,732
Total Current Assets	$387,674	$433,303
Property, Plant, and Equipment	142,194	177,237
Less: Accumulated Depreciation	(47,977)	(70,154)
Net Property, Plant, and Equipment	$ 94,217	$107,083
Total Assets	$481,891	$540,386
Liabilities and Stockholders' Equity:		
Notes Payable	$ 0	$ 26,697
Accounts Payable	41,145	40,576
Accrued Compensation and Benefits	9,337	12,957
Federal, State and Foreign Taxes	44,186	26,860
Other Current Liabilities	21,267	25,006
Total Current Liabilities	$115,935	$132,096
Long-Term Debt	117,270	110,489
Total Liabilities	$233,205	$242,585
Stockholders' Equity		
Common Stock, $0.02 Par	76	80
Paid-in Capital	76,183	94,684
Retained Earnings	172,427	203,037
Total Stockholders' Equity	$248,686	$297,801
Total Liabilities and Stockholders' Equity	$481,891	$540,386

EXHIBIT 8.2

Computal

Income Statement for the Year Ending March 31, 1987
(In Thousands)

Revenues	
Equipment Sales	$441,394
Service	121,606
Total Revenues	$563,000
Costs and Expenses	
Equipment Sales and Service	$287,320
Research and Development	55,929
Marketing	101,021
General and Administrative	47,306
Total Costs and Expenses	$491,576
Income from Operations	$ 71,424
Interest Expense	14,760
Income Before Taxes	$ 56,664
Federal and State Income Taxes	22,664
Net Income After Taxes	$ 34,000

Note: Interest on long-term debt = $14,000,000.

EXHIBIT 8.3

Computal

Selected Ratios for Electronic Computing Equipment
Manufacturers for the Following Calendar Periods

	1983	*1984*	*1985*	*1986*
Liquidity:				
1. Current Ratio	1.8	2.3	2.1	2.1
2. Acid Test	1.0	1.1	1.0	1.1
3. Current Assets/Total Assets (%)	74.2	74.7	72.1	69.7
Activity:				
4. Receivables Turnover	5.1	5.4	5.7	5.6
5. Cost of Goods Sold/Inventory	2.8	2.6	2.9	3.1
6. Net Sales/Net Working Capital	4.7	4.1	4.1	4.5
7. Net Sales/Total Assets	1.6	1.6	1.5	1.5
Leverage:				
8. Total Debt/Total Assets (%)	61.4	53.7	52.9	52.1
9. Debt/Net Worth	1.6	1.2	1.1	1.1
10. EBIT/Interest	5.2	5.4	3.5	3.1
Profitability:				
11. COGS/Net Sales (%)	60.0	59.8	58.8	59.7
12. Operating Profit/Net Sales (%)	9.4	10.1	7.0	5.8
13. Profit Before Taxes/Net Sales (%)	8.2	8.8	6.1	4.9
14. Profit Before Taxes/Total Assets (%)	14.7	13.5	10.3	8.6
15. Profit Before Taxes/Net Worth (%)	34.9	30.3	23.7	21.3

QUESTIONS

1. Calculate earnings per share using the fiscal 1988 sales estimate:
   (a) Under the bond plan.
   (b) Under the stock plan.
2. Calculate the degree of operating leverage, the degree of financial leverage, and the degree of combined leverage using the fiscal 1988 sales estimate:
   (a) Under the bond plan.
   (b) Under the stock plan.
3. Graph earnings per share against earnings before interest and taxes:
   (a) Under the bond plan.
   (b) Under the stock plan.
   Interpret the chart in terms of financial risk.
4. Choose an appropriate financing plan for Computal; support your choice with sound reasoning.

PART II

WORKING CAPITAL MANAGEMENT

Vista World, Inc.
WORKING CAPITAL
MANAGEMENT

Vista World, Inc. manufactured major home appliances such as gas and electric ranges, refrigerators, freezers, trash compactors, waste disposals, and dishwashers. The firm was founded by Zachary Hester in 1956 near Fort Pierce, Florida, to supply components to the housing industry. Although growth was slow the first few years, sales had climbed to $30,000,000 by 1974. Since Mr. Hester was approaching retirement, he wanted to diversify his asset holdings. To do this, he needed to find a buyer for the company. Balance sheets and an operations statement are included as Exhibit 9.1 and Exhibit 9.2.

In 1975, Controlls, Inc., a large conglomerate specializing in industrial heating and air conditioning, bought Vista World, adding it as a division. The arrangement did not prove to be economically sound. In 1977, the Vista World Division was sold to a group of investors, who immediately sold stock to the general public. The decision was then made to sell appliances to the home consumer market. By 1982, Vista World was established as a significant force, especially in the Sun Belt area of the country.

Dorothea Jackson, vice-president for finance, had just completed a stormy meeting with Zane Hill, vice-president for marketing, and Samuel Licante, vice-president for production. These corporate officers were responsible for formulation of a policy that covered working capital assets: cash, marketable securities, accounts receivable, inventory, and prepaids, along with the financing of those assets. Going into the meeting, Ms. Jackson was aware of different viewpoints among the three vice-presidents, but she felt any disagreements could be resolved with a minimum of difficulty. She was clearly wrong.

Ms. Jackson realized it was important to understand the viewpoints of Mr. Hill and Mr. Licante and to improve her own knowledge of working capital management. To accomplish this, she authorized a meeting in which her staff assistants, Jarvis Levine, Sally Haas, and Selma Haydn, would present the arguments of the three vice-presidents. Mr. Levine was the surrogate for Mr. Hill and would present the case for aggressive working capital management. Ms. Haas represented Ms. Jackson and would explain why a conservative approach would be best. Ms. Haydn took the position of Mr. Licante and demonstrated why a middle-of-the-road approach was sound. To this end,

Ms. Jackson prepared Exhibit 9.3, which provided parameters for aggressive, middle-of-the road, and conservative working capital policies. It also provided interest rate data for those policies.

The working capital policy of Vista World applied to the composition of the current assets and to the manner in which they were to be financed. Any working capital position, be it aggressive, conservative, or middle-of-the-road, should be explained not only in terms of working capital, but also in terms of how it might impact other areas of the firm. For fiscal 1988 (July 1987–June 1988), Ms. Jackson told the preparers that total assets would be estimated at $180,000,000 and that earnings before interest and taxes would be estimated at $22,000,000.

Selected ratios for household electric appliance manufacturers are presented in Exhibit 9.4.

EXHIBIT 9.1

Vista World, Inc.

Condensed Balance Sheets as of June 30 (In Millions)

	1986	1987
Assets:		
Cash and Near-Cash Items	$ 12	$ 12
Accounts Receivable, Net	51	55
Inventory	63	66
Other Current Assets	2	2
Total Current Assets	$128	$135
Net Fixed Assets	41	40
Other Assets	1	1
Total Assets	$170	$176
Liabilities and Stockholders' Equity:		
Trade Accounts Payable	$ 20	$ 21
Notes Payable to Banks	6	6
Product Warranty	7	7
Current Maturity, Long-Term Debt	2	2
Accruals and Other	9	9
Total Current Liabilities	$ 44	$ 48
Long-Term Debt, Less Current Maturity	43	41
Stockholders' Equity		
Preferred Stock	18	18
Common Equity	65	72
Total Stockholders' Equity	$ 83	$ 90
Total Liabilities and Stockholders' Equity	$170	$176

EXHIBIT 9.2

Vista World, Inc.

*Condensed Operations Statement for the Year Ending
June 30, 1987 (In Millions)*

Net Sales	$340
Cost of Goods Sold	282
Gross Profit	$ 58
Operating Expenses	
Marketing and Administrative	29
Operating Income	$ 29
Interest Expense	5
Income Before Taxes	$ 24
Federal and State Income Taxes	8
Net Income	$ 16
Preferred Dividends	$ 2
Earnings Available to Common Shareholders	$ 14
Common Dividends	$ 7

EXHIBIT 9.3

Vista World, Inc.

Information for the Preparation of Working Capital Policies

Policy	Current Assets/ Total Assets	Current Liabilities/ Total Claims	Interest Rate on Debt
Aggressive	0.40 to 0.50	0.50 to 0.60	12%
Middle of the road	0.50 to 0.60	0.40 to 0.50	11
Conservative	0.60 to 0.70	0.30 to 0.40	10

EXHIBIT 9.4

Vista World, Inc.

Selected Ratios for Household Electric Appliance
Manufacturers for the Following Calendar Periods

	1984	1985	1986	1987
Liquidity:				
1. Current Ratio	1.9	1.8	1.9	2.4
2. Acid Test	0.8	0.9	0.9	1.1
3. Current Assets/Total Assets (%)	71.9	71.9	73.3	73.2
Activity:				
4. Receivables Turnover	7.9	6.8	7.7	7.4
5. Cost of Goods Sold/Inventory	3.9	4.1	3.8	3.7
6. Net Sales/Net Working Capital	6.7	6.3	5.5	5.2
7. Net Sales/Total Assets	2.1	1.8	2.0	1.8
Leverage:				
8. Total Debt/Total Assets (%)	40.0	40.5	41.0	44.3
9. Debt/Net Worth	1.6	1.4	1.2	1.3
10. EBIT/Interest	4.2	4.2	3.8	2.4
Profitability:				
11. COGS/Net Sales (%)	73.4	71.6	72.5	68.8
12. Operating Profit/Net Sales (%)	6.7	8.1	7.6	6.6
13. Profit Before Taxes/Net Sales (%)	5.5	6.8	5.6	4.9
14. Profit Before Taxes/Total Assets (%)	10.1	10.8	12.0	9.1
15. Profit Before Taxes/Net Worth (%)	26.1	28.1	25.6	26.1

QUESTIONS

1. Prepare the case for an aggressive approach to working capital policy for fiscal 1988 from the point of view of Mr. Levine.

2. Prepare the case for a middle-of-the-road approach to working capital policy for fiscal 1988 from the point of view of Ms. Haydn.

3. Prepare the case for a conservative approach to working capital policy for fiscal 1988 from the point of view of Ms. Haas.

4. Choose an appropriate working capital policy for Vista World. (Be prepared to explain what factors are significant in making your choice.)

Case 10

Universal Electronics
CASH AND MARKETABLE SECURITIES

Universal Electronics was a medium-sized manufacturer of small electronics parts including capacitors, resistors, relays, and switches for sale to manufacturers, wholesalers, and electronics parts dealers. A balance sheet and income statements are included as Exhibit 10.1 and Exhibit 10.2. The company was founded by George Patrick in Syracuse, New York in 1939. With the advent of World War II, and subsequently the Korean conflict, sales had increased dramatically. However, by the 1970s, competition from Japanese firms had left Universal Electronics in a less secure position. This led to cost-reduction programs and pressure to reduce working capital.

With the outbreak of the war in Korea, George Patrick's son, Michael, enlisted in the United States Army and was assigned to the Signal Corps. After three years as an electronics technician, Michael returned home to work for his father. College was not in his plans. Michael assumed the presidency of the company upon the retirement of his father in 1971.

Barbara Peterson had been hired by Universal Electronics as a financial analyst. She had an undergraduate degree in business administration from Tuskegee Institute and an MBA from Indiana University. As part of her training program, she was assigned as an assistant to the president.

Michael Patrick believed that cash management was an area that needed improvement. Since he was more interested in the technical aspects of production, he had not concentrated on this problem in the past, but increased competition was forcing him to consider all aspects of the company's operations. He felt that Ms. Peterson's business administration background would be beneficial in analyzing the cash requirements of the firm.

Ms. Peterson studied the company's cash management problem. After much thought, she arrived at the following three basic approaches:

1. Pay bills as late as possible without damaging the company's credit rating.
2. Manage the inventory-production cycle efficiently to maximize the inventory turnover rate.
3. Collect accounts receivable quickly.

Improvement in these areas would lead to a shorter cash cycle, allowing a higher cash turnover and a lower minimum level of operating cash.

To stretch the average age of accounts payable, currently 30 days, Ms. Peterson considered the first approach to cash management: paying bills as late as possible without damaging the company's credit rating. She found, however, that Universal Electronics was not in a position to stretch accounts payable. The company's suppliers were able to dictate credit terms, and tight money prevailed during the period. Ms. Peterson felt it could not be an area for improvement in the near future.

The second approach required efficient management of the inventory-production cycle to maximize the inventory turnover rate. That included investigation of the raw materials, work-in-process, and finished goods inventories. Ms. Peterson found the raw materials inventory to be unusually high in some areas, which had resulted from a fear of supplier strikes the previous year. Supply contracts had been signed, but stocks remained high. She calculated that the average age of raw materials could safely be reduced from 49 to 27 days. The age of work-in-process inventory, equal to the production cycle, averaged 5 days. After talking with the industrial engineers, she concluded that the time could not be significantly changed. The finished goods inventory had an average age of 62 days. Ms. Peterson knew from a survey in *Electronics Age* that the industry average was 42 days. She learned that the large finished goods inventory resulted from Mr. Patrick's determination not to dismiss workers while an international union was in the process of organizing.

The third approach involved the collection of accounts receivable. After intensive study, Ms. Peterson felt that the credit standards and collection policies could be tightened to reduce the average collection period from 51 to 45 days. There would not have to be a revision in credit terms because they seemed to be in line with the industry, and to make more stringent terms might weaken their competitive position.

Universal Electronics spent approximately $21,000,000 in fiscal 1988 on operating costs. With an opportunity cost of 9 percent, a significant reduction of minimum cash requirements would lead to a large annual savings. Ms. Peterson wanted to show Mr. Patrick how various proposals would affect the firm's profitability.

In studying the cash management problem, Ms. Peterson found that the company was keeping more cash in checking accounts than was necessary for compensating balances. She felt that the cash could be converted into marketable securities and planned to determine the necessary facts to convince Mr. Patrick that such a decision was justified.

Selected ratios for electronic components and accessories manufacturers are presented as Exhibit 10.3.

EXHIBIT 10.1

Universal Electronics

Balance Sheet as of November 30, 1988 (In Thousands)

Assets:	
Cash and Marketable Securities	$ 1,227
Accounts Receivable	3,422
Inventory	3,536
Prepaids	323
Total Current Assets	$ 8,508
Fixed Assets, Net	3,537
Other Assets	361
Total Assets	$12,406
Liabilities and Stockholders' Equity:	
Accounts Payable	$ 1,787
Accruals	980
Notes Payable	1,040
Current Maturities of Long-Term Debt	410
Total Current Liabilities	$ 4,217
Long-Term Debt	1,750
Stockholders' Equity	
Common Stock, $1 Par	762
Paid-in Capital	1,296
Retained Earnings	4,381
Total Stockholders' Equity	$ 6,439
Total Liabilities and Stockholders' Equity	$12,406

EXHIBIT 10.2

Universal Electronics

Income Statement as of November 30 (In Thousands)

	1987	1988
Net Sales	$21,913	$22,654
Cost of Sales	14,539	15,020
Gross Profit	$ 7,374	$ 7,634
Operating Expenses	5,667	5,992
Operating Profit	$ 1,707	$ 1,642
Other Expenses, Including Interest	316	311
Net Profit Before Taxes	$ 1,391	$ 1,331
Federal and State Income Taxes	555	525
Net Income After Taxes	$ 836	$ 806

EXHIBIT 10.3

Universal Electronics

Selected Ratios for Electronic Components and Accessories
Manufacturers for the Following Calendar Periods

	1984	1985	1986	1987
Liquidity:				
1. Current Ratio	1.8	1.9	1.9	1.8
2. Acid Test	0.9	1.0	1.0	1.0
3. Current Assets/Total Assets (%)	71.3	69.7	67.0	64.9
Activity:				
4. Receivables Turnover	6.1	6.6	6.4	6.8
5. Cost of Goods Sold/Inventory	3.9	3.6	4.0	4.6
6. Net Sales/Net Working Capital	5.7	5.6	6.6	7.2
7. Net Sales/Total Assets	1.8	1.8	1.8	1.8
Leverage:				
8. Total Debt/Total Assets (%)	57.6	54.8	55.6	55.9
9. Debt/Net Worth	1.3	1.2	1.2	1.3
10. EBIT/Interest	5.6	5.2	3.7	3.1
Profitability:				
11. COGS/Net Sales (%)	65.1	65.5	65.9	66.6
12. Operating Profit/Net Sales (%)	8.2	8.5	7.5	6.0
13. Profit Before Taxes/Net Sales (%)	7.8	7.1	6.0	4.3
14. Profit Before Taxes/Total Assets (%)	13.1	12.5	10.2	9.3
15. Profit Before Taxes/Net Worth (%)	33.5	30.7	24.7	21.0

QUESTIONS

1. What proposals could Ms. Peterson present to Mr. Patrick that would reduce the minimum operating cash requirements?

2. Calculate the cash cycle, cash turnover, and the minimum level of operating cash for each of the combinations proposed.

3. Explain how each proposal would affect profitability per cycle.

4. What other approaches to the cash management problem were available to Ms. Peterson?

5. What types of marketable securities could Ms. Peterson suggest to Mr. Patrick?

Harbenger's
ACCOUNTS RECEIVABLE

Harbenger's of St. Paul, Minnesota was a producer of flexible packaging materials for the foods industry. Traditionally, the company had concentrated on the packaging of snack foods such as potato chips, corn chips, and crackers, but within the last 10 years, the nonsnack business was increasing at a faster rate. A balance sheet and an income statement are included as Exhibit 11.1 and Exhibit 11.2. Exhibit 11.3 provides a sales comparison for the two kinds of business.

Production of flexible packaging products was accomplished through coating paper, cellophane, foil, or films with materials such as polyethylene, waxes, and plastics. The firm's customers determined the specifications of the products, such as the ability to seal out moisture, resistance to light rays, and strength. In addition, all packaging material was constructed so that clear graphic and color presentation of the customer's product was possible.

The production facilities of Harbenger's were located in Mason City, Iowa and Austin, Minnesota. In addition, they had a plant near corporate headquarters in St. Paul. The St. Paul plant produced half the firm's output, with the rest divided evenly between the other two facilities. The company was operating between 80 and 85 percent of capacity, with a backlog of close to $10,000,000.

Cory Esken, treasurer at Harbenger's, was reviewing the company credit and collection policies in both the sales and credit departments. In his initial investigation, he found that sales of flexible packaging were made by salaried sales representatives and that the firm had approximately 275 customers. He noted that 40 customers accounted for 60 percent of sales, with the largest customer providing 8 percent of total sales.

Credit terms and collection policies were established by a three-person committee: Calvin Hinson, the vice-president for sales; Betty Jean Delorme, the vice-president for production; and Cory Esken, the treasurer. At the previous meeting the group had decided to investigate the possibility of revamping the firm's credit terms, which were now 2/10, net 30. Mr. Hinson believed Harbenger's should change both credit terms and collection policies. He proposed to extend terms to 3/15, net 45. As far as collections were concerned, he wanted no past-due letter sent to the customer until 75 days from the date of sale. The current policy required a letter to be sent after 45 days. In addition, Mr. Hinson wanted no threat of legal action until the account was 90 days past due. This was in contrast to the prevailing policy of strong, intimidating litigation after 60 days.

Ms. Delorme's thoughts on credit terms and collection policies were completely opposite to those of Mr. Hinson. She wanted credit terms tightened since the manufacturing plants were operating at near practical capacity. (Harbenger's defined practical capacity as utilization in excess of 85 percent.) Ms. Delorme noted the backlog was $10,000,000, an all-time high. She suggested that terms of 1/10, net 20 be employed, but had no desire to change the collection procedure.

Mr. Esken did not favor changing either credit terms or collection policy. However, after questioning, the committee concluded that he should gather more information to analyze the competing proposals.

In a few days, Mr. Esken was able to compile the information as presented in Exhibit 11.4. Although the committee had asked for data on collection policy, Mr. Esken was not able to find a quantitative basis for showing the sales response to changes in collection policy. However, he was fairly confident that the internal costs of administering the credit policy would not change with the particular policy adopted.

Selected ratios for paperboard containers and box manufacturers are presented in Exhibit 11.5.

EXHIBIT 11.1

Harbenger's

Balance Sheet as of June 30 (In Thousands)

	1986	1987	1988
Assets:			
Cash	$ 1,030	$ 1,404	$ 1,581
Accounts Receivable	7,558	7,716	7.764
Less: Allowances	(743)	(804)	(769)
Inventory	7,718	8,441	8,220
Prepaids	302	389	367
Total Current Assets	$15,865	$17,146	$17,163
Property, Plant, and Equipment	28,302	29,592	30,542
Less: Depreciation	(14,462)	(15,201)	(15,708)
Total Fixed Assets	$13,840	$14,391	$14,834
Other Assets	406	400	386
Total Assets	$30,111	$31,937	$32,383

EXHIBIT 11.1 (Continued)

	1986	1987	1988
Liabilities and Stockholders' Equity:			
Accounts Payable	$ 5,431	$ 6,013	$ 5,845
Notes Payable	333	319	440
Accruals	986	759	1,014
Taxes Payable	390	410	427
Current Maturity, Long-Term Debt	450	950	450
Total Current Liabilities	$ 7,590	$ 8,451	$ 8,176
Long-Term Debt	4,500	4,050	3,300
Stockholders' Equity			
Common Stock, $1 Par	3,200	3,200	3,200
Paid-in Capital	2,914	2,914	2,914
Retained Earnings	11,907	13,322	14,793
Total Stockholders' Equity	$18,021	$19,436	$20,907
Total Liabilities and Stockholders' Equity	$30,111	$31,937	$32,383

EXHIBIT 11.2

Harbenger's

Income Statements for the Years Ending June 30 (In Thousands)

	1986	1987	1988
Gross Sales	$47,253	$50,547	$52,033
Sales Discounts	(940)	(830)	(1,027)
Net Sales	$46,313	$49,717	$51,006
Cost of Goods Sold	37,863	40,263	41,832
Gross Profit	$ 8,450	$ 9,454	$ 9,174
Operating Expenses			
Selling, General, and Administrative Expenses	3,838	4,444	4,038
Earnings Before Interest and Taxes	$ 4,612	$ 5,010	$ 5,136
Interest Expense	967	992	1,005
Net Income Before Taxes	$ 3,645	$ 4,018	$ 4,131
Federal and State Income Taxes	1,458	1,600	1,652
Net Income After Taxes	$ 2,187	$ 2,418	$ 2,479

EXHIBIT 11.3

Harbenger's

Net Sales by Division, for the Years Ending June 30
(In Thousands)

Year	Snack Food	Nonsnack Food
1979	$16,429	$ 615
1980	20,672	1,314
1981	23,506	2,164
1982	27,796	3,305
1983	29,344	11,411
1984	30,936	12,275
1985	31,666	12,683
1986	33,449	12,864
1987	35,753	13,964
1988	36,278	14,728

EXHIBIT 11.4

Harbenger's

Comparison of Proposed Changes in Credit Terms

	Hinson Proposal	Delorme Proposal	Esken Proposal
Normal growth grate in net sales (July 1, 1988– June 30, 1989)	6%	6%	6%
Growth rate in net sales due to the change in credit terms (July 1, 1988–June 30, 1989)	+2%	−2%	0%
Receivables turnover	6.00	7.20	6.55
Variable cost as a percentage of gross sales, not including bad debts	75%	75%	75%
Bad-debt expense in relation to gross sales	2.0%	1.0%	1.5%
Percentage of customers taking discounts as measured by dollars of gross sales	55%	45%	50%

EXHIBIT 11.5

Harbenger's

*Selected Ratios for Paperboard Containers and Box
Manufacturers for the Following Calendar Periods*

	1983	1984	1985	1986
Liquidity:				
1. Current Ratio	1.7	1.7	1.5	1.7
2. Acid Test	0.9	1.0	0.9	0.9
3. Current Assets/Total Assets (%)	57.3	57.8	58.6	58.5
Activity:				
4. Receivables Turnover	9.5	9.9	9.1	9.5
5. Cost of Goods Sold/Inventory	7.2	7.7	8.7	9.4
6. Net Sales/Net Working Capital	10.8	10.2	12.5	11.3
7. Net Sales/Total Assets	2.3	2.2	2.3	2.4
Leverage:				
8. Total Debt/Total Assets (%)	59.2	57.8	60.2	59.9
9. Debt/Net Worth	1.4	1.3	1.6	1.5
10. EBIT/Interest	3.1	2.9	2.2	2.2
Profitability:				
11. COGS/Net Sales (%)	75.7	74.9	74.8	75.7
12. Operating Profit/Net Sales (%)	4.5	4.5	4.3	3.6
13. Profit Before Taxes/Net Sales (%)	3.2	3.3	2.6	2.2
14. Profit Before Taxes/Total Assets (%)	7.0	7.2	5.3	4.6
15. Profit Before Taxes/Net Worth (%)	18.2	17.4	16.7	12.6

QUESTIONS

1. Prepare an analysis of the data presented in Exhibit 11.4 for the purpose of determining which plan would produce the greatest rate of return to Harbenger's. (Assume a 16 percent opportunity cost on the investment in receivables.)

2. Discuss the assumptions made by Mr. Esken in preparing Exhibit 11.4.

3. What information would you require to make an informed decision on collection policy?

4. Explain your decision in regard to both credit and collection policy.

5. How could Mr. Esken use the technique of sensitivity analysis to improve the decision-making process?

The Lane Corporation
INVENTORY MANAGEMENT

The Lane Corporation was founded in Paducah, Kentucky in 1907. The company, through its principal subsidiaries, was engaged in the specialty retailing of toys and leisure products and in the manufacture and sale of electronic components and industrial equipment. Although the company no longer manufactured toys, it did receive royalties in connection with their sale. A balance sheet and an income statement are included as Exhibit 12.1 and Exhibit 12.2.

The Specialty Retailing Division was involved in the mass merchandising of toys, games, hobby products, bicycles, pools, and sporting goods. With 50 retail toy supermarkets, Lane Corporation was the fourth largest toy supermarket chain in the United States. This division had historically been seasonal, with a large percentage of profits generally realized in the fourth quarter of each year.

The Electronic Components Division consisted of the manufacture and sale of discrete wirewound and film resistors and microcircuits. These were used in the electronic instrument, aerospace, computer, and telecommunications industries. The company was the second largest producer of precision wirewound and film resistors in the country. Output was manufactured at 10 plants in the United States, 1 plant in Mexico City, Mexico, and 1 plant in Lyon, France.

The Industrial Equipment Division was engaged in the manufacture and sale of power transmission equipment, including mechanical varible speed drives, gear motors, electric motors, worm gear speed reducers, as well as self-service car wash equipment. Unlike the Specialty Retailing Division, Industrial Division's operation was not seasonal and had generally shown a profit each quarter for the last five years. Nevertheless, the cumulative profits from the Electronic Components and Industrial Equipment Divisions had not been sufficient to offset the cumulative loss from the Specialty Retailing Division during the first three quarters of each year.

The newest of the four plants in the Industrial Equipment Division was located in Greenville, South Carolina. Management considered transportation facilities, access to raw materials, and a favorable labor market as significant factors in choosing that site. The facility functioned as both a manufacturing location and as a distribution center.

Start-up of that plant had been slow due to construction delays and numerous equipment failures that led to higher than expected costs. Management was thus anxious to employ tighter financial controls. In that environment, inventory was considered an important area for study.

Jim Anderson, an industrial engineering graduate from Georgia Tech, was assigned the task of writing standard operating procedures for inventory control. In accomplishing this, he wanted to prevent the loose practices frequently encountered during the start-up period. Procedures for finished product, work-in-process, raw materials, and operating supplies had to be written in a clear and concise manner.

He decided to start with the operating supplies procedure. His first step was to check with the planning department to find information about the items carried in inventory. An estimate of the annual usage and current cost per item is included as Exhibit 12.3.

Mr. Anderson felt that the basic economic order quantity (EOQ) model would be a good starting point for writing procedures, although he was aware of more sophisticated approaches. He sensed, however, that the particular type of inventory control employed would depend upon annual dollar usage.

Mr. Anderson needed additional information to apply the EOQ model. Carrying costs, totaling about 23 percent of acquisition cost, included such elements as storage, materials handling, obsolescence, insurance, pilferage, breakage, depreciation, taxes, and the marginal cost of capital. Ordering costs, amounting to $55 per order, took into account the managerial and clerical costs of preparing the order. He found lead times for each product by averaging past performance. (See Exhibit 12.4.) Daily usage was determined by dividing annual usage, in units, by 365. Reorder points were calculated by multiplying lead times by daily usage.

Selected ratios for industrial equipment manufacturers are presented in Exhibit 12.5.

EXHIBIT 12.1

The Lane Corporation

Balance Sheet as of December 31, 1988 (In Thousands)

Assets:	
Cash	$12,654
Receivables	14,072
Inventories	37,818
Prepaid Expenses	1,236
Deferred Income Taxes	52
Total Current Assets	$65,832
Land	263
Buildings and Improvements	10,246
Machinery and Equipment	18,666
Furniture and Fixtures	5,412
	$34,587
Less: Accumulated Depreciation	(16,091)
Total Fixed Assets	$18,496
Other Assets	
Notes Receivable	3,361
Other	2,247
Total Other Assets	$ 5,608
Leased Property Under Capitalized Leases	4,929
Goodwill	837
Deferred Charges	168
Total Assets	$95,870
Liabilities and Stockholders' Equity:	
Current Debt Maturities	$ 1,400
Obligations Under Capitalized Leases	682
Accounts Payable	30,865
Salaries and Wages	1,719
Sales and Other Taxes	3,528
Income Taxes	2,263
Accrued Expenses	4,519
Total Current Liabilities	$44,976
Long-Term Debt	
Debt Due After One Year	16,898
Obligations Under Capitalized Leases	5,162
Total Long-Term Liabilities	$22,060
Deferred Income	23
Deferred Income Taxes	616
Stockholders' Equity	
Common Stock, $0.10 Par Value	569
Paid-in Capital	16,296
Retained Earnings	13,196
	$30,061
Less: Treasury Stock	(1,866)
Total Stockholders' Equity	$28,195
Total Liabilities and Stockholders' Equity	$95,870

EXHIBIT 12.2

The Lane Corporation

Income Statement for the Year Ending December 31, 1988
(In Thousands)

Net Sales	$187,408
Other Income	1,049
	$188,457
Cost of Goods Sold	127,562
Gross Profit	$ 60,895
Operating Expenses	
Selling, General, and Administrative	43,550
Depreciation and Amortization	3,582
Operating Income	13,763
Interest Expense	3,903
Income Before Taxes	$ 9,860
Federal and State Income Taxes	3,769
Other Taxes	850
Net Income	$ 5,241

EXHIBIT 12.3

The Lane Corporation

Operating Supplies Inventory

Item Number	Annual Usage	Cost/Item
3595	$ 1,800	$ 5
7303	55,500	25
3695	45,000	20
9839	48,000	15
4508	162,000	75
2362	13,725	5
4790	97,500	50
7466	21,000	500
9044	3,675	5
5725	28,500	95
1650	5,550	50
6899	24,000	60
4058	138,000	300
6281	42,000	14
3514	51,000	1,000
7677	12,450	50
4462	16,500	30
6301	132,500	500
6735	52,500	25
4570	27,000	90

EXHIBIT 12.4

The Lane Corporation

Lead Times for Individual Items

Item Number	Lead Time (Days)	Item Number	Lead Time (Days)
3595	36	1650	18
7303	26	6899	28
3695	17	4058	10
9839	21	6281	21
4508	31	3514	31
2362	33	7677	28
4790	15	4462	12
7466	39	6301	23
9044	35	6735	16
5725	30	4570	16

EXHIBIT 12.5

The Lane Corporation

*Selected Ratios for Industrial Equipment Manufacturers for
the Following Calendar Periods*

	1984	1985	1986	1987
Liquidity:				
1. Current Ratio	1.8	1.7	1.8	1.9
2. Acid Test	0.9	0.9	1.0	1.0
3. Current Assets/Total Assets (%)	69.5	69.2	68.2	65.6
Activity:				
4. Receivables Turnover	6.9	7.3	6.8	7.4
5. Cost of Goods Sold/Inventory	4.1	4.3	4.2	4.4
6. Net Sales/Net Working Capital	6.7	6.8	6.4	6.4
7. Net Sales/Total Assets	1.9	1.8	1.8	1.8
Leverage:				
8. Total Debt/Total Assets (%)	59.8	56.4	56.5	55.5
9. Debt/Net Worth	1.3	1.3	1.4	1.3
10. EBIT/Interest	5.5	3.9	3.2	2.2
Profitability:				
11. COGS/Net Sales (%)	69.6	70.4	69.6	69.2
12. Operating Profit/Net Sales (%)	8.0	7.8	7.1	4.9
13. Profit Before Taxes/Net Sales (%)	6.7	6.0	5.4	3.0
14. Profit Before Taxes/Total Assets (%)	12.1	10.2	9.0	5.3
15. Profit Before Taxes/Net Worth (%)	29.5	24.9	22.6	13.9

QUESTIONS

1. Which items should be controlled by the EOQ model?
2. Determine the annual demand, in units, for each controlled item.
3. Determine the annual carrying cost, in dollars, for each controlled item.
4. Calculate the EOQ for each controlled item.
5. Explain how a safety stock would be useful.
6. Find the reorder point, with and without a safety stock.
7. How could the inventory procedures be improved?

Diane's of Virginia
TRADE CREDIT

Diane's of Virginia, headquartered in Norfolk, Virginia, was a retailer of women's apparel. The firm had grown from the original store, opened in Norfolk in 1955, to 85 locations: Virginia (40), North Carolina (28), Maryland (14), and Delaware (3). Much of Diane's growth and subsequent success could be traced to the decision to concentrate new stores in suburban shopping malls, with the emphasis on name-brand quality apparel. A balance sheet and an income statement are included as Exhibit 13.1 and Exhibit 13.2.

This approach meshed well with the emergence of large numbers of women into the work force. With the addition of contemporary, suburban housewives upscaling their apparel purchases, Diane's was able to take full advantage of the move toward trendier clothes.

Jason Kirlyman, vice-president for finance, was analyzing a pro forma balance sheet for fiscal 1988. He had requested the new statement in light of the planned increase in new stores. The rapid projected growth in population and income in Diane's primary market area had led to the decision to open 10 new stores during fiscal 1988. (See Exhibit 13.3.)

The projection distressed Mr. Kirlyman for a number of reasons. First, profits for fiscal 1988 were being projected at significantly lower levels than originally forecasted. This was due to higher start-up costs and greater competition than expected. Diane's planned to counter the latter problem by a policy of offering continuous merchandise sales to encourage customers to shop at their stores. Second, additions to gross fixed assets were about $250,000 higher than projected. Third, the buildup of accounts receivable and inventories was more than $1,000,000 in excess of previous estimates.

These conditions, if not corrected, would cause a liquidity situation that was unacceptable. Mr. Kirlyman therefore began to explore a number of possibilities, prior to presenting his case to Horace Waring, Diane's president, and the Board of Directors.

The most obvious way to show improvement was to reduce the number of new stores to be built during fiscal 1988. On the average, a new store required about $300,000 in assets. By reducing the number of new stores from 10 to 5, asset requirements would be cut by $1,500,000. In the short run, that option seemed most attractive, but the longer-run effects were detrimental. Curtailing expansion required the company to abandon prime locations that would then be seized by major competitors. Future expansion would also be hurt, as Diane's would be forced to accept less desirable sites at some later time. Therefore, cutting back was an unsatisfactory alternative.

The projected 40 percent increase in 1988 accounts payable over the previous year implied an 87-day average payables period. This was in contrast to the 62 days of 1987 and the 60 days of 1986. Mr. Kirlyman found that assumption unacceptable. If payables were to remain outstanding for nearly 90 days, suppliers would retaliate by delaying shipments and possibly even refusing to ship. In the past, suppliers complained whenever the average payment approached 62 days but still considered Diane's an excellent customer. In addition, the projection prevented the firm from taking cash discounts.

From its beginning, the firm had banked with First Norfolk of Virginia, a local institution serving only the immediate area. Additional short-term funds were available from the bank at a rate of 12 percent; however, Diane's was reluctant to increase its borrowing. It would do so only if no other sources could be located. One possibility Mr. Kirlyman wished to explore was commercial paper. He also considered factoring receivables or pledging them as security for a loan.

Diane's contractual agreement with its long-term lender, Tidewater Insurance, precluded any additional long-term borrowing without prior approval. The insurance company indicated it would not look favorably on such an increase at this time.

The Board of Directors of Diane's had flatly stated that there would be no new issuance of common stock. With the price at a four-year low, they were convinced it would take 18 months for the stock to rebound. They had discussed selling preferred shares, but had abandoned the idea due to the nondeductibility of preferred dividends.

Selected ratios for the women's ready-to-wear industry are presented in Exhibit 13.4.

EXHIBIT 13.1

Diane's of Virginia

Balance Sheet as of January 31 (In Thousands)

	1986	1987	1988
Assets:			
Cash	$ 1,504	$ 1,515	$ 1,100
Accounts Receivable	5,664	6,213	8,200
Less: Bad-Debt Allowance	(169)	(173)	(200)
Inventories	8,064	9,314	11,500
Prepaid Expenses	408	438	400
Total Current Assets	$15,471	$17,307	$21,000
Gross Fixed Assets	12,695	13,231	17,000
Less: Accumulated Depreciation	(5,634)	(6,012)	(7,000)
Total Fixed Assets	$ 7,061	$ 7,219	$10,000
Other Assets	309	412	300
Total Assets	$22,841	$24,938	$31,300
Liabilities and Stockholders' Equity:			
Accounts Payable	$ 8,617	$ 9,667	$15,500
Notes Payable, Bank	1,857	1,817	2,000
Current Maturity, Long-Term Debt	275	275	275
Accruals, Including Taxes	404	646	225
Total Current Liabilities	$11,153	$12,405	$18,000
Long-Term Debt	4,850	4,575	4,300
Total Liabilities	$16,003	$16,980	$22,300
Stockholders' Equity			
Common Stock, $1.00 Par	$ 360	$ 360	$ 360
Paid-in Capital	460	460	460
Retained Earnings	6,018	7,138	8,180
Total Stockholders' Equity	$ 6,838	$ 7,958	$ 9,000
Total Liabilities and Stockholders' Equity	$22,841	$24,938	$31,300

Note: Data for 1988 are on a pro forma basis.

EXHIBIT 13.2

Diane's of Virginia

Income Statements for the Years Ending January 31
(In Thousands)

	1986	1987	1988
Gross Sales	$70,878	$76,564	$86,000
Sales Discounts	569	596	800
Net Sales	$70,309	$75,968	$85,200
Cost of Sales	51,276	55,848	63,900
Gross Profit	$19,033	$20,120	$21,300
Operating Expenses			
General, Selling, and Administrative (Including Interest)	13,654	14,946	16,600
Net Income Before Taxes	$ 5,379	$ 5,174	$ 4,700
Federal and State Income Taxes	1,994	1,870	1,800
Net Income	$ 3,385	$ 3,304	$ 2,900
Depreciation	$ 575	$ 633	$ 700

Note: Data for 1988 are on a pro forma basis.

EXHIBIT 13.3

Diane's of Virginia

Number of Stores at the End of the Fiscal Year

Year	Number	Year	Number
1988 (est.)	95	1982	70
1987	85	1981	68
1986	80	1980	66
1985	77	1979	66
1984	75	1978	64
1983	72		

EXHIBIT 13.4

Diane's of Virginia

Selected Ratios for the Women's Ready-to-wear Industry for the Following Calendar Periods

	1984	1985	1986	1987
Liquidity:				
1. Current Ratio	2.0	2.0	2.0	2.1
2. Acid Test	0.7	0.7	0.7	0.7
3. Current Assets/Total Assets (%)	75.9	75.1	76.0	76.1
Activity:				
4. Receivables Turnover	18.0	19.6	21.8	24.3
5. Cost of Goods Sold/Inventory	3.9	3.5	3.4	3.5
6. Net Sales/Net Working Capital	4.0	6.7	7.3	7.0
7. Net Sales/Total Assets	2.6	2.5	2.6	2.6
Leverage:				
8. Total Debt/Total Assets (%)	55.2	54.5	57.6	56.6
9. Debt/Net Worth	1.2	1.2	1.4	1.3
10. EBIT/Interest	3.3	2.4	2.4	2.0
Profitability:				
11. COGS/Net Sales (%)	59.2	59.1	59.5	60.5
12. Operating Profit/Net Sales (%)	2.7	2.6	3.2	2.5
13. Profit Before Taxes/Net Sales (%)	2.7	2.6	2.5	2.3
14. Profit Before Taxes/Total Assets (%)	6.3	5.6	5.8	4.9
15. Profit Before Taxes/Net Worth (%)	15.7	13.3	14.4	12.2

QUESTIONS

1. Discuss the use of the firm's accounts receivable as a source of financing. (In answering this question, consider what amount of funds the firm is likely to receive, assuming it does not presently pledge accounts receivable.)

2. Explain the characteristics of the commercial paper market. (In answering this question, consider the viability of commercial paper as a source of funds.)

3. Describe the advantages and disadvantages of inventory financing. (In answering this question, consider what problems might arise should Diane's inventory be used for secured loans.)

4. Discuss the advantages and disadvantages of Diane's projected buildup of accounts payable.

5. Assume that Mr. Kirlyman has decided to take advantage of cash discounts of 3 percent if paid in 15 days and that suppliers allow Diane's 45 days on average to pay its bills. Answer the following:

   (a) What savings will Diane's realize in fiscal 1988 from taking the discount?

   (b) Calculate the amount of funds the firm will need if Mr. Kirlyman takes all discounts and the cost in dollars of these funds. (In answering this question, assume an unsecured borrowing rate of 12 percent.)

   (c) Discuss whether or not Diane's would be able to obtain the short-term bank financing necessary to take advantage of the cash discounts.

6. Comment on the policy of the Board of Directors prohibiting the issuance of either common or preferred stock at the time of the case.

7. What specific proposals should Mr. Kirlyman propose for fiscal 1988?

Case 14

Border Battery and Cable, Inc.
BANK LENDING

In late February 1988, Denise Myerson, loan officer and assistant vice-president of the Second United National Bank of El Paso, Texas, was reviewing and evaluting the financial statements of Border Battery. The bank, the largest in West Texas, had just completed a merger. However, with fast-breaking changes in the industry, management was determined to maintain an aggressive stance in securing new business. Comparative balance sheets and a statement of income and retained earnings are included as Exhibit 14.1 and Exhibit 14.2. Exhibit 14.3 is a statement of changes in financial position.

The owner of Border Battery, Carlos Hitera, had contacted Ms. Myerson about transferring the firm's bank accounts to Second United National. The change was contingent upon the bank granting a loan of between $250,000 and $300,000. The proceeds were to be used to finance inventory and equipment. Ms. Myerson had known Mr. Hitera for eight years, and during that time, she found him to be honest and reliable. She also knew he was the driving force behind Border Battery and that the firm was a success due to his efforts. Since Mr. Hitera was in excellent health and in his late thirties, she felt he was fully capable of running the firm for another 20 years.

Border Battery was a manufacturer of battery terminals and cable sets for the automotive replacement parts industry. The company had been in operation since 1976 and had enjoyed reasonable success with relatively strong growth in terms of both physical units and sales dollars. The firm's major competition came from national as well as regional manufacturers, with two competitors located in Texas, one in Oklahoma, and one in New Mexico. The dealers representing national firms handled a full line of automotive parts. Since Border Battery did not produce a full line and was not known nationally, the firm was forced to sell at lower prices even though the quality of its products was on a comparable level. Since all the manufacturers in the region produced a nonbranded product, their competition was based entirely on price.

Border Battery sold its output over the western half of the United States, primarily through warehouse distributors or large merchandising houses. The warehouse distributors marketed through parts jobbers, who, in turn, sold to service stations, the retail trade, and wagon distributors. The large merchandising houses were called on by company sales people.

The major manufacturing process, structured as an assembly line, was die casting. In addition, there were wire processing and punch press operations.

Ms. Myerson noted that the firm was moderately profitable through the first quarter of 1986 but had encountered difficulties during the second quarter. By the end of the third quarter, Border Battery was operating at a loss, which greatly accelerated during the fourth quarter.

In the face of this deteriorating situation, Mr. Hitera decided to take action: finished goods inventory was reduced to a minimum; overhead costs were cut to the bone; and some employees were dismissed. One problem that continued to plague Mr. Hitera was the level of raw materials inventory. During 1986, the company had taken advantage of the opportunity to purchase raw materials at low prices. Anticipating strong sales in 1987, it reasoned that the low prices would more than offset the greater carrying costs. With sluggish sales in 1987, the firm was unable to liquidate the inventory quickly. Mr. Hitera wanted to sell off a portion of it but could not find buyers willing to pay a reasonable price. Mr. Hitera defined a reasonable price as at least 80 percent of cost. Net profit before taxes, fourth quarter 1987, and a projected balance sheet for December 31, 1988 are included as Exhibit 14.4 and Exhibit 14.5.

Conversations with industry officials revealed that the last year had been characterized by excess production in the industry. Any attempt by Border Battery to raise prices was thwarted by its competitors. It was difficult to determine how long this condition would last. The last time this occurred, it took about 18 months to bring demand and supply into a more reasonable balance.

Ms. Myerson promised Mr. Hitera that she would have a decision on his loan request within one week. In making that decision, it was important that she take into consideration the personal wealth of Mr. Hitera. In all probability, if granted the loan, he would shift his personal bank balances to Second United National.

Selected ratios for motor vehicle parts and accessories manufacturers are presented as Exhibit 14.6.

EXHIBIT 14.1

Border Battery and Cable, Inc.

Comparative Balance Sheets as of December 31

	1986	1987
Assets:		
Cash on hand and in banks	$ 29,910	$ 27,465
Accounts Receivable	22,185	35,337
Inventory		
Raw Materials	174,444	406,965
Work-in-Process	46,066	21,411
Finished Goods	36,593	16,341
Supplies	3,501	1,836
Prepaid Expenses	3,261	3,927
Total Current Assets	$315,960	$513,282
Machinery and Equipment	$261,552	$270,714
Vehicles	12,387	34,797
Furniture and Fixtures	8,004	8,970
Leasehold Improvements	16,014	17,322
Less: Accumulated Depreciation	(88,092)	(131,388)
Total Fixed Assets	$209,865	$200,415
Total Assets	$525,825	$713,697
Liabilities and Stockholders' Equity:		
Accounts Payable	$134,207	$288,474
Notes Payable, Bank	115,000	215,000
Accruals	16,560	14,680
Total Current Liabilities	$265,767	$518,154
Stockholders' Equity		
Capital Stock ($1.00 Par,	$170,000	$170,000
180,000 shares authorized,		
170,000 shares outstanding)		
Retained Earnings	90,058	25,543
Total Stockholders' Equity	$260,058	$195,543
Total Liabilities and Stockholders' Equity	$525,825	$713,697

EXHIBIT 14.2

Border Battery and Cable, Inc.

Statement of Income and Retained Earnings for the Year Ending December 31, 1987

Sales	$1,998,156
Returns and Allowances	4,998
Net Sales	$1,993,158
Cost of Goods Sold	1,665,588
Gross Profit	$ 327,570
Operating Expenses	
Selling and Administrative	372,966
Net Loss from Operations	$ (45,396)
Interest	19,119
Net Loss	$ (64,515)
Retained Earnings, Beginning of Year	90,058
Less: Net Loss, 1987	(64,515)
Retained Earnings, End of Year	$ 25,543

EXHIBIT 14.3

Border Battery and Cable, Inc.

Statement of Changes in Financial Position for the Year Ending December 31, 1987

Additions to Working Capital:		
Amounts deducted in arriving at net income that require no outlay of working capital		
Depreciation		$ 43,296
Deductions from Working Capital:		
Net Loss for the Year	$64,515	
Amount Expended for the		
Purchase of Fixed Assets	33,846	$ 98,361
Net Decrease in Working Capital		$(55,065)

The Position of Working Capital on December 31, 1986 and December 31, 1987 Is Indicated by the Following Tabulation:

	1986	1987	Change
Current Assets	$315,960	$513,282	$197,322
Current Liabilities	265,767	518,154	252,387
Net Working Capital	$ 50,193	$ (4,872)	$ (55,065)

EXHIBIT 14.4

Border Battery and Cable, Inc.

Net Profit before Taxes, Fourth Quarter 1987

	Actual	Projected
Net Sales	$429,954	$558,000
Less: Cost of Goods Sold	372,255	451,980
Gross Profit	$ 57,699	$106,020
Operating Expenses		
Selling	$ 32,943	$ 30,747
General and Administrative	55,566	46,119
Operating Income (Loss)	$(30,810)	$ 29,154
Other Income (Loss)	(9,486)	7,200
Other Expenses	20,298	15,840
Income (Loss) Before Taxes	$(60,594)	$ 20,514

EXHIBIT 14.5

Border Battery and Cable, Inc.

Projected Balance Sheet as of December 31, 1988
(As Forecasted by Mr. Hitera)

Assets:	
Cash	$ 35,500
Accounts Receivable, Net	32,400
Inventory	270,000
Other Current	22,700
Total Current Assets	$360,600
Fixed Assets, Net	237,000
Total Assets	$597,600
Liabilities and Stockholders' Equity:	
Accounts Payable	$123,400
Notes Payable, Bank	225,000
Accruals	7,200
Total Liabilities	$355,600
Stockholders' Equity	
Common Stock	$170,000
Retained Earnings	72,000
Total Stockholders' Equity	$242,000
Total Liabilities and Stockholders' Equity	$597,600

EXHIBIT 14.6

Border Battery and Cable, Inc.

*Selected Ratios for Motor Vehicle Parts and Accessories
Manufacturers for the Following Calendar Periods*

	1985	1986	1987	1988
Liquidity:				
1. Current Ratio	1.9	2.0	2.0	1.8
2. Acid Test	0.9	0.8	0.8	0.8
3. Current Assets/Total Assets (%)	69.7	66.5	68.4	64.8
Activity:				
4. Receivables Turnover	8.8	8.1	8.5	8.7
5. Cost of Goods Sold/Inventory	4.2	4.4	4.2	4.7
6. Net Sales/Net Working Capital	6.9	6.6	6.3	7.7
7. Net Sales/Total Assets	2.2	2.0	1.9	1.9
Leverage:				
8. Total Debt/Total Assets (%)	55.1	52.9	54.6	56.3
9. Debt/Net Worth	1.3	1.2	1.1	1.3
10. EBIT/Interest	4.4	2.5	2.8	2.2
Profitability:				
11. COGS/Net Sales (%)	72.6	73.7	74.7	73.2
12. Operating Profit/Net Sales (%)	6.4	4.8	5.7	4.2
13. Profit Before Taxes/Net Sales (%)	5.3	3.2	4.4	2.7
14. Profit Before Taxes/Total Assets (%)	11.0	6.4	7.0	5.3
15. Profit Before Taxes/Net Worth (%)	24.2	15.4	17.2	12.5

QUESTIONS

1. Summarize the information, favorable and unfavorable, to Border Battery, that is available to Ms. Myerson. (Data from the exhibits should be included.)
2. Discuss the pros and cons of making the loan from the point of view of Second United National.
3. Specify the terms of the loan, if it is made, and prepare a plan for its payback.
4. What reasons would Ms. Myerson give to Mr. Hitera if the loan is rejected?
5. Explain in detail whether or not the account should be accepted and the loan granted.

The Music Shop
LOAN STRATEGY

Harley Rosen, a vice-president in charge of the commercial loan department at Marin National Bank, San Rafael, California, was reviewing correspondence and financial data from The Music Shop. In a letter to Igor Kipple, president and owner of the firm, Mr. Rosen had suggested a meeting to discuss the firm's operating situation and to determine if the firm should restructure its bank debt. At that time, debt consisted of short-term notes payable, with maturities ranging from 90 to 120 days.

The Music Shop was founded in 1954 by Ivan Kipple, the father of the current owner. The company was a retailer of organs and pianos as well as a complete line of other musical instruments. The elder Mr. Kipple operated the business until he died suddenly of a heart attack in 1979. His 35-year-old son, Igor, who was sales manager, then assumed the presidency. The younger Mr. Kipple had worked in all phases of company operations since graduating in 1966 as a fine arts major from the University of California at Davis. The company had banked with Marin National since its inception. The Kipple family had also banked there for more than 40 years.

In checking the records, Mr. Rosen noted the bank had committed significant sums of money to The Music Shop over the last 10 years. As of December 31, 1983, $400,000 was owed to the bank. Of that amount $300,000 was in short-term notes, half to be used to finance the accounts receivable generated by the sale of pianos and organs. The other $100,000 was unsecured and utilized for a home music center. With this financial backing, the company had attained high levels of profitability through fiscal 1984.

The Music Shop was well established in both San Rafael and Marin County, carving out a significant market in its major project lines, especially pianos and organs. Marin County, located directly north of San Francisco, had one of the highest per capita incomes in the country. During the previous six years, several large shopping malls had been built in the area. Included in those malls were two competitors, but still the company continued to be successful.

In fiscal 1985, the firm experienced a turnaround and suffered an operating loss, its first since 1960. Mr. Rosen's analysis revealed a number of causes. First, there was a marked increase in salaries. He doubted that this could be justified in light of narrowing profit margins. Second, advertising costs increased by about $45,000. Mr. Kipple had said, however, that those additional costs were necessary to meet the increased competition, but would not expand sales.

In making his study, Mr. Rosen noted that depreciation and out-of-pocket expenses were normal. Accounts receivable also had remained at the same level for the past two years. Due to the fact that the ratio of sales to total receivables was below the industry average, there was apprehension on the part of Mr. Rosen that the total receivables figure included an increasing percentage of contracts rejected by lenders but carried on the company books. Mr. Rosen mentioned that fact to Mr. Kipple.

In regard to the inventory account, Mr. Rosen concluded that the extra inventory added in fiscal 1984 was not justified by the increase in sales. The overall industry turnover seemed reasonable, but Mr. Rosen believed it would be better if turnover ratios were calculated for each of the major project lines. He suspected that this would indicate that some lines carried a large amount of dead stock. Mr. Kipple said the new system of inventory control should improve the turnover situation.

It seemed to Mr. Rosen that trade payables were satisfactory in fiscal 1985. He knew, however, that any decrease in the collection of receivables would cause uncertainties with payables.

Even with these problems, Mr. Rosen believed that, as of April 30, 1985, the firm was operating on a sound basis, with good depth of management and a solid financial foundation. He knew The Music Shop marketed quality products and maintained a mutually beneficial relationship with Marin National Bank.

During 1986 Mr. Kipple reported that the firm would close one of two major locations. The proceeds were to be applied to reducing the outstanding bank debt. He also stated that The Music Shop was current with all suppliers and was only in debt to the bank. Mr. Kipple felt the 1986 slump could be weathered and the firm would be stronger than ever.

Operating losses actually increased in fiscal 1986, but the company rebounded the next year to produce a slight profit. However, other income (the net earnings from carrying customer receivables less interest costs) declined drastically in fiscal 1987. The decrease occurred due to higher interest rates and to the fact that customers chose to finance big-ticket items at financial institutions instead of the firm. By the beginning of fiscal 1988, almost no customer financing was taking place.

In May 1988, Mr. Rosen received the information included in Exhibit 15.1, Exhibit 15.2, Exhibit 15.3, Exhibit 15.4, Exhibit 15.5, and Exhibit 15.6. In light of these statements, Mr. Rosen wrote to Mr. Kipple, commenting on the condition of the firm and on the steps needed to return The Music Shop to a profitable basis.

Selected ratios for muscial instruments and supplies retailers are presented as Exhibit 15.7.

EXHIBIT 15.1

The Music Shop

Aging of Accounts Receivable and Inventory as of
April 30, 1988

Accounts Receivable		*Current Inventory When Bought*	
Current to 30 days	45%	January to November 1987	60%
30 to 60 days	12%		
60 to 90 days	5%	1986	33%
90 to 120 days	4%		
over 120 days	34%	1985 or older	7%
	100%		100%

EXHIBIT 15.2

The Music Shop

Balance Sheets as of April 30

	1985	1986	1987	1988
Assets:				
Cash	$ 93,972	$ 7,365	$ 10,815	$ 21,417
Accounts Receivable	129,024	142,386	156,903	155,433
Merchandise Inventory	686,028	712,986	677,160	536,805
Prepaid Expenses	5,550	4,401	3,405	2,256
Cash Value, Insurance	8,034	11,076	13,758	20,292
Total Current Assets	$ 922,608	$ 878,214	$ 862,041	$ 736,203
Fixed Assets, Net	395,070	535,587	488,766	458,199
Due from Officers	2,244	453	13,605	52,158
Finance Reserves	20,232	18,891	18,993	14,166
Total Assets	$1,340,154	$1,433,145	$1,383,405	$1,260,726
Liabilities and Stockholders' Equity:				
Accounts Payable	$ 181,935	$ 137,760	$ 175,809	$ 174,057
Notes Payable, Banks	178,959	407,286	321,207	271,544
Income Taxes Payable	14,550	9,261	7,614	0
Accruals	130,770	0	21,060	10,698
Due Officers	24,144	46,941	9,708	0
Total Current Liabilities	$ 530,358	$ 601,248	$ 535,398	$ 456,299
Stockholders' Equity				
Common Stock	225,000	225,000	225,000	225,000
Retained Earnings	584,796	606,897	623,007	606,427
Treasury Stock	0	0	0	(27,000)
Total Stockholders' Equity	$ 809,796	$ 831,897	$ 848,007	$ 804,427
Total Liabilities and Stockholders' Equity	$1,340,154	$1,433,145	$1,383,405	$1,260,726

EXHIBIT 15.3

The Music Shop

Income Statements for the Years Ending April 30

	1985	1986	1987	1988
Sales	$2,588,619	$2,886,999	$2,468,490	$2,321,448
Cost of Goods Sold	1,772,958	1,961,817	1,543,017	1,498,506
Gross Profit	$ 815,661	$ 925,182	$ 925,473	$ 822,942
Operating Expenses	816,627	943,857	919,044	820,665
Operating Profit	$ (966)	$ (18,675)	$ 6,429	$ 2,277
Other Income (Expense)	59,034	51,837	18,825	(23,004)
Net Income Before Taxes	$ 58,068	$ 33,162	$ 25,254	$ (20,727)
Federal and State Taxes	14,547	11,061	9,144	(4,147)
Net Income	$ 43,521	$ 22,101	$ 16,110	$ (16,580)
Depreciation	$ 68,800	$ 89,200	$ 77,200	$ 73,200

EXHIBIT 15.4

The Music Shop

Selected Company Ratios as of April 30

	1985	1986	1987	1988
Quick	0.24	0.25	0.33	0.39
Current	1.74	1.46	1.61	1.61
Debt to Worth	0.65	0.72	0.63	0.57
Sales to Receivables	20.06	20.28	15.73	14.94
Cost of Sales to Inventory	2.58	2.75	2.28	2.79
Profit to Sales	0.017	0.007	0.006	(0.007)
Profit to Worth	0.054	0.027	0.019	(0.021)
Officers' Compensation to Sales	0.058	0.052	0.061	0.065

EXHIBIT 15.5

The Music Shop

Balance Sheet Projections, Proposed by Management, as of
April 30 (In Thousands)

	1989	1990	1991	1992
Assets:				
Cash	$ 84	$ 87	$ 69	$ 102
Receivables, Net	198	204	222	234
Inventory	567	567	567	597
Cash Value, Life Insurance	21	21	21	21
Total Current Assets	$ 870	$ 879	$ 879	$ 954
Fixed Assets, Net	420	384	348	312
Miscellaneous Assets	69	69	69	69
Total Assets	$1,359	$1,332	$1,296	$1,335
Liabilities and Stockholders' Equity:				
Accounts Payable	$ 129	$ 134	$ 147	$ 153
Notes Payable, Bank	348	296	201	174
Accruals	12	12	12	12
Total Current Liabilities	$ 489	$ 442	$ 360	$ 339
Stockholders' Equity				
Capital Stock	$ 225	$ 225	$ 225	$ 225
Retained Earnings	645	665	711	771
Total Stockholders' Equity	$ 870	$ 890	$ 936	$ 996
Total Liabilities and Stockholders' Equity	$1,359	$1,332	$1,296	$1,335

EXHIBIT 15.6

The Music Shop

Income Projections, Proposed by Management, for the Year
Ending April 30 (In Thousands)

	1989	1990	1991	1992
Net Sales	$2,330	$2,475	$2,650	$2,800
Cost of Goods Sold	1,520	1,610	1,725	1,825
Gross Profit	$ 810	$ 865	$ 885	$ 927
Operating Expenses	798	845	885	927
Net Operating Profit	$ 12	$ 20	$ 40	$ 48
Interest Expense	34	30	21	18
Other Expense (Income)	(38)	(30)	(27)	(30)
Net Income Before Taxes	$ 16	$ 20	$ 46	$ 60
Depreciation	$ 70	$ 60	$ 50	$ 50

EXHIBIT 15.7

The Music Shop

*Selected Ratios for Musical Instruments and Supplies Retailers
for the Following Calendar Periods*

	1984	1985	1986	1987
Liquidity:				
1. Current Ratio	1.65	1.67	1.72	1.70
2. Acid Test	0.34	0.41	0.42	0.42
3. Current Assets/Total Assets (%)	82.3	79.7	83.2	83.4
Activity:				
4. Receivables Turnover	20.2	21.0	17.2	18.7
5. Cost of Goods Sold/Inventory	2.00	2.22	2.24	2.16
6. Net Sales/Net Working Capital	7.0	7.6	6.4	6.8
7. Net Sales/Total Assets	2.0	2.2	2.2	2.0
Leverage:				
8. Total Debt/Total Assets (%)	66.7	66.5	64.0	63.7
9. Debt/Net Worth	2.00	2.22	1.91	1.98
10. EBIT/Interest	2.1	2.0	2.0	2.0
Profitability:				
11. COGS/Net Sales (%)	61.5	60.7	61.0	59.9
12. Operating Profit/Net Sales (%)	3.0	3.0	4.2	2.9
13. Profit Before Taxes/Net Sales (%)	3.6	3.8	4.0	4.0
14. Profit Before Taxes/Total Assets (%)	5.6	4.5	4.6	4.5
15. Profit Before Taxes/Net Worth (%)	9.0	9.4	10.7	10.8
16. Officers' Compensation/Sales (%)	4.3	5.1	5.2	4.4

QUESTIONS

1. List the major characteristics of the operating situation at The Music Shop from the viewpoint of Harley Rosen.
2. List the major characteristics of the operating situation at The Music Shop from the viewpoint of Igor Kipple.
3. How should Mr. Rosen prepare for the meeting with Mr. Kipple?
4. How should Mr. Kipple prepare for the meeting with Mr. Rosen?
5. What type of plan should Mr. Rosen devise for restructuring the firm's bank debt? (Be sure to include the most crucial variables in the plan.)
6. What limits are imposed on Mr. Rosen in dealing with Mr. Kipple?

PART III

CAPITAL
BUDGETING

Case 16

Autin Industries
MATHEMATICS OF FINANCE

Autin Industries was a large, diversified manufacturer of industrial machinery headquartered in Houma, Louisiana. Plants and sales offices were located throughout the United States and in several foreign countries. Machinery manufactured included paper, stitching, wrapping, and special-purpose machines for industry.

Each spring, the board of directors of Autin Industries reviewed investment proposals for the following year. Their decisions were critical to the future of the firm.

Robert Johnson, a recent business administration graduate from the University of Mississippi, was helping to prepare the annual review. The first step in the process was to assemble from each plant a list of proposals, including the supporting raw data.

The second step involved converting the raw data into relevant data. To accomplish this, Mr. Johnson had to determine the net investment and the after-tax cash flows for each proposal. Net investment not only took into account the initial outlay, but also installation costs, salvage values, and taxes as well. After-tax cash flows were determined by subtracting corporate income taxes from the revenues generated by the proposals. The next step was to discount the after-tax cash flows and to combine the result with the net investment.

Proposal 348 involved installation of a new machine at the Knoxville, Tennessee plant. It was anticipated that labor savings from the proposed machine would result in increased productivity. The net investment amounted to $51,500. After-tax cash flows had been calculated as $20,400 for the first four years and $30,800 in the fifth year. The discount rate in all cases was 12 percent. The relevant data are shown in Exhibit 16.1.

Proposal 730 involved a cost-reduction program at the Valdosta, Georgia plant, in which the employee responsible for the idea was given a percentage of the total savings for the first five years. The lump-sum payment was included in the net investment of $44,300. The after-tax cash flows were $18,500 per year for the first five years and $20,300 for the next five years. The relevant data are shown in Exhibit 16.2.

Proposal 937 and Proposal 949 were two possibilities for a new machine at the Conway, Arkansas plant. The net investment for Proposal 937 was $40,500. After-tax cash flows were $7,600 for the first nine years and $9,600 in year 10. The net investment for Proposal 949 was $28,500. After-tax cash flows were $6,600 for the first nine years and $9,000 in year 10. Since the proposals were mutually exclusive, Robert decided to subtract Proposal 949 from Proposal 937. The incremental net investment was $12,000. Incremental after-tax cash flows were $1,000 for the first nine years and $600 in year 10. The relevant data are shown in Exhibit 16.3.

Proposal 710 required expenditures for pollution control equipment at the Syracuse, New York plant. The proposal called for an immediate cost of $200,000 and after-tax cash flows of −$50,000, −$70,000, −$150,000, −$92,000, and −$176,000, respectively, during a five-year period. No specific revenues were associated with this proposal. The relevant data are shown in Exhibit 16.4.

A balance sheet and an income statement are included as Exhibit 16.5 and Exhibit 16.6. Selected ratios for special industry machinery manufacturers are presented as Exhibit 16.7.

EXHIBIT 16.1

Autin Industries

Projected Cash Flows for
Proposal 348 (In Dollars)

Year	Cash flows
0	−51,500
1	+20,400
2	+20,400
3	+20,400
4	+20,400
5	+30,800

EXHIBIT 16.2

Autin Industries

*Projected Cash Flows for
Proposal 730 (In Dollars)*

Year	Cash flows
0	−44,300
1	+18,500
2	+18,500
3	+18,500
4	+18,500
5	+18,500
6	+20,300
7	+20,300
8	+20,300
9	+20,300
10	+20,300

EXHIBIT 16.3

Autin Industries

Projected Cash Flows for Proposals 937 and 949 (In Dollars)

Year	Proposal 937	Proposal 949	Proposal (937 − 949)
0	−40,500	−28,500	−12,000
1	+7,600	+6,600	+1,000
2	+7,600	+6,600	+1,000
3	+7,600	+6,600	+1,000
4	+7,600	+6,600	+1,000
5	+7,600	+6,600	+1,000
6	+7,600	+6,600	+1,000
7	+7,600	+6,600	+1,000
8	+7,600	+6,600	+1,000
9	+7,600	+6,600	+1,000
10	+9,600	+9,000	+600

EXHIBIT 16.4

Autin Industries

*Projected Cash Flows for
Proposal 710 (In Dollars)*

Year	Cash flows
0	−200,000
1	−50,000
2	−70,000
3	−150,000
4	−92,000
5	−176,000

EXHIBIT 16.5

Autin Industries

Balance Sheet as of September 30, 1988

Assets:	
Cash	$ 60,834
Accounts Receivable	218,525
Inventory	279,539
Other Current Assets	16,850
Total Current Assets	$575,568
Fixed Assets, Net	$189,118
Other Assets	35,772
Total Assets	$800,458
Liabilities and Stockholders' Equity:	
Accounts Payable	$ 71,208
Accruals	63,156
Notes Payable	45,500
Current Maturities of Long-Term Debt	20,800
Total Current Liabilities	$200,664
Long-Term Debt	$110,770
Stockholders' Equity	
Common Stock, $2 Par	$ 25,360
Paid-in Capital	79,370
Retained Earnings	384,364
Total Stockholders' Equity	$489,094
Total Liabilities and Stockholders' Equity	$800,458

EXHIBIT 16.6

Autin Industries

Income Statements for the Years Ending September 30
(In Thousands)

	1987	1988
Net Sales	$1,406,000	$1,432,200
Cost of Goods Sold	1,036,219	1,010,846
Gross Profit	$ 369,781	$ 421,354
Operating Expenses	300,043	344,026
Operating Profit	$ 69,738	$ 77,325
Other Expenses, Including Interest	22,776	25,769
Net Profit Before Taxes	$ 46,962	$ 51,559
Federal and State Income Taxes	18,178	20,602
Net Profit	$ 28,784	$ 30,957

EXHIBIT 16.7

Autin Industries

Selected Ratios for Special Industry Machinery Manufacturers
for the Following Calendar Periods

	1984	1985	1986	1987
Liquidity:				
1. Current Ratio	1.7	1.8	1.8	1.9
2. Acid Test	0.8	0.8	0.9	0.9
3. Current Assets/Total Assets (%)	69.9	69.3	68.4	65.4
Activity:				
4. Receivables Turnover	6.6	6.9	7.2	8.1
5. Cost of Goods Sold/Inventory	3.3	3.5	3.8	4.0
6. Net Sales/Net Working Capital	6.3	6.1	6.4	6.3
7. Net Sales/Total Assets	1.7	1.7	1.7	1.7
Leverage:				
8. Total Debt/Total Assets (%)	57.7	56.6	56.9	55.5
9. Debt/Net Worth	1.4	1.2	1.3	1.2
10. EBIT/Interest	4.4	3.9	3.3	2.2

EXHIBIT 16.7 (Continued)

	1984	1985	1986	1987
Profitability:				
11. COGS/Net Sales (%)	70.1	70.1	70.0	69.5
12. Operating Profit/Net Sales (%)	6.7	7.1	6.3	4.3
13. Profit Before Taxes/Net Sales (%)	5.7	6.0	5.0	2.9
14. Profit Before Taxes/Total Assets (%)	9.4	10.0	7.8	5.5
15. Profit Before Taxes/Net Worth (%)	24.2	22.8	19.8	13.3

QUESTIONS

1. For Proposal 348, calculate the present value of the stream of cash flows:
   (a) Using present value factors for each of the 5 years.
   (b) Using a present value of an annuity factor for the first 4 years and a present value factor for year 5.
   (c) Using a present value of an annuity factor for the 5 years and a present value factor for year 5.
2. For Proposal 348, determine the interest rate such that the present value for years 0 through 5 is approximately equal to zero.
3. For Proposal 730, calculate the present value of the stream of cash flows:
   (a) Using present value factors for each of the 10 years.
   (b) Using a present value of an annuity factor for the first 5 years and present value factors for years 6 through 10.
   (c) Using a present value of an annuity factor for the first 5 years and a present value of an annuity factor for years 6 through 10, discounting the second annuity to year 0 with a present value factor.
4. For Proposal 937, calculate the present value of the stream of cash flows using a present value of an annuity factor for the first 9 years and a present value factor for year 10.
5. For Proposal 937, calculate the present value of the stream of cash flows using a present value of an annuity factor for the first 9 years and a present value factor for year 10.
6. For Proposal 937 − 949, calculate the present value of the stream of cash flows using a present value of an annuity factor of the first 9 years and a present value factor for year 10.
7. Compare the present values calculated for Proposals 937 and 949 with the present value for Proposal 937 − 949.

8. For Proposal 710, calculate the present value of the stream of cash flows using present value factors for each of the 5 years.

9. For Proposal 348, Proposal 730, Proposal 937, and Proposal 710, calculate the present values of the streams of cash flows using Lotus 1-2-3.

Dalton Textile Corporation
CAPITAL BUDGETING,
CERTAINTY-BASIC

Dalton Textile Corporation was a medium-sized manufacturer of nylon yarns. In a wide denier range the product was used in the production of clothing, carpet, and tires. Founded in Dalton, Georgia, in 1926, the company had grown to 10 locations in the Southeast and Southwest by 1988. With increased imports of foreign textiles into the United States, the profitability of the company had declined, motivating management to implement profit improvement programs.

Kathy Smith accepted a management trainee position at the Greenville, South Carolina plant after receiving a business administration degree from the University of Alabama. Her first assignment was to spend a week or two in each of the main areas of the plant. She felt uncomfortable at first wearing a hard hat and safety glasses, but she was determined not to let that, or the heat and the noise, bother her.

In the spinning department she watched the hot nylon being forced through spinnerettes into individual filaments. The nylon was then wound by the spinning machine onto large sleeves. After trying it herself, she was amazed at the dexterity of the machine operators. In the next operation, the sleeves were removed from the machine and sent to the denier check station.

Sally Lett was the senior denier checker, having been with the company for eight years. She approached Kathy with an idea. "I can save $50,000 a year," she said.

"How, Sally?" Kathy asked.

"Easy. All you have to do is rig up a machine to reel one cart while I'm checking the other," she replied proudly.

"Where do you get those machines?" Kathy wondered.

"How should I know? You went to college, didn't you?"

The drawtwist department drew, twisted, and wound the nylon yarn onto bobbins. After only a week, Kathy was convinced that earplugs were necessary in noisy areas.

At the professional services department, Kathy met the engineers and technicians for the plant. Sitting at a desk most of the time, she began to think about Sally Lett's idea. "Maybe she wasn't joking." She decided to ask one of the mechanical engineers if the idea was feasible.

"Could be. I'll have to think about it," he replied. Two days later he told her it could be done for about $40,000.

In the meantime, she asked an industrial engineer how much the savings would be. Using the wage rate plus fringes, he came up with a labor savings of $20,160 per year.

At the end of the training program, Kathy began her initial assignment as a financial analyst. With so much to learn in her new job, she forgot all about Sally Lett's idea. But one day at lunch, she remembered and mentioned the proposal to her boss, Pat Jackson.

"You'll need to collect all the data first. Then I would like you to figure the payback period, the average rate of return, the internal rate of return, and the net present value."

A week later Kathy Smith had collected all the necessary data. (See Exhibit 17.1.) The initial estimates had changed somewhat.

Over coffee, she found out that the plant manager liked the payback method, but that he would discourage most projects with a payback greater than two years. This was due to the fact that he was evaluated on present earnings, not earnings projected into the future. She also learned that the business manager gave his approval to all projects with an internal rate of return 15 percent or greater.

Kathy wanted to show that the proposal should be accepted, but she was afraid the payback period would be too long to suit the plant manager. She knew another way to convince him would have to be found.

A balance sheet and an income statement are included as Exhibit 17.2 and Exhibit 17.3. Selected ratios for yarn manufacturers are presented as Exhibit 17.4.

EXHIBIT 17.1

Dalton Textile Corporation

Denier Check Proposal Data

Item	Data
Cost of equipment installed	$42,240
Net labor savings (yearly)	$19,640
Project life	5 years
Salvage value	$2,000
Tax rate	40%
Cost of capital	12%
Depreciation method	Straight line

EXHIBIT 17.2

Dalton Textile Corporation

Balance Sheet as of October 31, 1988 (In Thousands)

Assets:	
Cash	$ 5,375
Accounts Receivable	26,735
Inventory	34,219
Other Current Assets	6,258
Total Current Assets	$ 72,587
Fixed Assets, Net	$ 42,768
Other Assets	4,083
Total Assets	$119,438
Liabilities and Stockholders' Equity:	
Accounts Payable	$ 5,833
Accruals	7,644
Notes Payable	5,595
Current Maturities of Long-Term Debt	3,750
Total Current Liabilities	$ 32,822
Long-Term Debt	$ 24,480
Stockholders' Equity	
Common Stock, $5 Par	$ 5,205
Paid-in Capital	16,418
Retained Earnings	40,513
Total Stockholders' Equity	$ 62,136
Total Liabilities and Stockholders' Equity	$119,438

EXHIBIT 17.3

Dalton Textile Corporation

Income Statement for the Year Ending October 31, 1988
(In Thousands)

Net Sales	$248,833
Cost of Goods Sold	206,531
Gross Profit	$ 42,302
Operating Expenses	30,027
Operating Profit	$ 12,275
Other Expenses, Including Interest	2,076
Net Income Before Taxes	$ 10,199
Federal and State Income Taxes	3,961
Net Income After Taxes	$ 6,238

EXHIBIT 17.4

Dalton Textile Corporation

Selected Ratios for Yarn Manufacturers for the Following
Calendar Periods

	1985	1986	1987	1988
Liquidity:				
1. Current Ratio	2.0	2.0	2.0	1.6
2. Acid Test	1.0	1.0	1.0	0.9
3. Current Assets/Total Assets (%)	61.0	58.3	61.6	54.5
Activity:				
4. Receivables Turnover	10.0	8.9	9.3	9.3
5. Cost of Goods Sold/Inventory	8.3	7.6	8.3	9.1
6. Net Sales/Net Working Capital	9.2	9.7	8.1	9.8
7. Net Sales/Total Assets	2.1	2.1	2.4	2.0
Leverage:				
8. Total Debt/Total Assets (%)	43.8	51.6	52.5	54.4
9. Debt/Net Worth	0.6	0.9	1.0	1.0
10. EBIT/Interest	3.8	2.3	3.0	2.0
Profitability:				
11. COGS/Net Sales (%)	86.9	84.6	83.3	82.4
12. Operating Profit/Net Sales (%)	4.5	3.6	6.3	3.2
13. Profit Before Taxes/Net Sales (%)	3.9	2.5	3.5	1.4
14. Profit Before Taxes/Total Assets (%)	6.9	4.7	5.4	3.3
15. Profit Before Taxes/Net Worth (%)	11.8	9.0	10.7	9.1

QUESTIONS

1. Calculate earnings after taxes and cash flows for each of the five years.
2. Calculate the payback period.
3. Calculate the average rate of return.
4. Calculate the net present value.
5. Calculate the internal rate of return.
6. How would you convince the plant manager and the business manager that the proposal was justified?
7. Calculate the net present value and internal rate of return using Lotus 1-2-3.

Strong Racquet, Inc.
CAPITAL BUDGETING,
CERTAINTY-INTERMEDIATE

Strong Racquet, Inc. was a small manufacturer of tennis and badminton racquets. Founded in Trenton, New Jersey, in 1946, the company operated one plant employing 75 workers, which was located about 3 miles from its original site. A balance sheet and an income statement are included in Exhibit 18.1 and Exhibit 18.2.

As a teenager during the late 1930s, Richard Strong was a tennis sensation. At age 13, he was the number one ranked player in New Jersey for his age group. After finishing high school, he worked nights at a local chemical company. This permitted him to practice tennis several hours each day. On weekends he often drove for hours to play in tournaments.

World War II changed his life. On January 2, 1942, Richard Strong enlisted in the United States Army. At the beginning of 1945, things seemed to be going well, but Richard Strong's tennis career ended on May 19, 1945. The jeep in which he was riding hit a land mine, killing the driver. Richard Strong's right leg was severely crushed, leaving him in a London hospital for two months.

While in bed, he spent a considerable amount of time thinking about a new type of racquet. He wanted a design that would give maximum power while retaining a high degree of control. Upon release from the hospital, he was assigned to Special Services as coach of the Army's touring tennis team. He used this opportunity to experiment with his new idea.

Richard Strong was discharged from the Army on January 31, 1946. He returned home and lived with his parents, working at his father's service station. He began making tennis racquets as a hobby in his father's garage. Demand was so great that within six months, he found it necessary to rent a vacant store to expand his operations. Strong Racquet, Inc. was in business.

In 1962 after graduating from Syracuse University with a degree in business administration, Bob Strong, the son of Richard's late brother, began working for his uncle. Richard Strong, still unmarried, was anxious for his nephew to learn the business, since Bob was his only heir. Bob learned about the company by starting at the bottom, sweeping floors. As time passed and Bob's knowledge grew, Mr. Strong began to incorporate Bob's judgment into his decisions.

This did not mean, however, that Mr. Strong and Bob agreed as to the future direction of the company. Mr. Strong took the conservative view that Strong Racquet should stick with wooden tennis racquets, while Bob felt that diversification into other types of racquets was necessary. In 1975 Bob convinced Mr. Strong to enter the small but profitable badminton market.

In September 1988 Richard Strong was considering the replacement of tennis line 1. He asked Bob to study the pros and cons of such a decision. Bob found that similar equipment could be purchased from Ludwig Industries, and he asked the vendor to visit the plant to explain what options were available. The current method of manufacture involved one machine and three workers. Two men were involved in the actual production of the racquets, while one man handled packaging and case packing. The nature of the work was such that the three men could go on breaks or to lunch together without disrupting operations. This practice resulted in lasting friendships.

The present machine was installed new at a cost of $11,000. No salvage value was anticipated at the end of the expected life of 20 years. After 15 years of use, the machine could be sold for book value. Strong Racquet always calculated depreciation on a straight-line basis. The assumed rate for federal and state income taxes was 40 percent.

Ludwig offered two alternatives for replacement of the machine. A similar machine could be purchased for $18,000, with installation adding $1,000 to the cost. The expected life of that machine was also 20 years, but a $1,000 overhaul would be necessary every 5 years. At the end of 20 years, the machine could be sold for $1,000, but it would cost $400 to remove it.

The second alternative involved a more automated machine. Replacement with this equipment would result in a savings of one man, since the line could be run by two men instead of three. The men on that line were paid $8.20 per hour. In addition, they received 20 percent in fringe benefits. The plant was open on a one-shift basis 50 weeks per year, but the workers were paid for the 2-week shutdown. Replacement of the machine would involve an expenditure of $30,730. Also $1,070 would be needed for installation. The expected life of the machine was 20 years, with a $2,000 overhaul necessary every 5 years. At the end of 20 years, the machine could be sold for $2,000, but it would cost $600 to scrap it. Bob felt that either possibility offered equal production quality and quantity.

Ludwig also offered a packaging/case packing machine that could be installed in the line and would result in an additional savings of one man. Thus, the line could be run with one, two, or three men depending on which combination of machinery was purchased. The packaging/case packing machine would cost $20,600 installed. The expected life of the equipment was 20 years, with a $1,400 overhaul necessary every 5 years. No net salvage value was anticipated.

Bob was concerned about Mr. Strong's reaction to terminating workers since this had not been necessary for years. Mr. Strong's reaction was as anticipated, "Hell, no! Fred Criddle is retiring in two years and Ed Watkins in about four. If we decide to buy this new stuff—and I'm not sure we will—we'll just have to keep the same number of people on the payroll till these boys retire."

Bob Strong wanted to evaluate the various capital expenditure alternatives and planned to begin by determining earnings after tax and by calculating cash flows. Before doing so he listed the replacement proposals:

Proposal A—purchase the similar machine but not the packaging/case packing machine.

Proposal B—purchase the similar machine and the packaging/case packing machine.

Proposal C—purchase the automated machine but not the packaging/case packing machine.

Proposal D—purchase the automated machine and the packaging/case packing machine.

Bob knew that proposals B, C, and D involved a reduction in personnel. Proposals B and C would reduce labor requirements by one man and proposal D by two men. He realized those reductions in labor requirements would not change cash flows until the affected workers retired.

Selected ratios for sporting and athletic goods manufacturers are presented in Exhibit 18.3.

EXHIBIT 18.1

Strong Racquet, Inc.

Balance Sheet as of August 31, 1988 (In Thousands)

Assets:	
Cash	$ 106
Accounts Receivable	554
Inventories	792
Other Current Assets	38
Total Current Assets	$1,490
Fixed Assets, Net	300
Other Assets	42
Total Assets	$1,832
Liabilities and Stockholders' Equity:	
Accounts Payable	$ 228
Accruals	125
Notes Payable	290
Current Maturities of Long-Term Debt	55
Total Current Liabilities	$ 698
Long-Term Debt	275
Stockholders' Equity	
Common Stock, $4 Par	56
Paid-in Capital	198
Retained Earnings	605
Total Stockholders' Equity	$ 859
Total Liabilities and Stockholders' Equity	$1,832

EXHIBIT 18.2

Strong Racquet, Inc.

Income Statements as of August 31 (In Thousands)

	1987	1988
Net Sales	$2,884	$3,405
Cost of Goods Sold	2,013	2,311
Gross Profit	$ 871	$1,094
Operating Expenses	771	912
Operating Profit	$ 100	$ 182
Other Expenses, Including Interest	64	106
Net Profit Before Taxes	$ 36	$ 76
Federal and State Income Taxes	13	30
Net Profit After Taxes	$ 23	$ 46

EXHIBIT 18.3

Strong Racquet, Inc.

*Selected Ratios for Sporting and Athletic Goods Manufacturers
for the Following Calendar Periods*

	1985	1986	1987	1988
Liquidity:				
1. Current Ratio	1.9	1.8	1.8	2.0
2. Acid Test	0.8	0.8	0.7	0.7
3. Current Asscts/Total Assets (%)	76.3	74.8	73.0	71.7
Activity:				
4. Receivables Turnover	7.0	6.8	7.4	7.9
5. Cost of Goods Sold/Inventory	3.2	3.3	3.0	3.2
6. Net Sales/Net Working Capital	5.5	6.2	6.2	5.4
7. Net Sales/Total Assets	1.9	1.7	1.8	1.7
Leverage:				
8. Total Debt/Total Assets (%)	58.7	60.7	60.9	57.0
9. Debt/Net Worth	1.3	1.7	1.6	1.5
10. EBIT/Interest	3.3	2.1	2.2	2.1
Profitability:				
11. COGS/Net Sales (%)	68.0	68.5	65.9	66.9
12. Operating Profit/Net Sales (%)	7.3	5.4	6.7	6.3
13. Profit Before Taxes/Net Sales (%)	5.0	3.1	3.9	3.3
14. Profit Before Taxes/Total Assets (%)	8.3	5.0	6.5	5.2
15. Profit Before Taxes/Net Worth (%)	24.5	16.4	19.4	12.7

QUESTIONS

1. For each proposal, calculate the net investment at time zero. Then specify the amount and timing of investment required in later years.

2. For each proposal, calculate the savings compared with the present equipment during each of the 20 years. What assumptions must be made about labor savings?

3. For each proposal, calculate the depreciation for the 20 years. Expense overhauls in the indicated years.

4. For each proposal, calculate earnings after taxes for the 20 years.

5. For each proposal, calculate the effect on cash flows for the 20 years. Include investments after time zero and salvage values as necessary.

6. For each proposal, calculate the net present value and internal rate of return using Lotus 1-2-3.

Swanson Shipyards Corporation
CAPITAL BUDGETING, CERTAINTY-COMPLEX

Swanson Shipyards Corporation was engaged in the repair of marine vessels at shipyard facilities located near Charleston, South Carolina. Services were marketed through direct contacts with present and prospective customers. A balance sheet and an income statement are included as Exhibit 19.1 and Exhibit 19.2.

The company owned or leased 64 acres comprised of piers, buildings, bulkheads, wharves, cranes, and equipment necessary for the repair and overhaul of ships. In addition, the company had two drydocks, one of wood and one of steel.

Repair work ranged from relatively minor repair and hull scraping to major overhauls that often involved the drydocking of the vessel. Although the company had experienced stability in this area of operations, its business was subject to fluctuating volume due to the location of marine accidents, the availability and scheduling of maintenance overhauls, and conditions within the maritime industry as a whole.

Contracts were obtained by competitive bidding, awarded by negotiation, or assigned by customers who had a preference for a specific shipyard. Frequently, however, an accident resulted in the necessity for immediate repair. In such cases the ability to repair quickly was the overriding consideration in choosing a shipyard. On jobs that were advertised for competitive bids, owners usually furnished a set of specifications and plans that became the basis for an agreed-upon contract. Bid jobs were usually awarded on a fixed-price basis, and any added work was negotiated. Because repair jobs were of a short duration, the contracts did not contain cost-escalation provisions. Terms of payments were determined by mutual agreement, but it was common industry practice that prices were not settled or final payment made until after a job had been completed.

Despite a somewhat depressed world maritime market, repair work sales during 1988 totaled in excess of $37 million. Approximately $17 million of the repair revenues represented work performed for the Navy. Repair work of this kind was obtained by formal bidding, usually against intense competition in the various naval districts. This work was done under terms of Standard

Master Ship Repair Contracts that Swanson Shipyards held with the Navy as well as with the other branches of the armed services. In most cases, contracts for commercial jobs were more profitable than Navy work.

Competition in the marine repair industry was intense. Swanson Shipyards competed with a large number of other shipyards that had substantially greater resources. Navy shipyards also competed for Navy business. Price competition was particularly acute, as many contracts were awarded by competitive bidding. Thus, profits were dependent upon effective cost controls and the ability to meet strict time schedules. To help in the planning of major overhauls, the company had subcontracted with Critical Path Systems to provide project planning with critical path methods.

A number of recent contracts, particularly with the Navy, had involved extensive work performed over a substantial period of time. Contracts of that magnitude generally involved the same risks inherent in construction contracts. In addition, damage resulting in the temporary or permanent loss of a drydock had in the past, and could in the future, adversely impact the company's business. With the exception of the U.S. government, no single customer provided revenues of more than 4 percent of the total for 1988.

Swanson Shipyards reported its income on major repair contracts on the percentage of completion accounting method. Under this method, the company recognized and recorded as income that percentage of the estimated total profit from a contract that was indicated by measuring on a worker-hour basis the progress toward completion. Estimated total profit was determined by estimating the final contract price and the total costs at completion of the contract based upon, among other things, actual performance to date. The principal risks inherent in the use of the percentage of completion method of accounting were that it was necessarily dependent on estimates of the amount of work remaining to be done and future costs to be incurred.

The company was founded in 1981 by William Swanson, Frank Lyden, and Thomas Lane. Mr. Swanson worked for another shipyard in the city and had extensive experience in estimating and negotiating contracts. Mr. Lyden had worked at the same shipyard, but he had been involved with the production side of the business. Mr. Lane provided the money. He was a wealthy Charlestonian whose family was among the first settlers to the area more than 300 years earlier. His numerous contacts with the banking community were of inestimable value to the company.

It was normal practice on Monday mornings for the three owners to get together to discuss business. But usually the conversation turned to sports.

"Hey, Tom, I see your team played another close one. You should have taken the 28 points on Friday," Frank began.

"You know, we really didn't play that bad. Without the 6 turnovers, it would have been a lot closer."

"Sure," Bill broke in. "You could have lost by 20 instead of 24."

"And we don't want to hear how hard it is to recruit for a military school," Frank added. "We have just as big a problem recruiting for an engineering school."

"Since when have any athletes at your school majored in engineering?" Tom retorted.

"I'll have you know we had one three years ago." At that, they all laughed.

"Look," Bill interrupted. "Let's get down to business."

"Speaking of business, how about that twenty dollars I won this weekend playing golf?" Frank asked.

"Don't worry, you'll get it."

Tom was ready to change the subject. "I was thinking about something yesterday. You know we lost a job last March because we only had one drydock in service. I was wondering whether we ought to consider buying another one."

"Yea, as rough as Frank is on drydocks, we had better buy a couple," Bill cheerfully added.

"It wasn't my fault. If that guy had been following safety procedures, it never would have happened."

"But in any event, the drydocks are getting a little old, especially the wooden one," Tom said. "When we bought them, we didn't have a lot of extra money, and they were a bargain, even considering how old they were."

"I think we all agree that we need a new one, but which is better in the long run, wood or steel?"

"Steel lasts longer. About 40 years compared to about 30 years for wood." It was obvious that Frank had already made up his mind as to which was better.

"Is there any difference as far as use is concerned?" Tom asked.

"Six of one, half of dozen of the other," Frank answered. "I could care less which one I use."

"Steel may last longer, but it costs more," Bill said. "I believe a woman gave me a quote last month." With that, he rolled his chair toward his file cabinet while making a smooth 360-degree turn. "If your school had players with moves like that, they would never lose."

"Let's stick to the subject," Tom added quickly. "Did you find out how much they cost?"

"Yes, but give me a couple of minutes to find the total." Bill leaned over, tapped the calculator on the desk, and began adding. Three minutes later he had finished. "The delivered price for the wooden one is $794,300 and for the steel one is $988,200."

"You know, another consideration is yearly maintenance," Tom said.

"You're right," Frank interjected. "Based on past history, I believe a new wooden one would require about $60,000 a year in maintenance and a new steel one about $40,000 a year."

At this point, Tom was looking out the window. "I was just thinking." He paused for emphasis. "Bill, you haven't said anything about your football team." He paused again. "Oh, that's right, you don't have a football team."

"We may not have a football team, but we do have baseball. Went to the Small College World Series last year. And speaking of baseball, you have a convenient memory. In case you have forgotten, we beat your school last spring. Of course, I realize it is difficult to hit a baseball with a rifle."

"Let's stick to the subject." This was a favorite phrase of Tom's when he could not think of a comeback.

"Well, the subject is business." Bill had finally warmed up. "And in business we have to consider taxes. I learned that at my little school. After looking at the new tax law, I have found that our company will have a combined federal and state marginal tax rate of 40 percent."

"What difference does that make?" Frank asked.

"It makes a lot of difference when you start to figure cash flow," Bill added.

"Cash flow has been one our biggest problems in the past." Tom seemed pleased that he was able to add to the conversation. "But the thing I don't understand is how can we decide which drydock to purchase when one lasts 30 years and the other lasts 40 years?"

"In school we learned two ways to approach the problem," Bill began. "The first way is called the replacement chain method. With this approach, the cash flows for each drydock are discounted back to the present. But the trick is to repeat the projects over the same number of years. In other words, you need to know the lowest common denominator of years."

"I understand what you are saying," Tom said. "But what about the second way?"

"The second way is called the equivalent annual annuity method. It's a bit more complicated. With this approach, you first discount the cash flows back to the present, using the 30 years for wood and 40 years for steel. But then you spread the result over the years to get each of them on an annual basis. This allows you to make a fair comparison."

"Which way do you like best?" Frank asked.

"I have no favorite since both methods should yield the same result," Bill continued. "Why don't I make all the calculations, and we can get together when I finish."

"One question." Tom always had one more question. "What discount rate do you use?"

"You should use the marginal cost of capital. And according to my calculations, 12 percent would be about right."

EXHIBIT 19.1

Swanson Shipyards Corporation

Balance Sheet as of the Year Ending December 31, 1988
(In Thousands)

Assets:	
Cash	$ 3,521
Accounts Receivable	3,196
Unbilled Costs	5,256
Materials and Supplies	921
Prepaid Expenses	162
Total Current Assets	$13,056
Land	409
Plant, Drydock and Equipment	4,120
Total Fixed Assets	$ 4,529
Other Assets	220
Total Assets	$17,805
Liabilities and Stockholders' Equity:	
Accounts Payable	$ 7,415
Excess Billings	391
Notes Payable	770
Current Maturities of Long-Term Debt	640
Taxes Payable	360
Total Current Liabilities	$ 9,576
Long-Term Debt	2,899
Total Liabilities	$12,475
Stockholders' Equity	
Common stock, $1 Par	211
Additional Paid-in Capital	3,064
Retained Earnings	2,055
Total Stockholders' Equity	$ 5,330
Total Liabilities and Stockholders' Equity	$17,805

EXHIBIT 19.2

Swanson Shipyards Corporation

Income Statement for the Year Ending December 31, 1988
(In Thousands)

Net Sales	$37,299
Cost of Goods Sold	32,503
Gross Profit	$ 4,796
Selling and Administrative Expenses	1,845
Other Expenses	866
Operating Profit	$ 2,085
Interest Expense	693
Net Profit Before Taxes	$ 1,392
Income Tax, Federal and State	552
Net Profit After Taxes	$ 840
Depreciation Expense	$ 328

EXHIBIT 19.3

Swanson Shipyards Corporation

*Selected Ratios for Ship and Boat Building and Repairing
for the Following Calendar Periods*

	1984	*1985*	*1986*	*1987*
Liquidity:				
1. Current Ratio	1.5	1.4	1.3	1.5
2. Acid Test	0.5	0.6	0.6	0.7
3. Current Assets/Total Assets (%)	65.2	63.1	59.9	61.0
Activity:				
4. Receivables Turnover	17.3	15.2	12.0	13.4
5. Cost of Goods Sold/Inventory	5.4	5.8	6.1	6.5
6. Net Sales/Net Working Capital	13.8	11.7	13.7	10.1
7. Net Sales/Total Assets	2.2	2.1	2.1	1.9
Leverage:				
8. Total Debt/Total Assets (%)	64.5	64.3	63.2	61.3
9. Debt/Net Worth	2.3	2.0	1.8	1.6
10. EBIT/Interest	3.2	2.3	2.5	2.2
Profitability:				
11. COGS/Net Sales (%)	77.5	76.5	76.1	75.5
12. Operating Profit/Net Sales (%)	5.4	3.4	4.6	5.7
13. Profit Before Taxes/Net Sales (%)	4.1	2.0	3.2	4.6
14. Profit Before Taxes/Total Assets (%)	8.1	7.2	7.8	9.2
15. Profit Before Taxes/Net Worth (%)	25.8	24.0	23.6	24.4

QUESTIONS

1. Determine the relevant cash flows for the wooden drydock and for the steel drydock projects.
2. What assumptions are made in identifying the relevant cash flows?
3. Determine which project should be accepted using the replacement chain approach.
4. Determine which project should be accepted using the equivalent annual annuity approach.
5. What are some weaknesses of the two approaches?
6. Determine which project should be accepted using Lotus 1-2-3.

Aetna Optical Company
CAPITAL BUDGETING,
RISK-BASIC

Aetna Optical Company was incorporated in Corpus Christi, Texas on March 9, 1975. The firm processed glass and plastic lenses to fill prescription orders from opthalmologists, optometrists, and dispensing opticians. Eyeglass frames, lenses, and related optical equipment were sold without processing. In addition, contact lenses accounted for about 5 percent of sales. Customers were dispersed throughout the country, with no customer representing more than 3 percent of sales. A balance sheet is included as Exhibit 20.1, and an income statement as Exhibit 20.2.

Exhibit 20.3 reflects the gross and net sales attributable to various product categories in recent years. Glass and plastic lens prescriptions processed were of the following types: single-vision or multifocal; tinted, clear, or photochromic; uncut, cut for mounting in frames supplied by the customer, or cut and mounted in frames sold by the company. The firm also distributed frames and optical equipment for major domestic manufacturers, including a line of high-fashion frames imported from Europe. When the company was first started, all contact lenses sold were of the hard plastic type, but they soon went into manufacturing soft lenses. A variety of colors were available for both single-vision and multifocal lenses.

The processing of lenses required either surfacing or finishing. Surfacing consisted of grinding one or both surfaces using automated lens generators to achieve the desired toric or spherical curves for proper refraction, and then polishing the lens for clarity. Finishing involved selecting the proper frame pattern and edging the lenses to achieve the proper shape, placement of axis, optical center, and multifocal segment for mounting; cleaning and inspecting the lenses; hardening either by heating and air-tempering or by a chemical process; and tinting, when ordered.

Hard contact lenses began as hard plastic buttons. The process required the button to be cut on a contact lens lathe, polished and inspected for the desired base curve, cut to the proper front curve and thickness, cut and polished to any secondary curves, and edged by hand. The company's plastic contact lens was thinner than some of the competitions', resulting in a more comfortable fit.

Aetna Optical Company used direct-mail advertising, distribution of catalogs, advertisements in trade journals, telephone calls, and sales representatives to stimulate sales. The company also offered a volume discount to its customers on a monthly basis. A customer normally received the goods within one week of submission of their order.

The firm was involved in a highly competitive business. In the United States, the industry was composed of two large companies having optical facilities in most of the large cities, 11 mail-order companies whose operations and pricing were similar to Aetna Optical, and many smaller companies operating on the local level. Aetna Optical believed it could compete with other companies on the basis of quality, service, and price.

The wholesale optical industry was regulated by the federal government. The Medical Device Amendments of 1976 to the federal Food, Drug, and Cosmetic Act gave the Federal Drug Administration (FDA) authority to regulate nearly every aspect of the manufacture, distribution, and sale of medical devices distributed through interstate commerce.

Robert Jackson had served as president and chairman of the board of directors since 1976. Prior to that time he had been employed by competitors, at various levels of the wholesale optical business. He was especially concerned with the growth of the company. The contact lens market offered steady sales, but instead of promoting hard contact lenses, he thought it best for Aetna to concentrate on the soft contact lens market. Those lenses, along with soaking solutions, cleaners, and disinfecting units, were sold to opthalmologists, optometrists, and opticians.

Soft contact lenses had been sold in the United States since 1971. Customers were attracted to them primarily for cosmetic reasons, convenience, and safety. Soft contact lenses were made of materials that conform to the eye, providing greater eye comfort than hard lenses. On the negative side, soft contact lenses had a higher cost, required daily cleaning and disinfecting of the lenses, were susceptible to tearing and splitting, and could not be worn by those people with severe astigmatisms.

To remain competitive in the soft contact lens market, Mr. Jackson knew it was necessary to expand Aetna's product line of lenses to meets its customers' demands. There was a new type of lens on the market that he thought was worth investigating. Mr. Jackson knew of a small company whose primary business was the manufacture and sale of soft lenses as well as soaking solutions, cleaners, and disinfecting units. They had developed a lens that was a combination of a hard and soft lens. It consisted of a semipermeable lens in the center surrounded by a "skirt" of soft plastic that adhered to the eye. This lens was very popular with patients who had severe astigmatisms, since with this lens, the wearer had the clarity of vision afforded by a hard lens, but the comfort of wear of a soft lens. They also did not require the daily disinfecting required by soft lenses.

Contact Lenses, Inc. had obtained clearance from the U.S. Food and

Drug Administration to manufacture and sell the contact lenses it had developed. The company agreed to lease the rights to the process to Aetna Optical for 10 years at a fixed sum of $500,000 per year.

In studying the proposal, Mr. Jackson had been advised that several risk factors were involved. First, legal action was being brought against the single supplier of the plastic. In the event the plaintiffs obtained an injunction against the use of the material, Aetna Optical might be unable to manufacture the new type of contact lenses. Second, it was anticipated that competition in this new lens market would increase. Finally, there was no assurance that the company would receive FDA approval to manufacture the new type lens.

James Woo had recently joined the company after receiving an undergraduate degree from the University of Houston. Following a training program, he was assigned to the New Contact Lens Project (NCLP).

Mr. Jackson explained to him that he needed financial justification for the project. He knew the first step would be to estimate the after-tax cash flows for the 10-year period. His results are recorded in Exhibit 20.4. The second step was to find the marginal cost of capital for the firm.

Mr. Woo then decided to estimate the cost of capital using the capital asset pricing model. Application of this method yielded a figure of about 20 percent. Even so, he felt that a new venture was more risky than a going concern. Twenty-three to 25 percent appeared reasonable, but he was unsure of the exact range.

Selected ratios for opthalmic goods manufacturers are presented in Exhibit 20.5.

EXHIBIT 20.1

Aetna Optical Company

Balance Sheet as of January 31, 1988 (In Thousands)

Assets:	
Cash	$ 158
Certificates of Deposit	1,260
Accounts Receivable	3,518
Inventories	4,876
Prepaid Expenses	100
Total Current Assets	$ 9,912
Land	34
Building and Leasehold Improvements	386
Equipment	3,454
Leasehold Interest	5,058
	$ 8,932
Less: Accumulated Depreciation	1,160
	$ 7,772
Other Assets	2,374
Total Assets	$20,058

Liabilities and Stockholders' Equity:	
Notes Payable, Bank	$ 438
Current Maturities of Long-Term Obligations	670
Accounts Payable	3,234
Accrued Liabilities	510
Federal Income Taxes	3,308
Total Current Liabilities	$ 8,160
Long-Term Obligations, Less: Current Maturities	6,680
Deferred Federal Income Taxes	256
Stockholders' Equity	
Common Stock, $5 par	138
Paid-in Capital	42
Retained Earnings	4,782
Total Stockholders' Equity	$ 4,962
Total Liabilities and Stockholders' Equity	$20,058

EXHIBIT 20.2

Aetna Optical Company

Income Statements for the Fiscal Year Ending June 30, 1987,
and Seven Months Ending January 31, 1988 (In Thousands)

	1987	1988
Net Sales	$23,764	$19,370
Cost of Goods Sold	14,703	11,810
Gross Profit	$ 9,061	$ 7,560
Operating Expenses	8,028	6,613
Profit Before Taxes	$ 1,033	$ 947
Other Expenses, Including Interest	405	283
Net Profit Before Taxes	$ 628	$ 664
Federal and State Income Taxes	222	254
Net Profit After Taxes	$ 406	$ 410

EXHIBIT 20.3

Aetna Optical Company

Gross and Net Sales by Product Categories for Fiscal Years
Ending June 30, Except for Seven Months Ending
January 31, 1988 (In Thousands)

	1985	1986	1987	1988
Glass Lens Prescriptions	$7,594	$13,446	$22,112	$16,530
Plastic Lens Prescriptions	806	1,956	4,954	5,094
Unprocessed Lenses, Frames, and Optical Equipment	186	464	1,014	1,464
Contact Lens Prescriptions	144	238	750	678
Total Gross Sales	$8,730	$16,104	$28,830	$23,766
Less: Discounts	1,578	2,710	5,066	4,396
Total Net Sales	$7,152	$13,394	$23,764	$19,370

EXHIBIT 20.4

Aetna Optical Company

*After-tax Cash Flows for
NCLP (In Dollars)*

Year	After-Tax Cash Flow
0	−722,200
1	+ 91,200
2	+134,000
3	+185,600
4	+185,600
5	+185,600
6	+185,600
7	+185,600
8	+185,600
9	+185,600
10	+213,400

EXHIBIT 20.5

Aetna Optical Company

*Selected Ratios for Opthalmic Goods Manufacturers for the
Following Calendar Periods*

	1984	1985	1986	1987
Liquidity:				
1. Current Ratio	1.7	1.9	1.8	1.9
2. Acid Test	0.9	1.0	1.0	1.0
3. Current Assets/Total Assets (%)	68.3	66.7	66.1	67.1
Activity:				
4. Receivables Turnover	7.6	8.6	8.6	8.5
5. Cost of Goods Sold/Inventory	4.1	4.6	5.6	5.1
6. Net Sales/Net Working Capital	8.0	8.3	9.9	7.6
7. Net Sales/Total Assets	1.9	2.2	2.5	2.2
Leverage:				
8. Total Debt/Total Assets (%)	69.5	57.0	62.5	60.2
9. Debt/Net Worth	2.0	1.3	1.3	1.2
10. EBIT/Interest	2.6	3.0	2.1	3.0

EXHIBIT 20.5 (Continued)				
	1984	*1985*	*1986*	*1987*
Profitability:				
11. COGS/Net Sales (%)	61.2	58.8	63.5	61.5
12. Operating Profit/Net Sales (%)	3.2	6.1	3.4	4.5
13. Profit Before Taxes/Net Sales (%)	2.7	3.9	2.8	3.4
14. Profit Before Taxes/Total Assets (%)	7.1	8.2	5.8	6.5
15. Profit Before Taxes/Net Worth (%)	21.4	14.2	14.0	13.3

QUESTIONS

1. Discuss how Mr. Woo would use the capital asset pricing model to find the cost of capital.
2. What factors cause the project to be of above average risk?
3. Calculate the internal rate of return for the project.
4. Should the project be accepted?
5. Calculate the internal rate of return using Lotus 1-2-3.

Inca, Inc.
CAPITAL BUDGETING,
RISK-INTERMEDIATE

Inca, Inc. operated and licensed others to operate quick service restaurants under the name "Pedro's." The menu featured chiliburgers along with a limited selection of Mexican foods.

The first "Pedro's" was opened in Santa Fe, New Mexico, on June 9, 1978. Ten years later there were 298 restaurants in operation in 27 states, of which 111 were operated by the company and 187 by franchisees. In addition, 4 restaurants were under construction by the company and 64 by franchisees. A balance sheet as of June 30, 1988 is included as Exhibit 21.1, and an income statement as Exhibit 21.2.

Each "Pedro's" restaurant was built to the same specifications as to exterior style and interior decor. The walls of each restaurant were decorated with the exploits of Mexican heroes. The buildings, constructed of yellow brick, were located on sites of approximately one acre. The parking lots, depending on the exact size and shape of the land, were designed for 30 to 35 cars. The standard restaurant contained about 1,900 square feet, seated 81 persons, and included a pickup window for drive-through service. Locations were chosen in heavily populated areas, since success depended upon serving a large number of customers.

All the restaurants offered the same menu. Three sizes of chiliburgers were featured: the Gaucho (quarter pound), the Soldado (half pound), and the Matador (three-quarter pound). The names were integrated into the company's advertising. Each television commercial gave special attention to one of the three themes.

The prospective franchisee signed a document that included the option of operating a specified number of "Pedro's" restaurants in a prescribed geographical area. Each new location required an initial payment of $18,000. In addition, a royalty of 5 percent of gross sales was specified. It was also stipulated that franchisees must spend at least 2 percent of gross receipts on local advertising.

Inca, Inc. believed that properly trained employees were the key to success; therefore, managers and company trainees were required to attend a three-week program covering all aspects of company operations. More than 600 people were graduated from the school during 1987.

Inca, Inc. planned to begin construction on five new company-owned restaurants during 1989. The exact size of the buildings had not been determined, although the specific sites had already been selected. Management believed that restaurants with a capacity of 144 persons would be more profitable than the present size of 81.

The company faced two choices: continuing with the smaller-sized units or going to the larger size. The initial cost for each of the five smaller restaurants was $2,100,000, and $3,700,000 for each of the five larger ones. Demand expectations over the years were 40 percent for high demand, 40 percent for medium demand, and 20 percent for low demand. The present values of cash flows for the two proposals are given in Exhibit 21.3.

John H. Porter had been president and chief executive officer of the Inca, Inc. since July 1982. Prior to that time he had worked for a competitor. He knew the decision concerning the size of new restaurants could be a major turning point for the company. Mr. Porter wondered if the potential higher returns for the larger units justified the increased risk. In any event, the strategy would have to be sold to the board of directors.

Selected ratios for restaurants are presented in Exhibit 21.4.

EXHIBIT 21.1

Inca, Inc.

Balance Sheet as of June 30, 1988 (In Thousands)

Assets:	
Cash	$12,026
Accounts Receivable	1,646
Inventory	512
Other Current Assets	1,872
Total Current Assets	$16,056
Buildings	10,208
Leasehold Improvements	4,826
Restaurant Equipment	11,630
Motor Vehicles	1,188
Office Equipment	464
Lease Rights	542
Less: Accumulated Depreciation	3,104
Net Fixed Assets	$25,754
Land	10,606
Construction in Progress	434
Other Assets	1,566
Total Assets	$54,416
Liabilities and Stockholders' Equity:	
Notes Payable, Banks	$ 316
Accounts Payable	3,846
Income Taxes	1,754
Accrued Liabilities	1,314
Current Portion, Long-Term Debt	1,564
Total Current Liabilities	$ 8,794
Long-Term Debt, Less Current Portion	17,742
Deferred Income Taxes	982
Deferred Franchise Fees	3,730
Total Deferrals	$ 4,712
Stockholders' Equity	
Common Stock, $0.10 Par	676
Capital in Excess of Stated Value	9,726
Retained Earnings	12,766
Total Stockholders' Equity	$23,168
Total Liabilities and	
Stockholders' Equity	$54,416

EXHIBIT 21.2

Inca, Inc.

Income Statements for the Year Ending June 30
(In Thousands)

	1987	1988
Net Sales	$132,618	$163,792
Cost of Goods Sold	61,667	75,356
Gross Profit	$ 70,951	$ 88,436
Operating Expenses	66,321	82,404
Net Operating Profit	$ 4,630	$ 6,032
Other Expenses, Including Interest	2,814	3,036
Net Profit Before Taxes	$ 1,816	$ 2,996
Federal and State Income Taxes	1,708	1,106
Net Profit After Taxes	$ 1,108	$ 1,890

EXHIBIT 21.3

Inca, Inc.

Present Value of Cash Flows

Restaurant Size	Level of Demand	Present Value of Cash Flows
	High	$3,150,000
Standard	Medium	2,730,000
	Low	1,900,000
	High	6,512,000
Expanded	Medium	4,440,000
	Low	2,800,000

EXHIBIT 21.4

Inca, Inc.

Selected Ratios for Restaurants for the Following
Calendar Periods

	1985	1986	1987	1988
Liquidity:				
1. Current Ratio	0.7	0.7	0.7	0.7
2. Acid Test	0.4	0.4	0.4	0.4
3. Current Assets/Total Assets (%)	36.9	34.9	35.3	36.7
Activity:				
4. Receivables Turnover	225.8	226.9	162.1	172.6
5. Cost of Goods Sold/Inventory	27.0	26.7	24.0	26.5
6. Net Sales/Net Working Capital	(29.1)	(33.2)	(35.9)	(32.6)
7. Net Sales/Total Assets	2.8	2.8	2.8	2.8
Leverage:				
8. Total Debt/Total Assets (%)	73.2	70.8	70.2	70.7
9. Debt/Net Worth	2.7	2.5	2.6	2.5
10. EBIT/Interest	2.8	2.5	2.3	2.2
Profitability:				
11. COGS/Net Sales (%)	46.1	47.0	45.8	45.2
12. Operating Profit/Net Sales (%)	3.8	5.3	5.0	5.2
13. Profit Before Taxes/Net Sales (%)	3.3	3.3	3.1	3.1
14. Profit Before Taxes/Total Assets (%)	7.7	7.7	6.9	7.3
15. Profit Before Taxes/Net Worth (%)	31.8	30.7	25.5	27.4

QUESTIONS

1. Express Mr. Porter's two basic choices as a decision tree.

2. Calculate the possible net present values for each branch of the tree.

3. Calculate the expected net present value for each alternative.

4. Calculate the standard deviation for each alternative.

5. Calculate the coefficient of variation for each alternative.

6. Which alternative should Mr. Porter choose?

7. What would be the effect of building a combination of large and small restaurants?

8. Express the combination alternative as a decision tree.

9. Calculate the expected net present value, standard deviation, and coefficient of variation for each combination alternative.

10. Calculate the expected net present value, standard deviation, and coefficient of variation for each combination alternative using Lotus 1-2-3.

Plastico
CAPITAL BUDGETING,
RISK-COMPLEX

In early 1988, Robert Peele, president of Plastico, was contemplating the acquisition of an additional piece of equipment from Wooten Industries. The expenditure would increase year-end assets of the firm by 6 to 7 percent. The proposed purchase was triggered by continued demand for the firm's products. By the end of 1987, Plastico was operating near full capacity. Year-end balance sheets and income statements are included as Exhibit 22.1 and Exhibit 22.2.

Plastico had been founded in 1969 by three brothers, William, John, and Robert Peele. The Peele brothers had been life-long residents of Boston, Massachusetts, the location of Plastico. Robert Peele served as the firm's president, while the two younger brothers were vice-presidents of production and accounting–finance, respectively. The three men were the only persons significantly involved in the managerial function and were the sole stockholders, each holding an equal number of shares.

Plastico fabricated plastic products for a wide variety of commercial and industrial applications, using the standard materials of the industry: acrylics, styrene, vinyls, and polyethylenes. The firm was also prominent in the manufacturing of fabricated fixtures and display counters for department stores. The company frequently landed contracts for refurbishing main stores or installation in new branches. In the recent past, Plastico had completed all the plastic fabrication work for two of the largest department stores in Boston. The company also performed engraving work for two national accounts as well as for several local manufacturing firms.

The piece of equipment that Plastico was considering acquiring was a vacuum forming machine. In the past, work requiring vacuum forming was subcontracted, even though it was frequently required in connection with the firm's fabrication orders. Robert Peele felt that the firm was somewhat limited in its growth potential because of this restriction. Plastico's engraving department was highly profitable, but it accounted for only about 15 percent of total sales. Mr. Peele believed growth in that area would be modest at best. He knew that if the firm could manufacture its own vacuum formed products, it could enter into a broad spectrum of industrial uses. The production technique would provide an entry into a business that was characterized by large orders of a repetitive nature, but was markedly more competitive than the firm's other markets.

Even though the opportunities were great, there were risks involved. The acquisition of this piece of equipment would greatly increase fixed costs, significantly raising the break-even point. That would make the firm even more sensitive to swings in demand. Robert Peele knew it would take time to penetrate the industrial market for vacuum formed products. He wondered whether or not the firm could absorb the additional fixed costs of the new machine while waiting for new orders. The purchase would also tie the company more closely to the fortunes of the plastics industry. He knew it might be better instead to make an investment that would diversify the firm's operating activities.

Each of the brothers prepared an independent estimate of the costs and benefits of the proposed machine, along with the probability of occurrence. (See Exhibit 22.3, Exhibit 22.4, and Exhibit 22.5.) From those estimates, John Porter, an outside financial consultant, was to provide an evaluation of the proposed capital investment. Although no exact calculation of the cost of capital had been prepared, Mr. Porter believed 12 percent was a reasonable figure. There was, however, some question whether that number would cover the risk inherent in the investment. The federal and state marginal tax rate was estimated at 40 percent.

Selected ratios for the plastic products manufacturing industry are presented in Exhibit 22.6.

EXHIBIT 22.1

Plastico

Year-end Balance Sheets (*In Thousands*)

	1986	1987
Assets:		
Cash	$ 10	$ 38
Accounts Receivable	156	274
Inventory	202	250
Other Current Assets	22	30
Total Current Assets	$390	$592
Machinery and Equipment	198	234
Furniture and Fixtures	12	14
Automotive Equipment	36	64
Leasehold Improvements	18	28
Less: Accumulated Depreciation	(88)	(126)
Total Fixed Assets	$176	$214
Other Assets	42	46
Total Assets	$608	$852
Liabilities and Stockholders' Equity:		
Accounts Payable	$ 90	$184
Notes Payable	0	94
Current Maturities, Notes Payable	50	70
Accrued Liabilities	12	20
Total Current Liabilities	$152	$368
Long-Term Debt, 8%, Less Current Portion	180	156
Stockholders' Equity		
Common Stock, $2 Par	$ 24	$ 24
Paid-in Capital	48	48
Retained Earnings	204	256
Total Stockholders' Equity	$276	$328
Total Liabilities and Stockholders' Equity	$608	$852

EXHIBIT 22.2

Plastico

Income Statements (In Thousands)

	1986	1987
Net Sales	$1,800	$2,156
Less: Cost of Goods Sold[1]	1,018	1,340
Gross Profit	$ 782	$ 816
Operating Expenses		
Direct Selling	72	102
General and Administrative[2]	540	578
Operating Income	$ 170	$ 136
Other Expense	16	24
Interest Expense	26	28
Income Before Taxes	$ 128	84
Federal and State Income Taxes	50	32
Net Income	$ 78	$ 52

[1] Includes depreciation of $16,000 in 1986 and $28,000 in 1987.

[2] Includes officer–owners' salaries of $150,000 in 1986 and $210,000 in 1987.

EXHIBIT 22.3

Plastico

Cost and Benefit Estimates of William Peele

Costs	
Invoice	$54,000
Freight	3,600
Total Costs	$57,600
Useful Life	10 years
Salvage Value	$5,600

Additional Benefits Before Depreciation and Taxes

Years	Benefits	Probability
1–10	$(10,000)	0.10
	0	0.20
	10,000	0.40
	20,000	0.20
	30,000	0.10

EXHIBIT 22.4

Plastico

Cost and Benefit Estimates of John Peele

Costs	
Invoice	$54,000
Freight	3,600
Installation	2,400
Total Costs	$60,000
Useful Life	10 years
Salvage Value	$4,000

Additional Benefits Before Depreciation and Taxes

Years	Benefits	Probability
1–5	$ 0	0.20
	12,000	0.25
	24,000	0.30
	36,000	0.15
	48,000	0.10
6–10	$ (4,000)	0.30
	0	0.25
	12,000	0.20
	16,000	0.15
	24,000	0.10

EXHIBIT 22.5

Plastico

Cost and Benefit Estimates of Robert Peele

Costs	
Invoice	$54,000
Useful Life	10 years
Salvage Value	$6,000

Additional Benefits Before Depreciation and Taxes

Years	Benefits	Probability
1–5	$12,000	0.15
	14,000	0.20
	16,000	0.30
	18,000	0.20
	20,000	0.15
6–10	6,000	0.15
	8,000	0.20
	10,000	0.30
	12,000	0.20
	14,000	0.15

EXHIBIT 22.6

Plastico

Selected Ratios for the Plastic Products Manufacturing Industry for the Following Calendar Periods

	1984	1985	1986	1987
Liquidity:				
1. Current Ratio	1.5	1.6	1.5	1.5
2. Acid Test	0.8	0.9	0.8	0.9
3. Current Assets/Total Assets (%)	59.4	57.5	57.2	57.3
Activity:				
4. Receivables Turnover	7.9	8.2	8.0	7.8
5. Cost of Goods Sold/Inventory	7.2	7.6	7.4	7.6
6. Net Sales/Net Working Capital	11.8	11.0	12.0	12.0
7. Net Sales/Total Assets	2.1	2.1	2.0	2.0
Leverage:				
8. Total Debt/Total Assets (%)	61.5	61.0	61.8	61.6
9. Debt/Net Worth	1.7	1.6	1.6	1.7
10. EBIT/Interest	3.7	2.4	2.4	2.1

EXHIBIT 22.6 (Continued)

	1984	*1985*	*1986*	*1987*
Profitability:				
11. COGS/Net Sales (%)	74.2	74.5	74.5	74.0
12. Operating Profit/Net Sales (%)	6.1	5.0	5.4	4.4
13. Profit Before Taxes/Net Sales (%)	4.6	3.5	3.7	2.8
14. Profit Before Taxes/Total Assets (%)	9.5	6.7	7.2	5.4
15. Profit Before Taxes/Net Worth (%)	26.4	19.4	21.0	16.5

QUESTIONS

1. Based on the various estimates, what amount should be used for the cost of the project?
2. Based on the various estimates, which of the three men believes the project to be of the greatest risk?
3. Using the estimates of John Peele, calculate the cash flows for years 1–10.
4. Using the cash flow estimates from Question 3, calculate the expected values of the cash flows.
5. Does 12 percent appear reasonable for the cost of capital?
6. Using the cash flow estimates from Question 3, calculate the internal rate of return.
7. Using the cash flow estimates from Question 3, calculate the net present value for a 12 percent cost of capital.
8. Calculate the standard deviation of the net present value for the project, assuming independent cash flows.
9. Using the cash flow estimates from Question 3, calculate the internal rate of return and net present value using Lotus 1-2-3.
10. Calculate the standard deviation of the NPV for the project, assuming independent cash flows, using Lotus 1-2-3.

American Travel Corporation
CAPITAL BUDGETING,
PROGRAMMING APPROACH

American Travel Corporation was engaged in owning, developing, operating, licensing, and supplying a chain of motels composed of 57 fully owned and 532 licensed units. The company was founded in Chicago, Illinois in 1976 by Jack Gibson. All operating units were presently in the United States, but an international expansion was planned within the next five years. A balance sheet and income statement are included as Exhibit 23.1 and Exhibit 23.2.

Each motel was a two-story structure designed with 45 guest rooms. All units measured 15 by 20 feet and included two double beds, four chairs, one table, a separate dressing area with vanity, and a full bath. The rooms also contained a color television set, as well as individually controlled heating and air conditioning units. The room rates were $29 for one person, $35 for two people, and $39 for three to six people.

American Travel Corporation exercised control over operations by the use of traveling inspectors. Unannounced monthly visits were made to each motel to inspect the premises with the resident manager. The managers were typically retired military personnel, married, without children at home.

The company assumed responsibility for all advertising, publicity, and promotion of the chain. With a small staff in the marketing area, the company chose to use an outside firm. The advertising campaign, featuring a vacationing family, used the slogan "American Travel for the American Traveler."

American Travel Corporation solicited qualified applicants as prospective licensees. After a complete investigation, the company would enter into an agreement, which set forth all the duties of the respective parties in connection with the construction, operation, and ownership of the motel. Each license agreement was for 25 years with a $5,000 deposit paid to the company upon execution of the contract. The deposit was applied against the cost of certain equipment and furnishings supplied by the company. If the licensee were unable to proceed with construction, the deposit would be retained for damages.

The company did not charge for the license, and no royalties were collected until the motel was open for business. The licensee then paid a royalty equal to 6 percent of the average room rate multiplied by the number of rooms actually occupied. The company also collected an advertising fee equal to $0.10 times the total number of guest units.

American Travel Corporation had considered several alternatives for expansion. One possibility involved development of an international resort division. Under this plan, hotels consisting of 88 guest rooms were to be built. Unlike the motels, a coffee shop, swimming pool, putting green, and tennis courts were to be included. The company anticipated direct investment in the first few hotels. Two initial locations in the Grand Bahamas were under consideration, one at Freeport and one at Nassau. The relevant data for each proposal is shown in Exhibit 23.3.

A second alternative involved a series of campgrounds located throughout the nation. The identifying feature of each facility would be a lake in the shape of the United States. Fifty weeks during the year were to be reserved for week-long celebrations of the states. The week of July 4th would be Independence Week and the fourth week of October, Veterans Week. Two initial sites in Florida were being considered, one near Orlando and one near St. Augustine. Exhibit 23.4 includes proposal data.

A third choice was a nationwide network of restaurants to be located along interstate highways. The unique feature of the restaurants would be the fast delivery of foods for the diet- and health-conscious traveler. The menu would be basically low fat, medium protein, and high fiber. Even with the emphasis on travelers, management expected that at least 40 percent of the business would come from local residents. Two locations on I-75 and I-85 near Atlanta, Georgia were being studied. The relevant data for each proposal is listed in Exhibit 23.5.

The company was planning an offering of stock after two years, but during the meantime, capital would have to be rationed. During the first year, the capital budget would be limited to $700,000, and during the second year, the maximum amount would be $500,000. Because of the operating risk of the firm, management had decided not to increase long-term debt at this time.

Jack Gibson, company president, was trying to decide which combination of projects to accept. He realized that the situation was not ideal, but that a practical approach had to be found.

Selected ratios for the motel and hotel industry are presented in Exhibit 23.6.

EXHIBIT 23.1

American Travel Corporation

Balance Sheets as of November 30 (In Thousands)

	1987	1988
Assets:		
Cash	$ 751	$ 936
Accounts Receivable, Net	396	556
Inventory	211	277
Other Current Assets	184	203
Total Current Assets	$ 1,542	$ 1,972
Fixed Assets, Net	9,306	10,002
Other Assets	1,575	1,724
Total Assets	$12,423	$13,698
Liabilities and Stockholders' Equity:		
Accounts Payable	$ 479	$ 686
Accrued Expenses	423	504
Notes Payable	607	736
Other Current Liabilities	492	516
Total Current Liabilities	$ 2,001	$ 2,442
Long-Term Debt	6,794	7,432
Stockholders' Equity		
Common Stock, $5 Par	1,005	1,005
Retained Earnings	2,623	2,819
Total Stockholders' Equity	$ 3,628	$ 3,824
Total Liabilities and Stockholders' Equity	$12,423	$13,698

EXHIBIT 23.2

American Travel Corporation

Income Statements for the Period Ending November 30 (In Thousands)

	1987	1988
Net Sales	$15,636	$17,687
Operating Expenses	13,306	15,141
Operating Profit	$ 2,330	$ 2,546
Other Expenses, Including Interest	1,594	2,227
Net Income Before Taxes	$ 736	$ 319
Less: Federal and State Income Taxes	280	123
Net Income After Taxes	$ 456	$ 196

EXHIBIT 23.3

American Travel Corporation

International Resort Investment Alternatives

| | Net Investment | | | |
Project	Year 1	Year 2	IRR	NPV of Cash Flows
Freeport	$225,400	$175,800	23%	$300,800
Nassau	$122,200	$ 80,600	20%	$152,000

EXHIBIT 23.4

American Travel Corporation

Campgrounds Investment Alternatives

| | Net Investment | | | |
Project	Year 1	Year 2	IRR	NPV of Cash Flows
Orlando	$190,000	$142,400	16%	$186,800
St. Augustine	$225,000	$157,600	17%	$181,800

EXHIBIT 23.5

American Travel Corporation

Diet Restaurant Investment Alternatives

| | Net Investment | | | |
Project	Year 1	Year 2	IRR	NPV of Cash Flows
I-75	$172,800	$131,400	16%	$171,200
I-85	$138,000	$ 93,800	19%	$130,200

EXHIBIT 23.6

American Travel Corporation

*Selected Ratios for the Motel and Hotel Industry for the
Following Calendar Periods*

	1985	1986	1987	1988
Liquidity:				
1. Current Ratio	0.6	0.6	0.6	0.7
2. Acid Test	0.4	0.4	0.4	0.4
3. Current Assets/Total Assets (%)	13.8	13.9	14.3	14.4
Activity:				
4. Receivables Turnover	34.5	38.6	37.3	39.4
5. Cost of Goods Sold/Inventory	—	—	—	—
6. Net Sales/Net Working Capital	(12.4)	(15.6)	(15.4)	(17.3)
7. Net Sales/Total Assets	0.8	0.8	0.8	0.8
Leverage:				
8. Total Debt/Total Assets (%)	82.1	77.5	77.2	77.0
9. Debt/Net Worth	5.7	4.4	4.2	4.7
10. EBIT/Interest	1.7	2.0	1.7	1.8
Profitability:				
11. COGS/Net Sales (%)	—	—	—	—
12. Operating Profit/Net Sales (%)	15.8	14.6	15.0	15.0
13. Profit Before Taxes/Net Sales (%)	6.5	7.6	6.6	5.8
14. Profit Before Taxes/Total Assets (%)	4.9	6.4	4.2	3.7
15. Profit Before Taxes/Net Worth (%)	28.7	27.6	21.4	19.3

QUESTIONS

1. Which projects should be accepted using internal rate of return? (Assume a 12 percent marginal cost of capital.)
2. Which projects should be accepted using net present value?
3. Would the decision change if each pair of proposals were considered mutually exclusive?
4. Set the problem up in integer programming format:
   (a) With any combination of projects possible.
   (b) With pairs of proposals considered mutually exclusive.
5. Solve the integer programming problem and compare the results with the previous solutions:
   (a) With any combination of projects possible.
   (b) With pairs of proposals considered mutually exclusive.

PART IV

CAPITAL STRUCTURE, COST OF CAPITAL, VALUATION, AND DIVIDEND POLICY

Defreu, Inc.
CAPITAL STRUCTURE

Defreu, Inc., founded in 1947 and headquartered in Laurel, Mississippi, was a manufacturer and marketer of office copying machines as well as a supplier of products and services for those machines. By 1960, it had outgrown its regional base and had begun selling to a national clientele. A balance sheet and an income statement are included as Exhibit 24.1 and Exhibit 24.2.

The firm was divided into three divisions: copy machine manufacturing, toner, and office systems. The copy machine manufacturing division had plant sites in Mississippi, Missouri, and Oregon. The toner division plants, producing for Defreu and several other large copying machine manufacturers, were located in Laurel, Mississippi and Des Moines, Iowa. The office systems division was responsible for marketing copy machines and supplies in the United States and Latin America, and operated out of corporate headquarters.

Mr. Harold Hawkins, treasurer of the firm, was responsible for securing the funds necessary to finance the firm's assets. His assistant, Mr. Arlie Lindskog, dealt with the banks on a daily basis, primarily in regard to short-term requirements.

Mr. Hawkins received a report from the finance committee detailing Defreu's long-term funds requirements for the next five years. Asset growth was targeted at a compound rate of 15 percent. If this objective were achieved, the company would double in size, resulting in an asset base of $0.5 billion. This would support a sales volume in excess of $1 billion. The report indicated that internal profits plus depreciation charges would generate approximately 40 percent of the necessary funds. The implication was that $150,000,000 would be raised externally in the form of long-term debt, preferred stock, and common stock.

Mr. Hawkins had devoted a large amount of time to the question of the appropriate capital structure for Defreu. To gain insight into the problem, he decided to gather information from five firms with business characteristics similar to Defreu. Exhibit 24.3 gives the capital structure of the five companies.

Immediately a problem arose as to which items should be included in the capital structure. He was sure that long-term debt, preferred stock, and common stockholders' equity should be included. It was not so clear how to treat the current liabilities and deferred income taxes for the five firms. After much consideration, he decided to consider current liabilities and deferred income taxes as short-term sources of funds and to transfer them to the left-hand side of the balance sheet. It was therefore apparent to Mr. Hawkins that the capital structure should consist of long-term debt, preferred stock, and common stockholders' equity. The breakdown of long-term debt as of December 31, 1987 is included as Exhibit 24.4.

Mr. Hawkins then decided to eliminate preferred stock as a source of funds since it was only a minor item in the capital structure for the five firms and had not been used at all by Defreu. He believed that the nondeductibility of preferred dividends had rendered that particular source of funds too costly relative to debt.

Mr. Hawkins realized that it was not necessary to raise $150,000,000 all at one time. After some thought he decided to make two $75,000,000 offerings over the next five years. Even with this time lag, he wanted to have recommendations ready within the month for presentation to the board of directors.

The next step in the process involved conversations with investment bankers. He concluded from his discussions that debentures could be issued at 10.5 percent. Transactions in the firm's common stock over the last few months had averaged $65 per share. Based on the price per share, it was believed that a stock issue could be sold to net the firm $60 per share.

Selected ratios for the systems and copier manufacturers are included as Exhibit 24.5.

EXHIBIT 24.1

Defreu, Inc.

Condensed Balance Sheet as of December 31, 1988
(In Thousands)

Assets:

Current Assets	$153,975
Other Assets	3,950
Fixed Assets, Gross	138,283
Less: Accumulated Depreciation	48,806
Net Fixed Assets	$ 89,477
Total Assets	$247,402

Liabilities and Stockholders' Equity:

Current Liabilities	$ 83,646
Current Maturities of Long-Term Debt	5,500
Total Current Liabilities	$ 89,146
Long-Term Debt	55,753
Stockholders' Equity	
Common Stock, $1 Par	3,106
Retained Earnings	99,397
Total Stockholders' Equity	$102,503
Total Liabilities and Stockholders' Equity	$247,402

EXHIBIT 24.2

Defreu, Inc.

Condensed Income Statement for the Year Ending
December 31, 1988 (In Thousands)

Net Sales	$508,843
Cost of Products Sold	329,486
Gross Profit	$179,357
Selling, Distribution, and Administrative Expenses	129,246
Research and Development	12,466
Income Before Interest and Taxes	$ 37,645
Interest Expense	8,021
Income Before Taxes	$ 29,624
Federal and State Income Taxes	11,790
Income After Taxes	$ 17,834

EXHIBIT 24.3

Defreu, Inc.

*Percentage Composition of Capital Structures for Selected
Manufacturers in the Systems and Copier Industries*

	Long-Term Debt	Preferred Stock	Stockholders' Equity
Galem Enterprises	30.5	4.1	65.4
CHW Corporation	24.9	0.0	75.1
Elston, Inc.	25.2	1.1	73.7
Compsol	25.0	0.0	75.0
International Office Equipment	12.0	6.8	81.7

EXHIBIT 24.4

Defreu, Inc.

*Breakdown of Long-term Debt as of December 31, 1987
(In Thousands)*

Interest Rate	Due Date	Amount	Terms
10.5%	1997	$13,000	Sinking fund of at least $1 million per year. Prepayment allowed.
12.0%	1992	18,000	Sinking fund of $3 million per year. No prepayment allowed.
11.5%	2000	10,753	No sinking fund. Payable in full by July 31, 2000.
11.0%	1996	14,000	Sinking fund payment of $1.5 million. Prepayment allowed.
		$55,753	

    The long-term borrowing agreement contains a group of restrictions on additional funded debt, working capital, the payment of dividends, and the purchase of the company's stock. As of December 31, 1987, the amount of retained earnings available for dividends under the most restrictive agreement was $15,000,000.

EXHIBIT 24.5

Defreu, Inc.

*Selected Ratios for the Systems and Copier Manufacturers
for the Following Calendar Periods*

	1985	1986	1987	1988
Liquidity:				
1. Current Ratio	1.60	1.62	1.64	1.61
2. Acid Test	1.20	1.19	1.23	1.20
3. Current Assets/Total Assets (%)	60.4	61.7	62.1	62.3
Activity:				
4. Receivables Turnover	7.31	7.24	7.43	7.50
5. Cost of Goods Sold/Inventory	6.20	6.22	6.24	6.27
6. Net Sales/Net Working Capital	7.47	8.01	8.04	8.00
7. Net Sales/Total Assets	2.00	2.04	2.08	2.10
Leverage:				
8. Total Debt/Total Assets (%)	56.3	56.3	57.1	57.9
9. Debt/Net Worth	1.34	1.64	1.52	1.48
10. EBIT/Interest	4.32	3.96	3.88	4.01
Profitability:				
11. COGS/Net Sales (%)	65.8	65.3	65.6	65.7
12. Operating Profit/Net Sales (%)	6.9	7.0	7.1	6.8
13. Profit Before Taxes/Net Sales (%)	5.6	5.7	5.8	5.5
14. Profit Before Taxes/Total Assets (%)	12.3	12.6	12.9	13.1
15. Profit Before Taxes/Net Worth (%)	24.3	25.2	26.1	26.0

QUESTIONS

1. Determine earnings per share assuming the issued securities are as follows:
   (a) Debenture bonds.
   (b) Common stock.
   (c) A 50-50 mix of debentures and common stock.

   (Prepare your answer with earnings before interest and taxes (EBIT) of $30,000,000, $50,000,000, and $70,000,000. Also assume that $75,000,000 of securities will be issued and that the marginal tax rate is 40 percent.)

2. Prepare a graph showing all financial plans. (Place EBIT on the X axis and earnings per share on the Y axis.)

3. Explain the major points of the three financing plans that can be determined from the graph in Question 2.

4. Explain how the necessity to add $75,000,000 in future securities would impact the financing decision.
5. Decide which plan Mr. Hawkins should choose and explain the reasoning behind your choice.

Welton Company
COST OF CAPITAL, BASIC

Don Hixon, a recent business administration graduate of Oklahoma State University, was in his office contemplating the task assigned by Jesse Queen, Welton's financial vice-president. He had been given the formidable responsibility of determining for the first time the firm's cost of capital.

The Welton Company, located in Enid, Oklahoma, manufactured radiators, pipes, valves, and a variety of tubing for use in the production of large heating and air conditioning units. George Welton, the firm's founder, had been employed for 13 years with a major producer of heating and cooling units. By 1968, he had risen to the position of vice-president for marketing. In 1972, he decided to organize his own firm, and he resigned his position. A balance sheet and income statement are included as Exhibit 25.1 and Exhibit 25.2.

To provide the necessary capital for the new venture, George Welton liquidated a series of successful investments in the stock market. The sale netted him just over $1,000,000 and became his capital for the new firm.

The company was an instantaneous success, as demand outstripped the firm's capacity to produce. By 1977, the Welton Company had expanded on two occasions, achieving annual sales in excess of $6,000,000. The company's early success was largely due to the marketing expertise Mr. Welton had acquired in his previous job as a marketing manager and to the wealth of personal contacts that he had developed in the company's major selling area of Oklahoma, Kansas, and North Texas.

Part of that success could also be traced to Mr. Welton's flexible manufacturing approach. He maintained a policy of filling customer orders in a very short time. Although this increased production costs, he thought it was necessary to remain competitive with the better established firms. By the end of fiscal year 1988, annual sales volume was about $50,000,000.

As the firm expanded, Mr. Welton realized it could not continue as a one-person operation. By the late 1970s, he knew that reorganization was an absolute necessity. He began the process by delegating decision making to a group of managers. He also hired business administration graduates from schools in the area to fill management positions and to form a pool of talent for future promotions. With that in mind, Mr. Hixon was hired as assistant to the financial vice-president. Within a short period of time, he capably performed a number of assignments, indicating his ability to handle the situation involving the cost of capital calculation.

Mr. Hixon knew he must first find an appropriate way to classify current liabilities in relation to the overall capital structure. He realized there would always be a certain level of current liabilities, but that in most finance textbooks, they were excluded in the definition of capital structure. He decided for simplicity's sake to follow that same pattern. A more crucial problem involved the question of the firm's optimal capital structure. Conversations with Mr. Welton and other executives indicated they were reasonably satisfied with the current structure. However, Peggy Higbee, an outside member of the board of directors, indicated she would like to see the firm employ a greater percentage of long-term debt. After much thought, Mr. Hixon rejected that idea and decided to consider the present structure as optimal.

To secure the costs of the various components of the capital structure, it was necessary for Mr. Hixon to contact a number of investment bankers in Oklahoma and North Texas. Their consensus was that a new long-term debt issue could be marketed with a 13 percent interest rate, while cumulative preferred would carry a rate of 14 percent. The firm's common stock, although not widely distributed, sold for $130 per share in the last group of transactions. An investment banking firm in Oklahoma believed it could sell a new issue that would net Welton $117 per share, but it was under the condition that the number of shares outstanding not increase by more than 20 percent. Mr. Hixon rejected the idea that retained earnings were costless, though he found it difficult to determine the appropriate cost. He calculated the net return on equity for similar firms and found it to be 18 percent. He decided to use that figure in his calculation.

Mr. Hixon estimated retained earnings for fiscal year 1989, July 1, 1988 through June 30, 1989, at $1,470,000. He believed that would be enough to finance a capital budget estimated at $3,500,000. He planned to use a marginal tax rate of 40 percent.

Selected ratios for air conditioning and warm air heating equipment manufacturers are presented as Exhibit 25.3.

EXHIBIT 25.1

Welton Company

Condensed Balance Sheet as of June 30, 1988
(In Thousands)

Assets:	
Current Assets	$12,000
Fixed Assets, Gross	20,000
Less: Accumulated Depreciation	9,800
Total Fixed Assets	$10,200
Total Assets	$22,200
Liabilities and Stockholders' Equity:	
Accounts Payable	$ 2,700
Accrued Expenses	1,600
Notes Payable	400
Total Current Liabilities	$ 4,700
Long-Term Debt (10.5%)	3,500
Stockholders' Equity	
Preferred Stock (12%)	1,750
Common Stock, $20 Par	1,500
Retained Earnings	10,750
Total Stockholders' Equity	$14,000
Total Liabilities and	
Stockholders' Equity	$22,200

EXHIBIT 25.2

Welton Company

Income Statement for the Period Ending June 30, 1988
(In Thousands)

Net Sales	$50,400
Cost of Sales	36,300
Gross Profit	$14,100
Operating Expenses	12,100
Operating Profit	$ 2,000
Other Expenses, Including Interest	400
Net Profit Before Taxes	$ 1,600
Federal and State Income Taxes	640
Net Profit	$ 960

EXHIBIT 25.3

Welton Company

*Selected Ratios for Air Conditioning and Warm Air Heating
Equipment Manufacturers for the Following Calendar Periods*

	1985	1986	1987	1988
Liquidity:				
1. Current Ratio	2.0	2.0	2.1	1.9
2. Acid Test	0.9	0.9	0.8	1.1
3. Current Assets/Total Assets (%)	73.1	74.0	72.5	71.4
Activity:				
4. Receivables Turnover	7.2	7.6	6.7	7.3
5. Cost of Goods Sold/Inventory	4.4	4.9	5.0	6.0
6. Net Sales/Net Working Capital	6.2	5.9	6.0	6.5
7. Net Sales/Total Assets	2.2	2.1	2.0	2.1
Leverage:				
8. Total Debt/Total Assets (%)	60.4	58.3	58.2	58.3
9. Debt/Net Worth	1.5	1.4	1.4	1.2
10. EBIT/Interest	5.4	4.2	3.2	2.7
Profitability:				
11. COGS/Net Sales (%)	72.6	72.1	71.1	72.8
12. Operating Profit/Net Sales (%)	7.7	6.4	7.0	5.9
13. Profit Before Taxes/Net Sales (%)	6.0	5.1	5.7	4.2
14. Profit Before Taxes/Total Assets (%)	11.2	10.3	8.5	8.2
15. Profit Before Taxes/Net Worth (%)	28.1	25.2	25.4	18.4

QUESTIONS

1. Calculate the cost of long-term debt, preferred stock, common stock, and retained earnings.
2. Determine the appropriate weights for each component of the capital structure.
3. Calculate the weighted average cost of capital.
4. Assume for fiscal 1989 that retained earnings is $2,450,000. What effect, if any, would that have on the cost of capital calculation?
5. Ms. Higbee believed the firm should use more long-term debt in the capital structure. Calculate the effect on the weighted average cost of capital if she were able to increase the percentage of debt to 30 percent. Can the cost of capital continually be reduced by substituting cheaper debt for costlier equity? Explain.

Cobb, Inc.
COST OF CAPITAL,
INTERMEDIATE

Francine Zablockie was involved in the most challenging experience of her brief career. Ms. Zablockie, a June graduate of Georgia State University, had presented the capital budget to the executive group of Cobb, Inc., a moderate-sized producer of stationery products and systems. The firm was headquartered in Marietta, Georgia, a suburb about 20 miles northwest of Atlanta. The executive group consisted of the president and five vice-presidents: finance, marketing, operations, human resources, and control. A balance sheet and an income statement are included in Exhibits 26.1 and 26.2, respectively.

Ms. Zablockie was hired by the company in July 1987 and had spent the next six months moving between functional areas to learn the basic operating procedures. In early 1988, she was assigned to the vice-president for finance, Clement Steiner. Mr. Steiner was impressed with the speed at which Ms. Zablockie learned the inner workings of the finance department.

For the past few years, Mr. Steiner had contemplated the idea of presenting a formal capital budget, but he never seemed to have the time to gather the information necessary to forward a proposal to the executive group.

Capital budgeting was always handled on an ad hoc basis. Whenever a vice-president, or one of his authorized employees, decided a capital item was necessary, he simply approached Mr. Steiner informally. Mr. Steiner then determined if cash were available or if it could be made available by borrowing. If so, the purchase was made. Mr. Steiner realized this method did not allow him to compare different capital items. He had to rely totally on each of the vice presidents. Mr. Steiner knew he needed a more rational way of evaluating their judgments.

In March 1988, Mr. Steiner told Ms. Zablockie he was going to make her responsible for reorganizing the capital budgeting process. He notified the executive group of his intention to modify the procedure. The members agreed that a change was necessary.

Ms. Zablockie decided to begin by gathering the capital budgeting needs of the functional executives. She prepared and sent each a form that, in essence, was a request for documentation. She asked that she receive this information by the middle of April, since her presentation was scheduled for late May.

Ms. Zablockie planned to complete the capital budget by July 1, 1988. She tried to anticipate problems that might arise. She felt that most difficulties would involve estimates of savings on capital projects. These numbers were greatly influenced by subjective estimates and were subject to wide differences of opinion. A second area of concern would be her calculation of the firm's cutoff rate, the marginal cost of capital. The idea of the cost of capital was straightforward, but the measurement problem was a difficult one.

Mr. Steiner called the meeting to order. Ms. Zablockie was nervous, but to her surprise, the executives accepted her savings estimates without question. Their expressions changed, however, when she explained her cost of capital calculations. (See Exhibit 26.3.)

After the presentation, Mr. Steiner called for questions. They came in rapid succession. Barry Lee, president of Cobb, asked why the firm needed a cost of capital. He was more concerned with how fast he could recover his investment. Lois Hall, vice-president for operations, wanted to know why retained earnings had a cost since the firm did not have to pay dividends. Del Hauceford, vice-president for control, wondered why common stock and retained earnings differed in cost inasmuch as both are sources of common equity. George Luther, vice-president for human resources, asked why there was a tax adjustment for debt but not for the other three components. He also was curious as to the origination of the component weights. Al Alter, vice-president for marketing, questioned why she did not simply calculate each component cost and match the cost against a specific capital budgeting project. That made more sense to him than calculating an overall cost of capital to be applied to all capital projects.

At that point, Mr. Steiner intervened and suggested that since there were so many questions about the cost of capital calculation, another meeting would be in order. After some discussion, they decided to meet again in two weeks. He suggested that at that time Ms. Zablockie should be able to explain the derivation of the numbers and to discuss the necessity of the cost of capital in the capital budgeting process. Mr. Steiner then praised Ms. Zablockie for her work and added that he was sure she would be able to answer all the questions from the executive group.

Selected ratios for stationery products manufacturers are presented in Exhibit 26.4.

EXHIBIT 26.1

Cobb, Inc.

Condensed Balance Sheet as of December 31, 1987
(In Thousands)

Assets:	
Current Assets	$20,000
Fixed Assets, Gross	66,000
Less: Accumulated Depreciation	32,000
Total Fixed Assets	$34,000
Total Assets	$54,000
Liabilities and Stockholders' Equity:	
Current Liabilities	$14,000
Long-Term Debt, 9%	12,000
Stockholders' Equity	
Preferred Stock, $10 Par, 10%	4,000
Common Stock, $5 Par	3,000
Retained Earnings	21,000
Total Stockholders' Equity	$28,000
Total Liabilities and	
Stockholder's Equity	$54,000

EXHIBIT 26.2

Cobb, Inc.

Income Statement for the Period Ending December 31,
1987 (In Thousands)

Net Sales	$137,700
Cost of Sales	99,944
Gross Profit	$ 37,756
Operating Expenses	30,776
Operating Profit	$ 6,980
Other Expenses, Including Interest	1,520
Net Profit Before Taxes	$ 5,460
Federal and State Income Taxes	2,160
Net Profit After Taxes	$ 3,300

EXHIBIT 26.3

Cobb, Inc.

Cost of Capital According to Source

Source of Funds	Amount	Before Tax	After Tax	Weights	Weighted Average
Bonds (15 year)	$ 3,000	11.0%	6.6%	0.30	1.98%
Preferred Stock	1,000	12.0	12.0	0.10	1.20
Common Stock	2,000	15.9	15.9	0.20	3.18
Retained Earnings[1]	4,000	15.0	15.0	0.40	6.00
	$10,000				12.36%

[1] Based on estimated retained earnings for 1988.

EXHIBIT 26.4

Cobb, Inc.

Selected Ratios for Stationery Products Manufacturers for the Following Calendar Periods

	1984	1985	1986	1987
Liquidity:				
1. Current Ratio	1.8	2.0	1.8	1.8
2. Acid Test	0.9	1.0	0.9	1.1
3. Current Assets/Total Assets (%)	66.9	65.2	66.0	65.9
Activity:				
4. Receivables Turnover	9.6	9.3	9.0	8.6
5. Cost of Goods Sold/Inventory	5.8	7.2	6.8	7.6
6. Net Sales/Net Working Capital	8.6	8.8	8.9	8.9
7. Net Sales/Total Assets	2.4	2.4	2.5	2.5
Leverage:				
8. Total Debt/Total Assets (%)	53.3	53.1	57.2	57.8
9. Debt/Net Worth	1.2	1.0	1.4	1.4
10. EBIT/Interest	5.3	3.7	3.2	2.5
Profitability:				
11. COGS/Net Sales (%)	74.5	73.9	74.3	72.1
12. Operating Profit/Net Sales (%)	6.8	5.6	5.1	4.4
13. Profit Before Taxes/Net Sales (%)	5.6	4.3	3.9	2.9
14. Profit Before Taxes/Total Assets (%)	11.7	10.4	9.0	6.9
15. Profit Before Taxes/Net Worth (%)	25.5	21.9	20.9	16.6

QUESTIONS

1. Prepare a report detailing how Ms. Zablockie found the information contained in Exhibit 26.3. Assume the following facts:
   (a) The company believes the present capital structure, consisting of long-term debt, preferred stock, and common equity is optimal.
   (b) Future bond issues will cost 11 percent.
   (c) Future preferred issues will cost 12 percent.
   (d) The common stock is currently selling for $50 per share.
   (e) Flotation costs are $5 per common share.
   (f) The marginal tax rate is 40 percent.
   (g) Dividends are expected to be $4 per share in the coming year and to grow at a rate of 7 percent indefinitely.

2. Answer Mr. Lee's question as to why it is necessary for a firm to calculate its cost of capital.

3. Answer Ms. Hall's question concerning retained earnings.

4. Answer Mr. Hauceford's question concerning the costs of retained earnings and common stock.

5. Answer Mr. Luther's questions concerning tax adjustments on component costs and why component costs are weighted.

6. Discuss Mr. Alter's idea of calculating a component cost and matching it against a specific capital budgeting project.

7. Assume that the firm has to raise an additional $10,000,000 and that debt will cost 12 percent, preferred stock 13 percent, and common stock 17.5 percent.
   (a) Calculate Cobb's marginal cost of capital.
   (b) Plot the marginal cost of capital from $0 to $20,000,000.

Yardley Brothers, Inc.
COST OF CAPITAL, COMPLEX

Yardley Brothers, Inc., a specialty food company headquartered in Dayton, Ohio, was recognized in the United States and Western Europe as a leader in the manufacture and distribution of seasonings and flavored products for the food industry. Processing facilities were found in 11 locations in the United States. The company was considering building a plant near Amsterdam as its first site in Western Europe. The company was organized into two divisions: Grocery Products, which accounted for 75 percent of sales, and Food Service, which was responsible for the remainder of the sales. A balance sheet and an income statement are included as Exhibit 27.1 and Exhibit 27.2. Selected statistics on Yardley Brothers are given as Exhibit 27.3.

During the 1980s, Yardley Brothers benefited tremendously from the increasing sophistication of American consumers. Since this group had both the means and the desire to try different types of foods, new and exotic seasonings were demanded. The product could also be used to spice up recipes that were low in cost when measured on a per serving basis. The company believed the willingness of consumers to experiment would continue during the 1990s. They felt that this would lead to more ethnic types of cooking and the use of more recipes from gourmet magazines. This line of thinking gave Yardley Brothers a solid base from which to expand its Grocery Products Division.

The Food Service Division manufactured and distributed seasonings and sauces as well as portion control and specialty products. This division had experienced only modest sales expansion during the 1980s, as growth was tied to fast-food outlets and they had grown at a relatively moderate rate. Management knew that for this division to expand, costs must be kept competitive. Management also realized that new products had to be developed to enable the division to experience growth, even if fast food remained a mature industry. Although studies had been done to determine whether the firm should move into activities distinctly apart from grocery products and food service, management had always decided to remain in those two areas. It believed that approach would allow profits to be earned without taking the risks associated with new projects.

During February, Laurie Benston, vice-president of finance, considered various ways to finance several investment projects. Included in her list were a new processing plant in Western Europe, modernization of present processing facilities, the addition of a new plant in Florida or Georgia, and a major addition to working capital. The addition to working capital alternative involved providing funds to finance inventory growth necessary to expand the firm's line of seasonings.

Since Ms. Benston had requested capital estimates from the two operating divisions, each of the division heads had submitted proposals. From their recommendations, Ms. Benston had decided on the four projects previously mentioned. Her job then was to assemble the best financial package and to present it to the president of Yardley Brothers, Jackie Calmire. Ms. Benston planned to have the report completed by March 15 for negotiations beginning in mid-April.

Ms. Benston believed the amount of funds needed would be about $30,000,000. Of the total, $10,000,000 would be required for the Amsterdam plant, $9,000,000 for the plant in the Southeast, $7,000,000 for modernization, and $4,000,000 for the inventory addition.

Her first contact was Irving Goldman, vice-president of the National Bank of Ohio, the firm's major banking connection. The bank was Yardley Brothers' principal source of short- and intermediate-type debt. In 1988, the bank was also instrumental in helping to secure, on favorable terms, $15,000,000 in bond funds to replace short-term bank notes.

Mr. Goldman informed Ms. Benston that the bank would lend a maximum of $15,000,000 at 8 percent over the prime rate, which was presently at 9 percent. The rate reflected the increased financial leverage incurred by the firm over the last 3 years. The loan, beginning on July 1, 1989, would mature in 10 years and would be payable in semiannual installments of $750,000, plus outstanding interest on the unpaid principal.

Certain requirements and restrictions would be imposed on the loan: (1) net current assets must be maintained at a level of $5,000,000, (2) the company would not declare cash dividends or purchase its own common stock in amounts in excess of 40 percent of net income in any one year, and (3) capital expenditures in any one year must not exceed 100 percent of depreciation charges, without the bank's approval. The covenant applied to the modernization of plant facilities, not to the two plants being constructed. The loan would be unsecured.

Mr. Goldman stated that for Yardley Brothers to receive these funds, the firm would have to raise the $15,000,000 from retained earnings and securities junior to the bank's position. Since earnings less dividend payout was estimated at $5,000,000 for the coming year, the remaining $10,000,000 would have to come from junior securities. Although Ms. Benston had some reservations about the bank package, especially the restriction on capital expenditures, she decided to accept informally the bank's commitment and to begin the search for other funds.

Although there were a number of ways to raise the needed funds, three possibilities seemed the most likely: preferred stock, common stock, and subordinated convertible debt. To discuss the type of financial package the firm might expect, Ms. Benston contacted Hargrow & Sacks, a regional underwriting organization located in Columbus, Ohio.

Craig Belton of the underwriting firm explained that a common stock issue would net the firm $60 per share. This was found by subtracting a $5 flotation cost from the current price of $65. Preferred stock, sold at $100 par, would have a 10.5 percent rate and would be cumulative. Convertible subordinated debentures would carry a rate of 9.5 percent, with a conversion price ranging between $72 and $78 per share. Ms. Benston believed that conversion would take place within one or two years, since forecasts for the firm and the stock market were favorable.

In preparing her report, Ms. Benston's job was to determine which of the following financial packages would produce the lowest cost of capital: (1) debt and common stock, (2) debt and preferred stock, or (3) debt and subordinated debentures. This presented her with difficult problems that needed resolution, if she were to be successful.

Ms. Benston knew two ways to calculate the cost of common equity: the Gordon model and the capital asset pricing model. There was also the question of the weights that should be assigned to each component of the cost of capital. Should the weights be based on the marginal funds being raised or based on the optimal mix of funds? If optimal weights were used, should she use book weights or market weights?

Ms. Benston wondered if the projects being financed would effect the cost of capital by changing the business risk of the firm. If this were the case, she knew the effect should be incorporated into the cost of capital calculation. While thinking about this, she was interrupted by one of her staff members asking how depreciation would figure in the calculation.

After much effort, Ms. Benston was able to compile some useful information. Exhibit 27.4, "Selected information concerning the cost of capital calculation," was the result.

Selected ratios for spices and seasonings manufacturers and wholesalers are presented in Exhibit 27.5.

EXHIBIT 27.1

Yardley Brothers, Inc.

Balance Sheets for Years Ending December 31 (In Thousands)

	1986	1987	1988
Assets:			
Cash	$ 2,291	$ 2,750	$ 2,839
Accounts Receivable	37,404	46,220	50,896
Inventories	77,776	92,443	93,291
Prepaid Expenses	1,727	2,295	3,090
Total Current Assets	$119,198	$143,708	$150,116
Land and Improvements	3,867	4,328	4,069
Buildings and Improvements	22,328	25,004	27,396
Machinery and Equipment	52,091	62,735	70,833
Construction in Progress	2,432	2,566	6,846
Less: Accumulated Depreciation	(35,077)	(42,218)	(46,756)
Total Fixed Assets	$ 45,641	$ 52,415	$ 62,388
Other Assets	12,207	7,424	4,570
Total Assets	$177,046	$203,547	$217,074
Liabilities and Stockholders' Equity:			
Accounts Payable and Accruals	$ 47,436	$ 49,441	$ 51,282
Notes Payable	12,089	20,620	5,675
Current Portion, Long-Term Debt	1,240	1,450	2,100
Income Taxes	3,351	3,210	3,550
Dividends Payable	1,166	1,452	1,410
Total Current Liabilities	$ 65,282	$ 76,173	$ 64,017
Long-Term Debt			
Bonds	21,300	31,300	48,800
Notes Payable	28,500	29,460	32,655
Total Long-Term Debt	$ 49,800	$ 60,760	$ 81,455
Stockholders' Equity			
Preferred Stock, $100 Par	$ 1,250	$ 1,250	$ 1,250
Common Stock, $1 Par	1,212	1,300	1,688
Retained Earnings	59,502	64,064	68,664
Total Stockholders' Equity	$ 61,964	$ 66,614	$ 71,602
Total Liabilities and Stockholders' Equity	$177,046	$203,547	$217,074

EXHIBIT 27.2

Yardley Brothers, Inc.

Income Statements for Years Ending December 31
(In Thousands)

	1986	1987	1988
Net Sales	$300,268	$342,873	$406,970
Operating Expenses			
Cost of Goods Sold	196,483	222,220	266,494
Selling, General, and Administrative	90,879	105,776	124,125
Profit from Operations	$ 12,906	$ 14,877	$ 16,351
Other Income	1,977	1,798	1,426
Other Expense	437	401	673
Interest Expense	4,538	4,278	4,344
Income Before Taxes	$ 11,206	$ 12,584	$ 12,817
Federal and State Income Taxes	4,538	4,278	4,344
Net Income After Taxes	$ 6,668	$ 8,306	$ 8,473

EXHIBIT 27.3

Yardley Brothers, Inc.

Selected Statistics on Yardley Brothers, Inc.

	1986	1987	1988
Gross Profit to Net Sales	34.6%	35.2%	34.6%
Net Income to Assets	3.8%	4.1%	3.9%
Profit from Operations to Assets	7.3%	7.3%	7.5%
Current Ratio	1.83%	1.89%	2.35%
Acid Test Ratio	0.61%	0.64%	0.84%
Net Sales to Assets	1.70%	1.69%	1.87%
Return on Common Equity	11.0%	12.9%	12.0%
Per Common Share			
Earnings	$5.54	$6.39	$5.14
Common Dividends	2.32	2.88	2.88
Book Value	50.43	50.28	42.64
Market Price (high)	63.25	68.875	75.50
Market Price (low)	38.50	40.00	43.125
Average P/E Ratio	9	10	12
Average Shares Outstanding	1,204	1,300	1,650
Average Number of Employees	312.0	336.0	340.5

EXHIBIT 27.4

Yardley Brothers, Inc.

Selected Information Used in Calculating the Cost of Capital

I. Estimated Dividend (per Share) in Coming Year	$3.50
II. Estimated Growth Rate in Earnings	8%
III. Estimated Beta of Yardley Brothers from Three Brokerage Houses	+1.20
	+1.30
	+1.40
IV. Estimated Risk-Free Rate Based on the 91-Day Treasury Bill Rate	6%
V. Estimated Market Rate of Return Based on Standard & Poor's 500	12%
VI. Current Capital Structure (book weights)	
Debt	52%
Preferred Stock	1%
Common Equity	47%
VII. Optimal Capital Structure (book weights)	
Debt	40%
Preferred Stock	5%
Common Equity	55%

EXHIBIT 27.5

Yardley Brothers, Inc.

*Selected Ratios for Spices and Seasonings Manufacturers and
Wholesalers for the Following Calendar Periods*

	1984	1985	1986	1987
Liquidity:				
1. Current Ratio	1.5	1.5	1.4	1.4
2. Acid Test	0.8	0.8	0.7	0.7
3. Current Assets/Total Assets (%)	49.8	49.4	55.0	52.6
Activity:				
4. Receivables Turnover	13.2	13.8	14.0	14.0
5. Cost of Goods Sold/Inventory	9.4	11.6	10.0	10.2
6. Net Sales/Net Working Capital	17.3	17.8	22.3	22.6
7. Net Sales/Total Assets	3.9	4.1	3.9	3.7
Leverage:				
8. Total Debt/Total Assets (%)	62.0	61.5	65.8	65.6
9. Debt/Net Worth	1.7	1.6	2.3	2.3
10. EBIT/Interest	2.9	2.5	2.5	2.7

	1984	1985	1986	1987
EXHIBIT 27.5 (Continued)				
Profitability:				
11. COGS/Net Sales (%)	77.7	77.4	79.6	78.7
12. Operating Profit/Net Sales (%)	3.7	2.4	2.8	2.7
13. Profit Before Taxes/Net Sales (%)	2.8	1.8	2.1	2.1
14. Profit Before Taxes/Total Assets (%)	8.5	5.9	5.0	5.7
15. Profit Before Taxes/Net Worth (%)	23.8	17.5	17.8	17.1

QUESTIONS

1. Compare the capital asset pricing model with the Gordon model in calculating the cost of equity.
2. Discuss the issues involved in using marginal weights and optimal weights in determining the cost of capital.
3. Discuss the use of book weights versus market weights in finding the optimal capital structure.
4. Explain whether or not depreciation charges should be included in the cost of capital calculation.
5. Explain what effect, if any, the business risk of projects in the capital budget will have on the cost of capital.
6. Calculate the cost of capital assuming that debt and common stock are issued. (Where there is a choice of models and techniques, state your assumptions and be able to defend your calculations.)
7. Recalculate Question 6 assuming that debt and preferred stock are issued.
8. Recalculate Question 6 assuming that debt and subordinate convertible debt are issued. (In answering this question, comment on the convertibility feature as it relates to the cost of capital.)
9. Select the most appropriate financing package for the firm, giving the reasons for your choice.

Case 28

Home Supplies, Inc.
VALUATION

How do you determine the value of a company? That question would dominate a meeting in late January 1989, between the Galenson brothers and Sally Blair, senior partner of a large Omaha brokerage house, Blair, Higgins, and Zorch. The Galenson brothers, Maxwell, Benjamin, George, and Paul each owned one-sixth of Home Supplies, Inc., a company that provided products and services for homeowners and contractors. The remaining ownership was represented by some 220 investors, with no one investor owning more than 4 percent of the outstanding shares. The firm was headquartered in Omaha, Nebraska, and operated 30 retail stores in Iowa, Kansas, Nebraska, and Missouri. A balance sheet and income statement are included as Exhibit 28.1 and Exhibit 28.2.

The value of the company needed to be ascertained since Maxwell, the oldest of the four brothers, wanted to sell his stock to the other three. Maxwell Galenson was nearing 70 and wished to retire from active participation in the firm. He believed that a family member who no longer wished to manage should not own a large portion of the stock in the company. Another consideration was that none of his three children were interested in being a part of the firm. Therefore, he preferred to leave in his estate a well-diversified group of listed stocks and bonds, not assets represented by ownership in the family business. Also, by diversifying in this way, he knew he would significantly reduce his portfolio risk. Additional financial information is included as Exhibit 28.3 and Exhibit 28.4. Selected ratios for the hardware retailing industry are presented as Exhibit 28.5.

Maxwell Galenson founded Home Supplies, Inc. in Omaha in 1952 as a neighborhood hardware store. Sales grew by an average of 10 percent, and by 1970, the firm had revenues in excess of $3,000,000. Between 1952 and 1968, Benjamin and George Galenson joined the firm. In 1970, Paul Galenson was hired as vice-president for marketing.

Paul Galenson brought a radically new approach to the business. He had previously been head of marketing for a regional lumber company. Influenced by what he had seen in that industry, he believed that Home Supplies, Inc., should begin developing a network of one-stop building products supermarkets. He conceived of these as self-service outlets designed to serve the do-it-yourself market. He knew this market would expand at a much faster pace than would that for the traditional hardware store. He was fairly confident that the superstore for hardware and building materials would dominate the retailing of these products. He proved to be a prophet, but it took over seven years for the other brothers to be convinced of the soundness of his idea.

In 1978, Home Supplies, Inc. opened its first superstore. For the next 10 years, an average of three outlets were added each year. By 1988, the firm operated in a five-state area, with sales in excess of $60,000,000.

Ms. Blair opened the meeting. "There are a lot of different ways of establishing value: book value, liquidation value, market value, and value based on what is known as capitalization of future income." She paused for a moment. "I personally believe that the market provides the best estimate of value because something is only worth what somebody else is willing to pay for it."

"Like trying to sell a house." It was Paul Galenson, arriving late and searching for a place to sit.

"Precisely," she continued. "Investors tell us what a company is worth by their willingness to buy and sell the firm's shares. As you know, our firm has been making a market in your stock since 1983. Yesterday, a block of 800 shares sold for $22 per share."

Maxwell Galenson squirmed in his chair. "Yes, but book value is the fairest. It relies on real numbers, the ones on the balance sheet. The people establishing book value have no ax to grind. They just record what really happens."

Benjamin Galenson leaned back, smiled, and added, "I agree that book value is the most objective, but there are still a few things that worry me about it. For example, we own the land that some of our stores are located on and that property is worth a lot more than it's recorded for on the books. To be fair, book value would have to be adjusted for that kind of situation."

"What in the world is capitalization of income?" It was George Galenson. Before Sally Blair could answer, he started to light a large cigar.

"George, can't that wait?" Maxwell Galenson began. "My doctor told me not even to get near smoke."

He slipped the cigar back in his pocket. "As I was saying, the way it's been explained to me, it sounds like some kind of fancy way to give you any number you want. I want to buy the shares from Maxwell at a fair price, fair to him, fair to us."

"We all want that." Paul Galenson spoke up again. "I really think market price is the only true price, but the question is what market price do you use? Is it the average market price over some period of time, or the price on the day we close? I really don't know."

"I gave up smoking ten years ago. I'll outlive all of you." The other brothers hoped Maxwell would get back to the subject. He had a habit of telling stories, anecdotes actually, from the early days. They were relieved when he continued. "I really don't know what you fellows ought to pay me for the stock. Just try to be fair." When Maxwell talked like that, the brothers knew to be careful. "If I have to put the shares on the open market, I'll lose a lot because that many shares at one time would cause the price to fall. It sounds like I'm knocking the value of my holdings, but I want to do the right thing."

The discussion continued in the same vein for more than an hour. Then Maxwell began telling stories. That brought the meeting to a fast conclusion.

George Galenson reached in his pocket for his cigar, stood up, and said, "Let's meet again in two weeks. By then we will have had time to think about the various ideas of value and will be in better shape to tell Maxwell how much his shares are worth."

EXHIBIT 28.1

Home Supplies, Inc.

Balance Sheet as of December 31 (In Thousands)

	1986	*1987*	*1988*
Assets:			
Cash	$ 819	$ 713	$ 1,004
Accounts Receivable	4,917	5,106	5,787
Inventory	8,627	9,447	10,213
Other Current Assets	499	456	310
Total Current Assets	$14,862	$15,722	$17,314
Property, Plant, and Equipment	15,102	16,755	19,439
Less: Accumulated Depreciation	6,834	7,823	8,647
Net Property, Plant, and Equipment	$ 8,268	$ 8,932	$10,792
Other Assets	647	450	392
Total Assets	$23,777	$25,104	$28,498
Liabilities and Stockholders' Equity:			
Accounts Payable	$ 4,190	$ 4,697	$ 5,749
Notes Payable, Bank	525	620	2,100
Accruals	718	556	752
Current Maturity, Long-Term Debt	850	850	850
Total Current Liabilities	$ 6,283	$ 6,723	$ 9,451
Long-Term Debt	8,450	7,600	6,750
Stockholders' Equity			
Common Stock $1 Par	480	480	480
Paid-in Capital	912	912	912
Retained Earnings	7,652	9,389	10,905
Total Stockholders' Equity	$ 9,044	$10,781	$12,297
Total Liabilities and Stockholders' Equity	$23,777	$25,104	$28,498

EXHIBIT 28.2

Home Supplies, Inc.

Income Statement for the Years Ending December 31
(In Thousands)

	1986	1987	1988
Net Sales	$55,777	$56,919	$60,702
Cost of Operations	46,028	47,925	50,702
Gross Profit	$ 9,749	$ 8,994	$10,000
Selling and Administrative	4,866	4,879	5,750
Operating Profit	$ 4,883	$ 4,115	$ 4,250
Interest Expense	940	921	966
Net Profit Before Taxes	$ 3,943	$ 3,194	$ 3,284
Federal and State Income Taxes	1,577	1,278	1,314
Net Profit After Taxes	$ 2,366	$ 1,916	$ 1,970

EXHIBIT 28.3

Home Supplies, Inc.

High and Low Stock Prices of Home
Supplies, Inc.

Year	High	Low
1983	14.500	6.750
1984	18.000	8.500
1985	27.000	13.750
1986	33.500	20.625
1987	30.000	21.500
1988	28.500	20.250

EXHIBIT 28.4

Home Supplies, Inc.

Earnings (EPS) and Dividends Per Share (DPS)

Year	EPS	DPS
1980	$2.17	$0.60
1981	2.40	0.60
1982	2.70	0.60
1983	2.90	0.60
1984	3.46	1.00
1985	3.70	1.00
1986	4.93	1.10
1987	3.99	1.10
1988	4.10	1.10

EXHIBIT 28.5

Home Supplies, Inc.

Selected Ratios for the Hardware Retailing Industry for the Following Calendar Periods

	1985	1986	1987	1988
Liquidity:				
1. Current Ratio	2.8	2.2	2.2	2.1
2. Acid Test	0.5	0.5	0.5	0.4
3. Current Assets/Total Assets (%)	76.7	76.4	75.4	74.6
Activity:				
4. Receivables Turnover	20.8	18.9	19.3	21.3
5. Cost of Goods Sold/Inventory	2.7	2.6	2.5	2.6
6. Net Sales/Net Working Capital	5.7	5.6	5.8	6.2
7. Net Sales/Total Assets	2.3	2.1	2.1	2.1
Leverage:				
8. Total Debt/Total Assets (%)	59.0	58.3	58.7	60.1
9. Debt/Net Worth	1.5	1.4	1.4	1.4
10. EBIT/Interest	3.5	2.6	2.1	2.0
Profitability:				
11. COGS/Net Sales (%)	67.0	66.8	66.2	66.3
12. Operating Profit/Net Sales (%)	3.7	4.0	3.2	2.5
13. Profit Before Taxes/Net Sales (%)	3.3	3.4	2.4	1.6
14. Profit Before Taxes/Total Assets (%)	7.5	6.0	4.9	3.7
15. Profit Before Taxes/Net Worth (%)	19.8	15.7	13.1	9.1

QUESTIONS

1. Determine the book value per share for 1986, 1987, and 1988.
2. Determine the value per share based on the capitalization of income method.
3. Determine and explain the market price you would use in valuing the firm.
4. How would you find the liquidation value? Is it a reasonable alternative in this case?
5. Are there any other concepts of value that are not stated in the case that you would choose? If so, discuss and compare them with the concepts stated in the case.
6. Which valuation model would you choose? Giver reasons for your choice.

Global Communications, Inc.
DIVIDEND POLICY

Leah Sternberg was preparing a paper on dividend policy for the Board of Directors' meeting at Global Communications, Inc. When they last met in December, there was a spirited discussion concerning the effectiveness of past dividend policy. The discussion was a prelude to establishing a set of guidelines for future dividend policy.

At that meeting, Miles Kinsky, the president of the firm, had instructed Ms. Sternberg, the company treasurer, to develop a working paper that would succinctly outline the major approaches to dividend policy. Mr. Kinsky expected Ms. Sternberg to be neutral in the upcoming policy debate, but he wanted her to be thoroughly prepared to answer any questions posed by the directors. To this end, Ms. Sternberg was pursuing material published in textbooks, financial journals, and financial magazines, to become as knowledgeable as possible about both the theoretical and applied issues that should be considered in developing a company's dividend policy.

Global Communications, Inc., located in New York City, was a large multinational corporation with diverse operating groups. The largest division, which accounted for approximately 45 percent of sales, was Consumer Products and Services. This division produced television sets, VCRs, stereos, records, and tapes. A balance sheet and income statement are included as Exhibit 29.1 and Exhibit 29.2.

In the fiscal year ending January 31, 1988, a company record was established for sales of VCRs and stereos. A new line of television sets called "Clearview" had spearheaded renewed interest in this major part of the company's product line. Profits on television and audio products had declined as a result of the highly competitive conditions that existed in the industry. The company found it difficult to pass on to the customer increased costs, but felt that anticipated price increases in fiscal 1989 should sufficiently cover any increased labor and material costs. Additional financial information is given as Exhibit 29.3 and Exhibit 29.4.

The Commercial Products and Services Division produced various solid-state devices and accounted for approximately 20 percent of total sales. The solid-state devices were sold mainly to the automobile and watch industries.

Other products in the division were broadcasting and aviation communications equipment, communications satellites, and telex switching systems. Due to a large and growing backlog of orders, facilities were being expanded by more than 10 percent.

Global Communications owned one of the major radio and television networks in the United States, the Standard Broadcasting System, which accounted for 30 percent of company revenues. However, during the 1970s and early 1980s, the television network, which provided the bulk of the group's revenues, had a mediocre performance, due to the steep decline in the ratings of its television programs. The drop in ratings precipitated major personnel changes, which culminated in the resignation of the president of the company. A new president, appointed in 1984, was able to reverse the ratings performance of the network. In fact, for the past two years, the network had earned, by a significant margin, the number one ranking. Also, the radio network had just experienced a record year in both sales and profits.

The Miscellaneous Products and Services Division, mostly consisting of government contract work, accounted for the remainder of Global's sales. This division's activities had shrunk in recent years, and this trend was expected to continue in the foreseeable future.

Ms. Sternberg's research into dividend policy uncovered two distinct approaches. One suggested that dividends be paid only if investment needs were met. This meant that if the firm had a large number of potentially profitable investments, it should employ all its internally generated funds to finance these projects. If funds remained after these requirements were met, then they would be paid out in the form of dividends. In this case, a firm generating high-return investment projects would have a dividend payout of zero, since all its internally generated funds would be reinvested. In fact, this type of firm might be forced to sell new common stock to finance its new projects.

With the second approach, the level of investment would not be the only determinant of dividend policy. Dividends would be paid even if some profitable projects had to be forgone. Thus, dividends would have a value in and of themselves. This meant that an equivalent amount of dividends was worth more than an equivalent amount of retained earnings. To induce investors to forgo a dollar of dividends, more than a dollar of capital gains must be promised. How much more was difficult to predict.

From her research, Ms. Sternberg noted that each of these approaches had strong advocates. She observed that the preponderance of supporters of the first approach were academicians, while financial executives supported the second approach.

From attending past directors' meetings, Ms. Sternberg could not determine if any one policy had been followed to the exclusion of another. She heard one director, Sonia Cann, say that dividends should be reduced only under the more dire circumstances, since a large number of Global Communications stockholders depended upon the income from dividends. She knew it would place a hardship on them to have their funds reduced. Another director, Jon O'Rourke, said that investors had no preference for dividends over capital gains. He felt that they wanted the highest possible return for a given level of risk. Directors Cartledge and Estobel argued that the firm could not establish a long-range policy, since dividend payout depended upon certain conditions, such as the state of the economy, cash needs of the firm, and the company's investment requirements. They contended that all the factors that entered into dividend policy were subject to such a high degree of variability that it was useless to chart a long-range plan. Both directors claimed that the formulation of a dividend policy had to be on a year-to-year basis.

Selected ratios for television, radio, and phonograph manufacturers are presented as Exhibit 29.5.

EXHIBIT 29.1

Global Communications, Inc.

Balance Sheets for Years Ending January 31 (In Millions)

	1985	1986	1987	1988
Assets:				
Cash	$ 210	$ 190	$ 229	$ 213
Short-Term Investments	146	147	105	375
Receivables, Less Reserves	813	885	815	1,007
Inventories, Net	600	569	631	643
Prepaid Expenses	411	414	410	426
Other Current Assets	301	312	243	46
Total Current Assets	$2,481	$2,517	$2,433	$2,710
Investments and Noncurrent Assets	588	288	245	262
Plant and Equipment, Net	1,040	1,149	1,168	1,157
Total Assets	$4,109	$3,954	$3,846	$4,129
Liabilities and Stockholders' Equity:				
Current Liabilities	$1,199	$1,374	$1,323	$1,269
Other Noncurrent Liabilities	270	243	250	297
Other Long-Term Debt	942	924	736	877
Total Liabilities	$2,411	$2,541	$2,309	$2,443
Stockholders' Equity				
10.0% Preferred Stock	$ 20	$ 20	$ 20	$ 20
Common Stock, $1.00 Par	75	75	75	75
Paid-in Capital	672	672	657	675
Retained Earnings	931	646	785	916
Total Stockholders' Equity	$1,698	$1,413	$1,537	$1,686
Total Liabilities and Stockholders' Equity	$4,109	$3,954	$3,846	$4,129

EXHIBIT 29.2

Global Communications, Inc.

Income Statements for the Years Ending January 31
(In Millions)

	1985	1986	1987	1988
Product Sales	$2,592	$2,859	$2,789	$3,135
Service Sales	2,382	2,436	2,320	2,621
Other Revenue	34	22	36	38
Total Revenue	$5,008	$5,317	$5,145	$5,794
Cost of Product Sales	1,986	2,168	1,928	2,313
Cost of Service Sales	1,473	1,500	1,457	1,641
Total Cost of Sales	$3,459	$3,668	$3,385	$3,954
Gross Profit	$1,549	$1,649	$1,760	$1,840
Selling, General, and Administrative Expenses	879	915	822	982
Depreciation	285	303	366	389
Interest	93	90	67	87
Total Operating Expenses	$1,257	$1,308	$1,255	$1,458
Net Profit Before Taxes	292	341	505	382
Federal and State Income Taxes	114	143	137	129
Extraordinary Charge	0	372	0	0
Net Profit for Year	$ 178	$ (174)	$ 368	$ 253

EXHIBIT 29.3

Global Communications, Inc.

Financial Data Ending January 31

	1985	1986	1987	1988
Earnings per Share	$2.37	($2.32)	$4.91	$3.37
Preferred Dividends (millions)	$2	$2	$2	$2
Common Dividends (millions)	$99	$111	$120	$120
Common Dividends per Share	$1.32	$1.48	$1.60	$1.60
Current Ratio	2.07	1.83	1.84	2.14
Additions to Plant and Equipment	$262	$251	$219	$216
Net Working Capital (millions)	$1,282	$1,143	$1,110	$1,441
Shareholders (thousands)	486	453	451	444
Average Stock Price	23.50	22.00	36.125	30.50

EXHIBIT 29.4

Global Communications, Inc.

Pro Forma Earnings Statement for Fiscal 1989, with Other Financial Data (In Millions)

Product Sales	$3,600
Service Sales	2,700
Total Revenue	6,300
Cost of Product Sales	2,700
Cost of Service Sales	1,620
Total Cost of Sales	$4,320
Selling, General, and	
Administrative Expenses	1,020
Depreciation	390
Interest	90
Total Operating Expenses	1,500
Net Profit Before Taxes	$ 480
Income Taxes	160
Net Profit After Taxes	$ 320
Additions to Plant	$ 350
Current Ratio	2:1
Earnings per Share	$4.67

EXHIBIT 29.5

Global Communications, Inc.

Selected Ratios for Television, Radio, and Phonograph
Manufacturers for the Following Calendar Periods

	1984	1985	1986	1987
Liquidity:				
1. Current Ratio	2.2	2.4	1.8	2.4
2. Acid Test	0.9	0.8	0.8	1.0
3. Current Assets/Total Assets (%)	34.7	35.9	44.6	35.3
Activity:				
4. Receivables Turnover	6.8	6.5	5.3	7.3
5. Cost of Goods Sold/Inventory	3.3	3.3	3.0	3.3
6. Net Sales/Net Working Capital	4.8	5.5	5.2	5.7
7. Net Sales/Total Assets	1.8	1.7	1.6	1.7
Leverage:				
8. Total Debt/Total Assets (%)	59.5	57.1	64.4	49.5
9. Debt/Net Worth	1.4	1.6	2.4	1.1
10. EBIT/Interest	1.8	2.1	2.5	3.2
Profitability:				
11. COGS/Net Sales (%)	61.0	65.2	69.5	65.9
12. Operating Profit/Net Sales (%)	5.7	5.5	2.9	7.3
13. Profit Before Taxes/Net Sales (%)	1.3	1.5	0.0	6.2
14. Profit Before Taxes/Total Assets (%)	5.1	5.4	2.8	8.2
15. Profit Before Taxes/Net Worth (%)	14.2	11.5	13.4	20.0

QUESTIONS

1. Discuss the two approaches to dividend policy found in the case.
2. Give specific examples of companies that have adopted the two approaches to dividend policy. (Annual reports should be used to prepare your answer.)
3. Defend or refute the statements concerning dividend policy made by Cartledge and Estobel.
4. Does the dividend policy of Global Communications correlate with the policies stated in Question 1?
5. Prepare a memo stating the dividend policy you would propose for the firm. (Reasons should be included in your response.)

Jarvis Incorporated
DIVIDEND POLICY

Lee Immerling, vice-president of finance for Jarvis Incorporated, was reviewing the dividend policy of the firm. A Board of Directors meeting was upcoming in mid-February 1989, and he intended to be ready to answer all inquiries as to the criteria for establishing an appropriate dividend policy for the company.

Jarvis Incorporated, headquartered in Huntington, West Virginia, was a producer of products serving the packaging markets. The company was organized into three divisions: Metal Container, Glass Container, and Plastics. Balance sheets and income statements are included as Exhibit 30.1 and Exhibit 30.2. Additional financial information is given in Exhibit 30.3 and Exhibit 30.4. Selected ratios for the packaging industry are presented as Exhibit 30.5.

The Metal Container Division, which accounted for 45 percent of sales in 1988, produced for the brewing and soft drink industry. This division had a strong year in 1988, with sales up 15 percent. All plants operated at capacity, and all achieved production records. If bookings for 1989 were any indication of customer interest, manufacturing facilities in Zanesville, Ohio, Fort Dodge, Iowa, and Montgomery, Alabama would be strained to satisfy demand.

The Glass Container Division, which accounted for 35 percent of total sales, experienced a moderate increase in profit in 1988 due to better plant utilization, reasonable price gains, and a 5 percent increase in sales. The division manufactured glass containers for commercial food processors and home preservation use. During the past year, a large portion of its excess manufacturing capacity disappeared. But Jarvis continued to emphasize customer service and quality. In addition, major capital expenditures improved productivity and automated many tasks.

The Plastics Division, which accounted for 20 percent of total sales, produced barrier plastic products that provided increased shelf stability and enabled food products to be shipped and stored at room temperature for up to one year. In addition, some sheet barrier plastic was sold to customers who formed and filled containers. This type of activity accounted for about 15 percent of division sales, but was growing faster than any other product line. This division manufactured, by the blow-molding process, squeezeable bottles for ketchup customers. Demand had been strong, and a new production facility was in the planning process.

During mid-January, Mr. Immerling received a letter from a friend, Dr. Ed Woodring. Both men had received bachelor degrees in 1964, and masters degrees in 1966, from West Virginia University. They then took jobs in industry, but Dr. Woodring left the industrial world in 1971 to go to Indiana University to pursue a doctorate in business administration with a major in finance. After completing the degree, he took a teaching position at a large university in the Midwest. One of his primary research areas involved how publicly held corporations formulated dividend policy.

Woodring and Immerling had kept in touch over the years on both a personal and a professional level. In the letter, Woodring said that he would be in Louisville, Kentucky in early February to attend a meeting and wanted to know if Immerling could come, since they had not seen each other for about a year. In reading the letter, Immerling thought it would be a good time not only to socialize with his old friend but also to review all aspects of dividend policy with an expert in the field. He called Woodring, and they arranged to meet in Louisville and spend a day discussing the subject.

When they found each other at the hotel, they went into the coffee shop and sat down. For more than an hour, they talked about the good old days at West Virginia, kids, and their philosophies of life. But finally the discussion turned toward dividend policy.

Immerling took the position that investment policy was the basic determinant of stock value and that investors were indifferent as to whether they received benefits in the form of dividends or capital gains. This meant that investment needs should be determined first, and if any equity funds remained, they should be paid out in the form of cash dividends. If future asset growth absorbed all internally generated funds, then no cash dividends should be declared. Under this concept, investors would not want the firm to pay dividends when this would cause the firm to forgo any future returns greater than its opportunity cost of retained earnings.

Woodring countered that although investment was an important determinant of stock value, it was not the only one. Investors were not indifferent between an equal amount of dividends and capital gains. He believed they actually preferred dividends over capital gains because dividends were certain, whereas capital gains were subject to uncertainty. He further stated that to get stockholders to forgo a dollar in dividends, they must believe they will get more than a dollar of capital gains appreciation. In closing his argument, Woodring emphasized that the firm's policy regarding retained earnings, whether distributed or retained, would have some effect on share price.

At this point, Woodring said that he had a session to attend and asked if Immerling could meet him for dinner. Woodring then noticed an old friend across the lobby and said goodbye.

When they met for dinner, Immerling suggested they go to an Indian restaurant a couple of blocks away that was famous for its lamb dishes. They left.

Again the conversation was light for a while with no reference to finance. Talk generally was about sports and politics, but once more the discussion turned toward dividend policy.

Woodring mentioned that the pattern of dividend payout was also important. He pointed out that investors paid attention to the dividend payout pattern established by Immerling's company. A regular pattern would imply a similar pattern in the future. An irregular pattern would imply a dividend that cannot be relied upon, one that may have frequent dividend reductions. Woodring suggested that stockholders desire to see, over the long road, dividends per share less variable than earnings per share.

Immerling pointed out that he considered a target payout ratio of less than 30 percent to be a small payout, between 30 and 65 percent in the average range, and above 65 percent a high payout. He had read that payout ratios of industrial companies since World War II had averaged between 50 and 55 percent.

This exchange motivated Woodring to point out that it is no longer possible simply to use historical payout data. It was now necessary to consider that the 1986 tax law reduced the corporate marginal federal tax rate to 34 percent and eliminated the difference in tax rates on dividends and capital gains.

Immerling found the discussion of dividend policy useful, but it did not answer all his questions. He knew he would have to do a lot of thinking in anticipation of the Board of Directors meeting in mid-February.

EXHIBIT 30.1

Jarvis Incorporated

Consolidated Balance Sheets as of December 31 (In Thousands)

	1987	1988
Assets:		
Cash and Marketable Securities	$ 13,110	$ 13,500
Accounts Receivable, Net	82,463	88,922
Inventories		
Raw Materials	69,416	61,470
Work in Process and Finished Goods	77,776	71,011
Prepaid Expenses	4,601	3,515
Total Current Assets	$247,366	$238,418
Plant, Property, and Equipment		
Land	8,820	9,455
Buildings	101,880	113,305
Machinery and Equipment	340,740	389,340
	$451,440	$512,100
Less: Accumulated Depreciation	177,300	208,530
Net Fixed Assets	$274,140	$303,570
Other Assets	38,796	35,550
Total Assets	$560,302	$577,538
Liabilities and Stockholders' Equity:		
Accounts Payable	$ 65,790	$ 57,152
Accrued Wages	11,880	11,158
Accrued Taxes	11,552	8,910
Current Portion of Long-Term Debt		
and Lease Obligations	9,360	7,200
Employee Benefits, Including Pensions	18,999	22,950
Other Current Liabilities	15,031	14,585
Total Current Liabilities	$132,612	$121,955
Long-Term Debt and Lease Obligations	103,320	80,820
Deferred Taxes on Income	44,820	62,733
Other Long-Term Liabilities	13,600	12,240
Total Long-Term Liabilities	$161,740	$155,793
Stockholders' Equity		
Common Stock	36,540	37,440
Retained Earnings	229,410	262,350
Total Stockholders' Equity	$265,950	$299,790
Total Liabilities and Stockholders' Equity	$560,302	$577,538

EXHIBIT 30.2

Jarvis Incorporated

Consolidated Income Statements for the Years Ending December 31 (In Thousands)

	1987	1988
Net Sales	$945,630	$995,680
Cost of Goods Sold	788,940	829,350
Gross Profit	$156,690	$166,330
Selling, General, and Administrative	74,790	74,880
Operating Profit	$ 81,900	$ 91,450
Interest Expense	8,370	8,010
Net Profit Before Taxes	$ 73,530	$ 83,440
Federal and State Income Taxes	29,410	33,375
Net Income After Taxes	$ 44,120	$ 50,065

EXHIBIT 30.3

Jarvis Incorporated

*Consolidated Statement of Changes in Financial Position for
Years Ending December 31 (In Thousands)*

	1987	1988
Sources (Uses) of Cash		
Operations		
Net Income	$ 44,120	$ 50,065
Noncash Items		
Depreciation	29,790	31,230
Deferred Taxes on Income	9,540	17,913
Other Items	8,100	0
Changes in Working Capital Items		
Accounts Receivable	(6,570)	(6,459)
Inventories	(18,270)	14,711
Accounts Payable	8,640	(8,638)
Other Working Capital Changes	2,340	(933)
Total from Operations	$ 77,690	$ 97,889
Financing Activities		
Proceeds From Long-Term Debt		
and Lease Obligations	$ 15,210	$ 5,000
Cash Dividends	(12,510)	(17,125)
Reduction of Long-Term Debt		
and Lease Obligations	(9,630)	(27,500)
Issuance of Common Stock		
Under Various Options	7,650	900
Other	(8,640)	(1,360)
Total Financing Activities	$ (7,920)	$(40,085)
Investment Activities		
Property, Plant, and Equipment	$(63,100)	$(60,660)
Other	(12,420)	3,246)
Total Investment Activities	$(75,520)	$(57,414)
Increase (Decrease) in Cash	$ (5,750)	$ 390
Cash and Temporary Investments		
at the Beginning of the Year	$ 18,860	$ 13,110
Cash and Temporary Investments		
at the End of the Year	$ 13,110	$ 13,500

EXHIBIT 30.4

Jarvis Incorporated

Selected Financial Information (Dollars in Thousands, Except Amounts Per Share)

	1984	*1985*	*1986*	*1987*	*1988*
Net Sales	$733,680	$800,002	$818,450	$945,630	$995,680
Net Income	$ 26,280	$ 31,050	$ 35,100	$ 44,120	$ 50,065
Property, Plant, and Equipment Additions	$ 53,360	$ 50,420	$ 36,080	$ 63,000	$ 60,660
Depreciation	$ 20,500	$ 25,400	$ 27,340	$ 30,000	$ 31,230
Net Working Capital	$103,950	$101,970	$108,720	$114,754	$116,463
Dividend Payout (%)	31.6	30.7	31.1	28.2	34.0
Return on Sales	3.6	3.9	4.3	4.7	5.0
Return on Equity	15.0	15.6	15.6	16.6	16.7
Debt-to-Total Assets (%)	58.8	58.3	57.4	52.1	48.1
Weighted Average Shares Outstanding (000s)	19,104	19,650	20,219	20,412	20,560
Per Share Data					
Net Income	$1.58	$1.77	$1.96	$2.16	$2.44
Dividends	$0.50	$0.55	$0.61	$0.61	$0.83
Book Value	$9.43	$10.40	$11.60	$13.01	$14.58
Market Value	$7.750	$12.875	$13.750	$20.000	$27.500

EXHIBIT 30.5

Jarvis Incorporated

Selected Ratios for the Packaging Industry for the Following Calendar Periods

	1985	1986	1987	1988
Liquidity:				
1. Current Ratio	1.7	2.5	2.2	2.0
2. Acid Test	0.8	1.3	1.1	1.1
3. Current Assets/Total Assets (%)	63.0	65.4	63.7	60.8
Activity:				
4. Receivables Turnover	8.5	9.5	8.7	8.5
5. Cost of Goods Sold/Inventory	6.2	6.1	5.9	4.8
6. Net Sales/Net Working Capital	9.7	6.8	6.9	6.0
7. Net Sales/Total Assets	5.4	5.7	5.8	4.1
Leverage:				
8. Total Debt/Total Assets (%)	45.3	46.6	49.8	49.1
9. Debt/Net Worth	1.0	0.8	0.9	1.0
10. EBIT/Interest	4.9	5.5	4.6	2.9
Profitability:				
11. COGS/Net Sales (%)	78.2	81.4	80.6	77.5
12. Operating Profit/Net Sales (%)	10.2	6.1	5.3	4.7
13. Profit Before Taxes/Net Sales (%)	6.9	5.1	4.6	3.5
14. Profit Before Taxes/Total Assets (%)	11.5	11.1	11.5	5.7
15. Profit Before Taxes/Net Worth (%)	28.6	19.1	20.4	14.9

QUESTIONS

1. What does the information in Exhibit 30.3 reveal about company operations during the years 1987–1988?
2. What can you learn about Jarvis Incorporated by examining the financial data in Exhibit 30.4?
3. Summarize the discussion between Dr. Woodring and Mr. Immerling concerning dividend policy, including relevant variables that were omitted.
4. Prepare a memo from Mr. Immerling for the mid-February Board of Directors meeting, articulating the appropriate dividend policy for Jarvis Incorporated.

PART V

LONG-TERM FINANCING

Low Country Industries
INVESTMENT BANKING

Low Country Industries, located in Charleston, South Carolina, was founded in 1962 by Melvin Gains and Evan Handell. Its business was slaughtering hogs and cows to provide a supply of fresh meat for supermarkets in the Charleston area. From its inception, the firm was careful to accept only the highest-quality animals, and it became known in the industry as a firm that competed more on quality than it did on price. Indeed, its sales pitch to customers was that no one could consistently supply high-quality beef and pork as well as Low Country Industries.

Growth was modest, but by 1970, sales were in excess of $10,000,000. The firm's market had expanded to include supermarket chains in North Carolina, South Carolina, Georgia, Tennessee, and Virginia. Between 1970 and 1976, sales grew at a compound rate of 20 percent, so that by the end of 1976, sales were about $30,000,000. This strong sales growth placed extreme pressure on the firm's financial position. A balance sheet and income statement are included as Exhibit 31.1 and Exhibit 31.2.

Mr. Gains and Mr. Handell had exhausted their own resources and decided that if growth was not to be curtailed, outside investment would be necessary. They were fortunate that Jarvis Levin, a respected businessman with experience in the meat processing industry, was interested in investing in the firm. For $1,000,000, he acquired 25 percent ownership, with the remaining 75 percent split evenly between Mr. Gains and Mr. Handell.

In 1977, Low Country Industries decided to expand its operations into the processed meat business. The firm bought high-quality beef and pork from its fresh meat division and processed it into high-quality sausage, bacon, and luncheon meats. These products were sold by supermarkets in the Southeast. They gained strong market acceptance even though they were priced 10 to 20 percent above the competition. Rising personal incomes in the region produced a growing demand for quality food products. Since the firm was already well known for quality fresh meats, the processed meats fit well with their overall market image.

In 1984, the three owners decided to sell a portion of their stock to the public. The major reason for doing so was to diversify their asset holdings.

They sold 25 percent of the firm's shares for $15,000,000. After the sale, the stock was held as follows: Mr. Gains (30 percent), Mr. Handell (25 percent), Mr. Levin (20 percent), and the public (25 percent). No member of the latter group held more than 2 percent of the outstanding shares.

In February 1988, the management of the firm decided to expand Low Country's activities into the West and Southwest. Management believed these areas would be receptive to the company's high-quality products. However, before expansion plans could be implemented, outside financing would have to be secured.

The vice-president for finance, Alvin Hingery, was instructed by the three owners to formulate a plan to determine the funds needed and to decide how the funds would be acquired. From consultations with operating management, he found out that $3,000,000 would be needed for fixed plant and equipment and an additional $2,500,000 for working capital. He made an estimate that between $1,500,000 and $2,000,000 would be available from retained earnings. Mr. Hingery decided to be conservative and use the lower figure. Therefore, approximately $4,000,000 in outside funds would be required.

In early March, Mr. Hingery placed a call to Earlene Withers, a partner in the Charleston investment firm of Hawkes and Withers. They decided to meet the next week concerning a new issue of stock for the firm. Mr. Hingery called Hawkes and Withers because that firm had been making a market in the stock since 1985. Ms. Withers had been especially helpful in assisting Mr. Gains in selling some of his shares. Although there were other local firms that could handle the underwriting, the three major owners decided to stick with Hawkes and Withers.

During the second week in March, a meeting between Mr. Hingery, Mr. Gains, and Ms. Withers took place in Ms. Withers's office. They discussed whether to issue debt or equity, but quickly rejected debt as producing a degree of financial leverage that was unacceptable to the owners.

The discussion, therefore, turned to some type of stock issue, either preferred or common. Ms. Withers stated that cumulative preferred stock could be marketed with a 12 percent dividend rate. It would be offered to the public at $108 per share, with net proceeds to the firm of $100 per share. Ms. Withers noted that the price of the common stock of the firm had been rising over the last several months (see Exhibit 31.3). She believed that common stock could be sold to net $29.00 per share. Another possibility, and one she favored, was to sell the stock to net $30.50 per share, with an option for the firm of Hawkes and Withers to buy up to 25,000 shares, at a price of $31.00 per share. The option would extend through December 31, 1989.

Mr. Hingery realized that if he could avoid the underwriting costs associated with a security issue, he could materially reduce the issue cost. He contacted acquaintances of his who were in the brokerage business, and they informed him that an issue sold on a best efforts basis would cost about 4 percent of the issue price. Mr. Hingery was well aware of the risks in selling on a best efforts basis, but was also cognizant of the significant reduction in costs.

Selected ratios for the meats and meat products industry are presented in Exhibit 31.4.

EXHIBIT 31.1

Low Country Industries

Balance Sheets as of January 31 (In Thousands)

	1987	1988
Assets:		
Cash and Marketable Securities	$ 538	$ 1,353
Accounts Receivable, Net	7,442	6,239
Inventories	4,863	3,598
Prepaid Expenses	215	274
Total Current Assets	$13,058	$11,464
Land	265	288
Buildings and Improvements	2,542	2,958
Machinery and Equipment	9,909	12,923
Delivery Equipment	1,618	2,036
Construction in Progress	252	243
Less: Accumulated Depreciation	(6,056)	(7,566)
Total Fixed Assets	$ 8,530	$10,882
Other Assets	318	354
Total Assets	$21,906	$22,700
Liabilities and Stockholders' Equity:		
Accounts Payable	$ 4,220	$ 5,628
Demand Notes Payable	3,096	0
Accruals	1,660	2,054
Current Portion of Long-Term Debt	385	370
Total Current Liabilities	$ 9,361	$ 8,052
Long-Term Debt	5,143	5,460
Stockholders' Equity		
Common Stock, $1.00 Par	940	940
Paid-in Capital	1,221	1,227
Retained Earnings	5,241	7,021
Total Stockholders' Equity	$ 7,402	$ 9,188
Total Liabilities and Stockholders' Equity	$21,906	$22,700

EXHIBIT 31.2

Low Country Industries

Income Statements as of January 31 (In Thousands)

	1987	1988
Net Sales	$154,548	$162,087
Operating Costs and Expenses		
Cost of Goods Sold	148,688	153,036
Selling	1,287	1,434
General and Administrative	1,815	2,369
Depreciation	1,151	1,331
Operating Income	$ 1,607	$ 3,917
Other Expenses (Income)		
Interest	872	720
Other	(265)	(408)
Net Income Before Taxes	$ 1,000	$ 3,605
Federal and State Income Taxes	392	1,442
Net Income	$ 608	$ 2,163

EXHIBIT 31.3

Low Country Industries

*Prices of LCI Common Stock from
August 1987 to February 1988*

	High	Low
August	29½	28¾
September	29⅜	28½
October	30	28¼
November	30⅛	30
December	31¼	30
January	32	30½
February	32¼	30⅞

EXHIBIT 31.4

Low Country Industries

Selected Ratios for the Meats and Meat Products Industry
for the Following Calendar Periods

	1984	*1985*	*1986*	*1987*
Liquidity:				
1. Current Ratio	1.3	1.4	1.4	1.4
2. Acid Test	0.9	0.9	0.9	1.0
3. Current Assets/Total Assets (%)	73.5	73.9	73.3	71.9
Activity:				
4. Receivables Turnover	19.3	18.2	19.1	20.7
5. Cost of Goods Sold/Inventory	29.5	28.4	27.2	28.0
6. Net Sales/Net Working Capital	43.9	38.4	36.5	37.3
7. Net Sales/Total Assets	7.3	7.3	7.1	7.1
Leverage:				
8. Total Debt/Total Assets (%)	68.7	64.8	65.0	65.8
9. Debt/Net Worth	2.5	2.0	2.0	2.1
10. EBIT/Interest	2.6	2.7	2.1	2.0
Profitability:				
11. COGS/Net Sales (%)	87.7	85.1	87.7	87.2
12. Operating Profit/Net Sales (%)	1.3	1.9	1.5	1.3
13. Profit Before Taxes/Net Sales (%)	1.0	1.4	1.0	1.0
14. Profit Before Taxes/Total Assets (%)	6.2	6.4	5.4	4.2
15. Profit Before Taxes/Net Worth (%)	22.6	19.5	16.6	14.1

QUESTIONS

1. Summarize the pertinent data concerning Low Country Industries.
2. Evaluate the costs and the risks of the plans involving the issuance of common stock, as proposed by Ms. Withers.
3. Evaluate the costs and risks of the preferred stock plan.
4. What is meant by issuing stock on a best efforts basis? Evaluate this strategy for Low Country Industries.
5. Which plan should Mr. Hingery favor? State the reasons supporting your decision.

Case 32

Datranix
LONG-TERM DEBT

Datranix, with home offices in Raleigh, North Carolina, was a world leader in the manufacture of electronic equipment and components. Production consisted of two-way radios and other forms of electronic communications systems; semiconductors, including integrated circuits and microprocessor units; electronic equipment for military and aerospace use; automotive electronic equipment; and data communication products, such as high-speed modems, multiplexers, and network processors. Plants were located in the United States, Canada, Western Europe, and the Far East. A balance sheet and income statements are included as Exhibit 32.1 and Exhibit 32.2.

The company, employing over 90,000 people, subdivided its business into five operating divisions. The Data Communications Division manufactured high-speed modems, multiplexers, network processors, and related integrated testing and monitoring equipment. These products handled the transmittal of digital information among dispersed business machines, terminals, other peripheral devices, and computer mainframes. In the late 1970s, they devoted capital resources in the development and marketing of minicomputers and since then have produced associated peripheral equipment, as well as related software and supplies. Customers were large international and frequently multinational organizations with extensive internal teleprocessing networks.

The Semiconductor Division processed semiconductors for a broad range of electronic products, including television receivers, VCRs, tape decks, minicomputers, calculators, and automatic controls. This group sold its products to original equipment manufacturers, primarily through its own sales force. The division's sales had been cyclical, reflecting the general economic conditions. However, the recent increase in consumer interest in televisions and VCRs promised a bright future for sales in this area.

The Government Electronics Division supplied military and space electronic equipment, including aerospace telecommunications systems, military communications equipment, radar systems, data links, display systems, positioning and navigation systems, instrumentation products, countermeasures systems, missile guidance equipment, electronic ordnance devices, and drone electronic systems. Although the division secured contracts through U.S. government agencies and their suppliers, no one contract accounted for a disproportionate percentage of sales. Ever since the *Challenger* space shuttle disaster of 1986, there had been greater scrutiny by the government toward contract holders, causing a considerable decrease in the profitability of this division.

The Communications Products Division provided the equipment and systems to meet the needs of many types of businesses, institutions, and governmental organizations. These included public safety agencies, such as police, fire, highway maintenance departments, and forestry services; petroleum companies; gas, electric, and water utilities; telephone companies; diverse industrial companies; railroads, taxicab operations, trucking firms, and other transportation companies; institutions, appliance sales and service, vending machines, fuel oil, heating, air conditioning, and auto towing. The products of this group were primarily sold or leased directly to users in the United States through a nationwide distribution force. Installation and maintenance were provided by a network of company service shops or by the individual customer.

The Automotive Products Division manufactured automobile radios, stereo cassette players, alternator changing systems, solid-state electronic ignition systems, citizen band radios, and other automotive electronic products. Demand for this group's products was also somewhat cyclical, reflecting not only the general economic conditions, but also the volume of automobile sales in the United States.

In 1989, Datranix was considering the sale of $108,000,000 in 10.0 percent sinking fund debentures due October 1, 2019. The net proceeds, estimated at $106,000,000 (after deduction of the underwriting discount and estimated expenses), were to be applied to the reduction of outstanding domestic commercial paper and to prepayment of a guaranteed sinking fund debenture March 1, 1999, of which $21,420,000 was outstanding on December 31, 1989. At the same time, total commercial paper outstanding was approximately $125,550,000. The proceeds from the sale of commercial paper had been utilized primarily for working capital purposes. The high growth in sales experienced in recent years by the Data Communications Division necessitated large amounts of working capital to remain competitive. The debenture redemption schedule is given as Exhibit 32.3.

The debentures were to be issued under an indenture to be dated October 1, 1989 between Datranix and Tarheel Trust and Savings Bank, Charlotte, North Carolina, as Trustee. The debentures were to be issued in denominations of $1,000 and integral multiples thereof and were to be issued in registered form only, without coupons.

The debentures were to be subject to redemption, in whole or in part, at any time or from time to time, at the option of Datranix. The company had only to give at least 30 days' notice at the redemption prices shown in Exhibit 32.3, if redeemed during the 12-month period beginning October 1 of the stated year. Datranix, however, would not have the option to redeem any of the debentures prior to October 31, 1999 from the proceeds or in anticipation of the issuance of any indebtedness for money borrowed at less than 10.0 percent.

The debentures could also be redeemed on at least 30 days' notice by mail through the operation of a sinking fund on October 1, 2000 and each October 1 thereafter until October 1, 2019, when they would be redeemed at 100 percent of their principal amount with accrued interest. The sinking fund provided for the redemption of $3,600,000 principal amount on each date. The company also has the right to redeem on each date an additional principal amount not exceeding 150 percent of the mandatory amounts.

The Board of Directors met during December 1988 to decide if the sinking fund debentures would be issued. However, before the step was taken, the chairman wanted to hear the opinions of the board members as to the benefits and drawbacks of this method of long-term financing.

Selected ratios for electronic components manufacturers are presented as Exhibit 32.4.

EXHIBIT 32.1

Datranix

Balance Sheet as of December 31, 1988 (In Thousands)

Assets:	
Cash	$ 37,303
Short-Term Investments	73,581
Accounts Receivable	369,678
Inventories	
Finished Goods	123,498
Work-in-Process	273,687
Future Tax Benefits	28,975
Other Current Assets	40,881
Total Current Assets	$ 947,603
Property, Plant, and Equipment	
Land	22,420
Buildings	276,602
Machinery and Equipment	425,234
Accumulated Depreciation, Property,	
Plant and Equipment	(286,440)
	$ 437,816
Other Assets	24,556
Total Assets	$1,409,975

EXHIBIT 32.1 (Continued)

Datranix

Balance Sheet as of December 31, 1988 (In Thousands)

Liabilities and Stockholders' Equity:	
Notes Payable	$ 136,712
Current Maturities of Long-Term Debt	5,311
Accounts Payable	117,920
Accrued Expenses	131,000
Income Taxes	34,780
Total Current Liabilities	$ 425,723
Long-Term Debt	$ 131,476
Deferred Income Taxes	19,361
Other Liabilities	27,953
Stockholders' Equity	
Common Equity, $3 Par	98,496
Additional Paid-in Capital	165,761
Retained Earnings	541,205
Total Stockholders' Equity	$ 805,462
Total Liabilities and Stockholders' Equity	$1,409,975

EXHIBIT 32.2

Datranix

Income Statements as of December 31 (In Thousands)

	1987	1988
Net Sales	$2,431,305	$2,653,621
Cost of Goods Sold	1,602,157	1,689,925
Gross Profit	$ 829,148	$ 963,696
Operating Expenses	652,680	784,998
Operating Profit	$ 176,468	$ 178,698
Interest Expense	26,394	27,015
Profit Before Taxes	$ 150,074	$ 151,683
Federal and State Income Taxes	58,453	60,007
Net Profit After Taxes	$ 91,621	$ 91,676

EXHIBIT 32.3

Datranix

Debenture Redemption Schedule as the Percentage
of the Principal Amount

Year	Percentage	Year	Percentage
1989	107.700	2004	103.080
1990	107.392	2005	102.772
1991	107.084	2006	102.464
1992	106.776	2007	102.156
1993	106.468	2008	101.848
1994	106.160	2009	101.540
1995	105.852	2010	101.232
1996	105.544	2011	100.924
1997	105.236	2012	100.616
1998	104.928	2013	100.308
1999	104.620	2014	100.000
2000	104.312	2015	100.000
2001	104.004	2016	100.000
2002	103.696	2017	100.000
2003	103.388	2018	100.000

EXHIBIT 32.4

Datranix

*Selected Ratios for Electronic Components Manufacturers for
the Following Calendar Periods*

	1985	1986	1987	1988
Liquidity:				
1. Current Ratio	1.8	1.9	1.9	1.8
2. Acid Test	0.9	1.0	1.0	1.0
3. Current Assets/Total Assets (%)	71.3	69.7	67.0	64.9
Activity:				
4. Receivables Turnover	6.1	6.6	6.4	6.8
5. Cost of Goods Sold/Inventory	3.9	3.6	4.0	4.6
6. Net Sales/Net Working Capital	5.7	5.6	6.6	7.2
7. Net Sales/Total Assets	1.8	1.8	1.8	1.8
Leverage:				
8. Total Debt/Total Assets (%)	57.6	54.8	55.6	55.9
9. Debt/Net Worth	1.3	1.2	1.2	1.3
10. EBIT/Interest	5.6	5.2	3.7	3.1
Profitability:				
11. COGS/Net Sales (%)	65.1	65.5	65.9	66.6
12. Operating Profit/Net Sales (%)	8.2	8.5	7.5	6.0
13. Profit Before Taxes/Net Sales (%)	7.8	7.1	6.0	4.3
14. Profit Before Taxes/Total Assets (%)	13.1	12.5	10.2	9.3
15. Profit Before Taxes/Net Worth (%)	33.5	30.7	24.7	21.0

QUESTIONS

1. Calculate the before-tax yield to maturity assuming that the initial public offering price is 98.1 percent of the face value of the debenture ($106,000,000/$108,000,000).
2. Calculate the after-tax cost of debt, assuming a 40 percent marginal tax rate.
3. In your opinion, will the company be able to meet interest payments and sinking fund requirements?
4. Discuss the rate of interest, sinking fund requirements, call feature, and other covenants as to their effect on long-term financing.
5. As a member of the Board of Directors, discuss the benefits and drawbacks using the 10.0 percent sinking fund debentures.
6. Calculate the before-tax yield to maturity as in Question 1 using Lotus 1-2-3.

Brown Tools Corporation
LEASING

Brown Tools Corporation manufactured and distributed high-quality tools and equipment for professional mechanics under the trademark "Pro-Tool." Over 6,000 items were sold, including open-end wrenches, socket wrenches, chisels, handles and attachments, screwdrivers, pliers, power tools, auto test equipment, and tool storage units. Most of the company's products were sold through 2,200 independent, self-employed dealers operating walk-in mobile units at the user locations. The company was incorporated under Kansas law in 1938. Executive offices were located in Topeka, Kansas. A balance sheet and income statement are included as Exhibit 33.1 and Exhibit 33.2.

The company considered the independent dealer network of crucial importance to its operations. The dealers provided services by solving unusual mechanical problems, by disseminating information about new methods used by professional mechanics, and by extending credit. Dealers maintained and improved their skills through periodic company training. Support was also provided by five tool repair centers. In addition, the dealers were assisted by 350 branch, sales, and field managers. Further backup was given by the company's product promotion staff, which furnished training in the use and application of tools and equipment.

Although the company's tools were used by a large number of auto mechanics, sales did not depend on the purchase of new cars. When auto sales were up, increased warranty work boosted demand. When new car sales declined, increased auto repair work (as car owners tried to keep old models running longer) supported strong tool sales.

Brown's earnings over its 50-year history grew at a constant rate until 1985 when a 2-year plateau was reached. This resulted from a number of factors, including an outbreak of price discounting that year, a rise in research spending in 1986, and the cost of relocating some manufacturing operations that same year. In 1987, costs of a new line of electric tools introduced the year before were realized. Since 1986, research spending had continued to rise because management felt that area needed to be broadened for Brown to continue to enjoy their favorable market share.

Brown's management had continued to modernize plants and equipment and, over the past few years, had started to see the cost savings due to improved manufacturing processes and increased efficiency. These factors led to a climb in earnings beginning in latter 1987 and continuing throughout 1988.

The independent dealer financed his customers for small-dollar purchases, but the company financed larger-dollar items by either purchase of the customers' installment receivables or purchase of the customers' 30-day receivables. Credit risks on purchased receivables were limited by full or partial recourse against the dealers in the event of customers' default. Further protection was provided by liens on the merchandise sold under installment receivables. Each dealer normally obtained advance credit approval from 1 of the 30 credit offices for the sale of an installment receivable to the company. Installment receivables were extended up to 36 months, with an average maturity of 15 months.

One hundred fifty sales representatives employed by the company handled sales to industrial customers. Operating out of 40 branch sales offices, the sales reps sold standard tools used in the maintenance of an extensive variety of production equipment and machinery. In addition, these salespersons worked with industrial customers to develop special tools for specific applications. They coordinated these activities closely with the research and development department.

Tools manufactured at the Topeka, Kansas plant were formed from cold rolled or hot rolled steel bar stock. Each product went through a number of forming and finishing operations, including forging, broaching, stamping, heat treating, grinding, polishing, and plating. The same basic manufacturing operations were carried out at the company's nine other plants. Although some components were shipped from one plant to another for final assembly, other components were purchased from outside sources.

Brown Tools required new electrical testing equipment at its Topeka plant. The company could choose either to design and make the equipment or lease it from an outside vendor. The component parts for electrical testing equipment were available from outside sources. Since plant engineers were already committed to projects, outside consultants would be needed for the construction job. The Industrial Engineering Department had calculated the cost of building the electrical testing equipment to be approximately $52,000.

Discussions with an outside vendor indicated that the leasing alternative required a five-year financial lease. The annual payments, to be made in advance, would amount to $15,000 per year. All maintenance, insurance, and other costs were the responsibility of the lessee. The company paid federal and state income taxes of 40 percent on its normal income.

The company wanted to compare the present values of the cash outflows associated with leasing and borrowing. The design of the electrical testing equipment required a 12 percent five-year loan, with equal end-of-year installment payments of $14,425. Depreciation would be taken on a straight-line basis without salvage value. It had also been decided that an after-tax cost of borrowing of 7 percent would be used to discount the cash outflows. A comparison would indicate which option—leasing or borrowing—was preferable.

Selected ratios for the handtools and hardware industry are presented in Exhibit 33.3.

EXHIBIT 33.1

Brown Tools Corporation

Balance Sheet for the Year Ending December 31 (In Thousands)

	1987	1988
Assets:		
Cash	$ 13,427	$ 12,112
Marketable Securities	1,710	2,052
Receivables	35,163	42,196
Inventories	46,847	50,216
Prepaid Expenses	2,649	3,179
Total Current Assets	$ 99,796	$109,755
Property, Plant, and Equipment		
Land	804	965
Buildings	12,812	15,375
Machinery and Equipment	24,703	29,644
Furniture and Fixtures	3,342	4,010
Auto, Trucks, and Other	586	703
	$ 42,247	$ 50,697
Accumulated Depreciation	14,808	17,770
	$ 27,439	$ 32,927
Other Assets	78	94
Total Assets	$127,313	$142,776
Liabilities and Stockholders' Equity:		
Current Maturities of Long-Term Debt	$ 338	$ 406
Accounts Payable	6,822	8,186
Accrued Liabilities	12,609	15,131
Income Taxes	2,782	3,338
Dealer Deposits	8,218	9,862
Total Current Liabilities	$ 30,769	$ 36,923
Long-Term Debt		
Senior Notes	18,000	21,600
Lease Obligations	4,172	5,006
	$ 22,172	$ 26,606
Current Maturities	338	405
	$ 21,834	$ 26,201
Stockholders' Equity		
Common Stock, $1 Par	8,750	8,750
Additional Contributed Capital	3,543	3,543
Retained Earnings	62,417	67,359
Total Stockholders' Equity	$ 74,710	$ 79,652
Total Liabilities and Stockholders' Equity	$127,313	$142,776

EXHIBIT 33.2

Brown Tools Corporation

Income Statement for the Year Ending December 31, 1988
(In Thousands)

Net Sales	$283,664
Cost of Goods Sold	199,012
Gross Profit	$ 84,652
Operating Expenses	62,415
Net Income Before Taxes	$ 22,237
Federal and State Income Taxes	8,947
Net Income After Taxes	$ 13,290

EXHIBIT 33.3

Brown Tools Corporation

Selected Ratios for the Handtools and Hardware Industry for
the Following Calendar Periods

	1985	1986	1987	1988
Liquidity:				
1. Current Ratio	2.2	2.3	2.1	2.2
2. Acid Test	0.9	1.0	0.9	1.0
3. Current Assets/Total Assets (%)	33.2	32.5	34.4	33.3
Activity:				
4. Receivables Turnover	7.8	8.5	8.0	8.9
5. Cost of Goods Sold/Inventory	3.6	3.6	3.9	4.0
6. Net Sales/Net Working Capital	5.3	4.9	5.5	5.4
7. Net Sales/Total Assets	1.9	1.9	1.9	1.9
Leverage:				
8. Total Debt/Total Assets (%)	50.0	49.5	41.5	40.7
9. Debt/Net Worth	1.0	1.0	1.2	1.0
10. EBIT/Interest	5.1	3.3	2.6	2.3
Profitability:				
11. COGS/Net Sales (%)	70.2	70.0	70.6	70.4
12. Operating Profit/Net Sales (%)	7.9	7.3	6.3	5.2
13. Profit Before Taxes/Net Sales (%)	6.9	5.2	4.5	3.7
14. Profit Before Taxes/Total Assets (%)	12.6	9.5	7.3	6.4
15. Profit Before Taxes/Net Worth (%)	23.9	20.0	16.7	13.8

QUESTIONS

1. Determine the cash outflows associated with leasing the electrical testing equipment. (For tax reasons, the payments cannot be deducted until one year from the date of payment.)
2. Calculate the interest components of the loan payments for each of the five years.
3. Determine the cash outflows associated with borrowing for the electrical testing equipment. (Depreciation must be considered.)
4. Compute the present values of cash flows for each alternative.
5. What subjective factors must be included in the decision-making process?
6. Calculate the present value of cash flows for each alternative using Lotus 1-2-3.

Hi Tech Supermarkets
PREFERRED STOCK

Hi Tech Supermarkets was a regional chain of stores headquartered in Baltimore, Maryland, with stores located in Maryland, Delaware, Pennsylvania, and New Jersey. Each location sold the standard items generally found in retail food stores. In addition, some of the larger stores stocked a line of hardware goods, drugs, and clothes as well as a delicatessen, bakery, and restaurant. These larger stores were conceived as one-stop shopping centers. Although more expensive to construct, management believed this was the store of the future and the only way for them to compete in such a dynamic industry. Balance sheets and income statements are included as Exhibit 34.1 and Exhibit 34.2. Selected financial data is shown in Exhibit 34.3.

The company was founded in 1957 by two brothers, Robb and Keith Davison. Since their father had owned a corner grocery store, they had grown up familiar with the retail food industry. Both brothers had served during the Korean conflict in the Quartermaster Corps, where they gained valuable experience in the buying of groceries on a large scale. After returning from the service, they became convinced that the chain store would be the food shopping wave of the future. With the profit margin on food items so low, they felt the only way to make a retail food business profitable was by buying in large quantities. Events proved them to be correct.

From the original store located in downtown Baltimore, the firm grew to include 85 stores in Maryland and Delaware. In 1980, the firm expanded into Virginia and West Virginia, and by 1988 Hi Tech Supermarkets included 185 stores with various distribution centers. All these facilities were owned by the company.

Management of the company had remained in the control of the Davison brothers until 1979, when they sold their shares to a group headed by Morgan McDuff, a local businessman. The new management team embarked on a program of expansion to meet the competition from national chains, which were seriously impinging on the firm's market area.

At that time, they also acquired the services of Select Services, Inc. (SSI). This company offered services to supermarket chains: a coupon-processing service and a check-cashing courtesy card program.

The job of processing the coupons at the retail level had become so overwhelming that retailers found it uneconomical to do the job themselves. The supermarket service company acted as the interface between the chain store and the manufacturers. The service company received a shipment of coupons every week from each individual Hi Tech store, which were then counted and sorted according to manufacturer. Information about each coupon was entered into a computer system that recorded the manufacturer and brand of the product, the face value of the coupon, and the store at which the coupon was redeemed. The data were then combined into several different reports and sent back to Hi Tech headquarters. These reports allowed Hi Tech to determine coupon redemption by store and by product.

The other service SSI offered, the courtesy card service, was tailored to the needs of Hi Tech. A courtesy card informs a cashier that the customer had been prescreened and permitted to cash checks at that store. Hi Tech was the first store in the Baltimore area to offer the service. Before receiving a check-cashing courtesy card, the customer was asked to fill out an application. The form generally asked for the customer's name, address, employer, bank name, and checking account number. Upon receipt of the courtesy card, customers were able to pay for their purchases without going through a lengthy check authorization process.

SSI provided all the necessary systems and supplies for a store to operate a courtesy card program. They processed applications, screened applicants, and issued the cards. Hi Tech Supermarkets did not get involved until the customer presented the check and the courtesy card at the checkout.

The courtesy card program provided marketing data as well as checkout efficiency. SSI used the information obtained from the card applications to develop mailing lists and demographic profiles of a store's customers. With this information, store management knew the areas from which it was drawing its customers and was able to mail promotional material to courtesy card customers. Mail surveys developed additional information on family size, eating habits, and the age of store customers. With this information, a store was able to adjust its merchandising techniques and send its courtesy card customers information consistent with their needs. Also, when a courtesy card was not used for an extended period of time, a notice was mailed encouraging the customer to shop at the store.

The innovative services performed by SSI had allowed Hi Tech not only to remain competitive in the retail food industry but also to be one of the most modern and fastest growing chain food stores. However, because of the increased costs involved with all the new projects and expansion of the number of stores, Hi Tech found it necessary to take on additional long-term debt and to issue common stock.

In early July 1988, Mr. McDuff called a meeting with the firm's vice-presidents to discuss a financial report prepared by the Philadelphia brokerage firm of Porter and Finn. The study concerned the type of securities the firm would need to issue to finance the company's asset requirements for the next five years. It was previously determined by management that profits generated from operations, less dividends, would not supply sufficient funds to finance Hi Tech's long-term needs. The firm had paid dividends for 10 consecutive years.

The report, presented at the meeting by Glenn Matteson, a partner of Porter and Finn, detailed the kinds of securities that the firm could issue to finance its additional $12,000,000 requirement. It concluded that term loans or bonds were not justified at this time since the firm's debt-to-equity ratio was at its outside limit relative to other firms in the industry. They feared that another debt issue would be perceived by the market as placing the company in an excessive risk position, and thus the firm's common stock would be devalued by investors.

The company's common stock was currently traded in the over-the-counter market; it was selling about 30 percent below its average price of the last two years. Mr. Matteson was not sure why the firm's stock was selling at such a large discount, although he believed the intense competition in the supermarket industry was the prime factor. Therefore, Mr. Matteson did not think it wise to sell common stock at this time, since the firm would probably suffer excessive dilution.

The report stated that the issuance of preferred stock would prove to be more feasible at this time. There were four types of preferred that could be issued: (1) cumulative preferred, $100 par, 9.5 percent dividend rate; (2) noncumulative preferred, $100 par, 11 percent dividend rate; (3) cumulative participating preferred, $100 par, 8 percent, participating equally on a per share basis; and (4) convertible cumulative preferred, $100 par, 9 percent dividend rate, convertible in five shares of common stock beginning January 1, 1990. The flotation cost under each plan would be approximately the same percentage.

Mr. McDuff asked Mr. Matteson to explain each kind of preferred stock and to state its advantages and disadvantages. Then he wanted Mr. Matteson to pick the best financing arrangement for Hi Tech Supermarkets.

Selected ratios for the food retailing industry are presented as Exhibit 34.4.

EXHIBIT 34.1

Hi Tech Supermarkets

Condensed Balance Sheet as of June 30 (In Thousands)

	1987	1988
Assets:		
Cash	$ 9,511	$10,164
Accounts Receivable	600	653
Inventories	21,626	23,411
Prepaids	1,084	1,135
Total Current Assets	$32,821	$35,363
Fixed Assets	76,645	78,852
Accumulated Depreciation	(45,553)	(47,941)
Other Assets	996	1,082
Total Assets	$64,909	$67,356
Liabilities and Stockholders' Equity:		
Current Liabilities	$ 9,092	$ 9,821
Long-Term Debt	33,413	32,426
Stockholders' Equity	22,404	25,109
Total Liabilities and		
Stockholders' Equity	$64,909	$67,356

EXHIBIT 34.2

Hi Tech Supermarkets

*Condensed Income Statements for the Years Ending
June 30 (In Thousands)*

	1987	1988
Net Sales	$322,045	$348,485
Cost of Sales	254,395	278,090
Gross Profit	$ 67,650	$ 70,395
Operating, Administrative,		
and Financial Expenses	60,316	62,814
Income Before Taxes	$ 7,334	$ 7,581
Federal and State Income Taxes	2,934	3,032
Net Income	$ 4,400	$ 4,549

EXHIBIT 34.3

Hi Tech Supermarkets

Selected Financial Data

	1987	1988
Common Shares Outstanding	1,844,000	1,844,000
Earnings per Share	$2.39	$2.47
Dividends per Share	$1.00	$1.00
Average Stock Price (high)	$22.75	$17.50
Average Stock Price (low)	$17.75	$14.55
Book Value per Share	$25.22	$25.90
Interest Expense (000s)	$2,278	$2,361
Depreciation Expense (000s)	$1,880	$1,950
Total Debt-to-Equity Ratio	1.9:1	1.7:1
Long-Term Debt-to-Equity Ratio	1.5:1	1.3:1
Current Market Price	—	$17.00

EXHIBIT 34.4

Hi Tech Supermarkets

*Selected Ratios for the Food Retailing Industry for the
Following Calendar Periods*

	1984	1985	1986	1987
Liquidity:				
1. Current Ratio	1.3	1.3	1.3	1.3
2. Acid Test	0.4	0.3	0.3	0.3
3. Current Assets/Total Assets (%)	52.4	50.4	49.4	48.9
Activity:				
4. Receivables Turnover	315.7	261.6	327.5	328.5
5. Cost of Goods Sold/Inventory	15.6	15.8	16.2	16.1
6. Net Sales/Net Working Capital	59.3	69.3	63.9	63.2
7. Net Sales/Total Assets	5.9	5.9	6.0	6.2
Leverage:				
8. Total Debt/Total Assets (%)	65.5	66.4	64.9	66.4
9. Debt/Net Worth	2.0	2.1	2.0	2.1
10. EBIT/Interest	4.0	2.9	3.1	2.7
Profitability:				
11. COGS/Net Sales (%)	77.2	78.5	77.9	78.6
12. Operating Profit/Net Sales (%)	2.6	1.8	2.0	1.7
13. Profit Before Taxes/Net Sales (%)	2.2	1.5	1.7	1.3
14. Profit Before Taxes/Total Assets (%)	10.0	7.3	7.6	6.9
15. Profit Before Taxes/Net Worth (%)	29.2	22.0	23.4	21.9

QUESTIONS

1. Discuss each of the four preferred stock plans from the point of view of Mr. Matteson.
2. Discuss the advantages and disadvantages of each plan from the point of view of Hi Tech.
3. How have the federal tax laws discouraged the issuance of preferred stock compared to bonds?
4. Which in your judgment is the best alternative for Hi Tech?

The Aumond Company
COMMON EQUITY
FINANCING

In late August 1988, Frank Simons, the treasurer of The Aumond Company, was trying to decide as to how a common stock offering would be made to the general public. The choice was between a straight common offering, under-written by a local brokerage house, and a rights offering to current stockholders.

The Aumond Company was founded in 1971 in Eau Claire, Wisconsin, and was operated as an individual proprietorship until its incorporation in 1975. The company provided claims-adjusting services mainly to casualty–property insurance companies. It specialized in all casualty, automobile, physical damage, and inland marine lines. In certain locations, Aumond provided service for straight fire, homeowners, and extended coverage claims. The firm had no contract or other arrangement with any insurance company, but depended on its ability to supply satisfactory service to the various insurance companies. A balance sheet and an income statement are included as Exhibit 35.1 and Exhibit 35.2.

The services rendered by The Aumond Company involved diverse elements. Its customers assigned claims to the company because they relied exclusively upon independent adjusters and maintained no force of field adjusters on their own, their own adjusters were overburdened at the time, or The Aumond Company's location made their services less costly. The company's adjusters then investigated to ascertain the obligation of the client to a third party or to its policyholder. After the client's liability had been determined, the adjuster attempted to settle the claim by negotiation with the damaged party. If negotiations were not successful and litigation ensued, the adjuster supplied information required to defend the action.

Exhibit 35.3 shows the approximate number of claims assigned to The Aumond Company in the period 1978 to 1987. The largest single account was 15 percent of the number of claims. From 1980 to 1987, a number of insurance companies, between 35 and 60, were the source of 65 percent of the claims assigned to the firm. The Aumond Company also received claims from certain self-insurers, but these contributed only slightly to volume. This portion of the business, however, had been growing steadily over the years, but still was a negligible percentage of their total business.

The firm charged its customers on the basis of the individual claims assigned. The charge for each case was calculated by the application of hourly rates for time worked by adjusters and clerical personnel. The company billed for expenses directly traceable to each case and charged a fixed amount per mile for automobile usage. Rates varied by geographical location. Periodically, the company made adjustments in hourly rates, with the most recent one implemented in July 1988, representing an increase of approximately 15 percent.

The independent casualty property claims adjusting industry was composed of a large number of companies of disparate size. Aumond faced competition from a number of local firms. Also, there were several independent adjusting firms operating branches and competing with the company nationally. In addition, certain stock companies owned an adjustment bureau, larger than The Aumond Company, which adjusted property and casualty claims. In the past the bureau functioned mostly in the property field, but in recent years it had moved into the casualty area. Management felt that this type of adjustment bureau would become an increasing source of competition in the future.

The executive staff, located in Eau Claire, consisted of principal corporate officers, a supervisory claims and management staff, and an educational staff. The company had 350 field offices, located in every state, employing 475 adjusters. It also had field offices in the Grand Bahamas, Puerto Rico, Vancouver, Toronto, Montreal, and London. A significant part of the company's growth was due to the expansion of field offices into new geographical areas. Generally, each field office covered an area of at least 50 miles in radius. Periodic trips were made to service routine claims, but any bodily injury case was handled by a special trip.

The company did not own any of the premises on which its offices were located. It leased 275 office locations, including that of the home office, with leases extending for an average of 2.5 years. Annual aggregate rentals of this type were approximately $725,000. The remaining locations were rented on a short-term basis. The company's 1,200 automobiles used by the field adjusters and certain management personnel were also leased.

Mr. Simons decided to contact the regional brokerage firm of Bucek and Carpenter, since they had marketed a common stock issue for the firm in 1983. Mr. Simons knew $1,800,000 was necessary to cover the investment needs of the firm. In speaking with Mr. Bucek, he found that the company would receive $14.00 per share. Control was not a consideration, since no one stockholder owned more than 15 percent of the outstanding stock and the new issue would receive a fairly wide distribution. Average weekly bid and ask prices on company stock are included in Exhibit 35.4.

Mr. Simons wondered whether the flotation cost was worth the benefit, and he began to consider a rights offering. Under this plan, each holder of five shares would receive the right to buy the company's stock at $15.25 per share. Since the stock price of The Aumond Company had been rising over the last four months, he felt the current shareholders would be eager to buy the stock at this price. Mr. Simons anticipated that the rights offering would be fully subscribed.

Selected ratios for the insurance industry are presented as Exhibit 35.5.

EXHIBIT 35.1

The Aumond Company

Condensed Consolidated Balance Sheets as of the Listed Dates

	December 31 1987	June 30 1988
Assets:		
Cash	$ 559,168	$ 612,990
U.S. Government Securities,		
Approximate Market	239,698	239,644
Accounts and Other Receivables, Net	5,133,474	5,157,550
Other Current Assets	124,298	137,656
Total Current Assets	$6,056,638	$6,147,840
Furniture, Fixtures, and Equipment	3,267,072	3,380,482
Leasehold Improvements	14,369	14,369
Total Fixed Assets	$3,281,441	$3,394,851
Accumulated Depreciation		
and Amortization	(1,678,981)	(1,792,522)
Net Fixed Assets	$1,602,460	$1,602,329
Other Assets	271,480	239,624
Total Assets	$7,930,578	$7,989,793
Liabilities and Stockholders' Equity:		
Accounts Payable	$ 477,498	$ 504,449
Accrued Liabilities	907,976	833,287
Accrued Income Taxes	837,676	672,424
Dividends Payable	68,948	68,948
Total Current Liabilities	$2,292,098	$2,079,108
Stockholders' Equity		
Common Stock, $1 Par	680,926	680,926
Paid-in Capital	1,923,289	1,923,289
Retained Earnings	3,034,265	3,306,470
Total Stockholders' Equity	$5,638,480	$5,910,685
Total Liabilities and		
Stockholders' Equity	$7,930,578	$7,989,793

EXHIBIT 35.2

The Aumond Company

Income Statements for the Periods Ending December 31, Except for the Six-month Period Ending June 30, 1988 (In Thousands)

	1986	1987	1988
Revenue for Services	$25,172	$27,250	$15,858
Costs and Expenses			
Cost of Services Rendered	19,800	22,115	13,615
Selling, General, and			
Administrative Expenses	2,558	2,843	1,361
Operating Income	$ 2,814	$ 2,292	$ 882
Other Expense (Income)	2	2	(4)
Before-Tax Income	$ 2,812	$ 2,290	$ 886
Federal and State Income Taxes	1,125	916	354
Net Income	$ 1,687	$ 1,374	$ 532
Dividends on Preferred Stock	31	16	0
Net Income Applicable			
to Common Stock	$ 1,656	$1,358	$ 532
Earnings per Share, Common	$2.43	$1.99	$0.78
Dividends per Share, Cash	$0.35	$0.50	$0.25

EXHIBIT 35.3

The Aumond Company

The Approximate Number of Claims Assigned to the Company (In Thousands)

Year	Claims	Year	Claims	Year	Claims
1987	497	1983	356	1979	260
1986	491	1982	342	1978	216
1985	458	1981	304	1977	192
1984	409	1980	284		

EXHIBIT 35.4

The Aumond Company

Average Weekly Bid and Ask Prices on Company Stock,
April–July 1988

Week Beginning		Average Ask	Average Bid
April	3	12½	11
	10	12¾	11¾
	17	12¾	11½
	24	12¾	11¾
May	1	13	11¾
	8	13⅛	11½
	15	13¼	12½
	22	13½	12½
	29	13¾	12½
June	5	14¼	13½
	12	14	13
	19	14	13
	26	14¾	13⅛
July	3	15	13¼
	10	15¼	13⅞
	17	15¼	13¼
	24	15½	13½
	31	15¾	14½

EXHIBIT 35.5

The Aumond Company

Selected Ratios for the Insurance Industry for the Following
Calendar Periods

	1984	1985	1986	1987
Liquidity:				
1. Current Ratio	1.0	1.0	1.0	1.0
2. Acid Test	1.0	1.0	1.0	0.9
3. Current Assets/Total Assets (%)	66.9	65.0	65.8	65.3
Activity:				
4. Receivables Turnover	2.1	2.0	2.3	2.6
5. Cost of Goods Sold/Inventory	—	—	—	—
6. Net Sales/Net Working Capital	58.8	55.1	INF	(55.6)
7. Net Sales/Total Assets	0.8	0.9	0.9	0.9
Leverage:				
8. Total Debt/Total Assets (%)	78.3	77.6	78.4	80.1
9. Debt/Net Worth	4.9	5.3	5.4	5.7
10. EBIT/Interest	4.7	3.6	2.5	2.0
Profitability:				
11. COGS/Net Sales (%)	—	—	—	—
12. Operating Profit/Net Sales (%)	11.4	8.4	9.1	5.2
13. Profit Before Taxes/Net Sales (%)	9.7	6.6	5.4	3.5
14. Profit Before Taxes/Total Assets (%)	5.9	4.1	2.9	2.5
15. Profit Before Taxes/Net Worth (%)	29.0	23.3	14.8	13.9

QUESTIONS

1. Evaluate the common stock plan as proposed by Bucek and Carpenter.
2. Evaluate the rights offering plan as proposed by Mr. Simons.
3. Devise a plan that would incorporate elements of the common stock and rights offering plans.
4. Choose an appropriate course of action for The Aumond Company.

Clymstrone Corporation
CONVERTIBLE SECURITIES

Bill Presley (chairman of the Board of Directors and president): Walter, which way do you think we should go on the new issue? I would like you to be ready at the next meeting.

Walter Richardson (treasurer and controller): I'll be ready. Most of the detail work has already been done. Perhaps I should give you a summary the day before the meeting.

Bill Presley: Good, set up an appointment with my secretary, and I'll see you then.

Clymstrone Corporation, incorporated in Dover, Delaware, in 1970, was engaged in furniture rental, sales, and equipment leasing. The company rented furniture to residents, owners, and operators of apartments. Rental return furniture and new furniture were sold through stores located throughout the southeastern United States. Management believed Clymstrone to be the largest in this area and one of the largest furniture rental companies in the country. The firm also leased industrial and commercial equipment, primarily on the East Coast. A balance sheet and income statement are included as Exhibit 36.1 and Exhibit 36.2.

In 1982, the company, by acquisition, entered the furniture rental and sales business, thus adding another line to the equipment leasing and consumer finance operations. Exhibit 36.3 gives the types of apartments utilizing rental furniture. When the acquired business did not meet profit expectations, a major reorganization of the new operation was initiated. During 1984, Clymstrone developed new operating procedures and controls, recruited the present management of the furniture rental and sales operations, and redefined its marketing strategy. For the next two years, the company closed a number of rental showrooms in unprofitable locations, reducing the total square footage by approximately 30 percent. In this same period, Clymstrone began new marketing programs and built its present sales organization.

The new marketing programs were implemented in 1985 and 1986. In its furniture rental activities, Clymstrone emphasized rentals directly to individual apartment residents, improved the quality of furniture offered for rental, and utilized incentive programs to encourage apartment owners to refer prospective customers to the company. Exhibit 36.4 shows the effect of this policy. In its furniture sales activities, Clymstrone began to sell, in addition to rental furniture, new furniture in its retail stores. A local area television advertising program was started. The results of these programs led the company in 1986 to sell its consumer finance business and other minor operations to concentrate financial resources on its furniture rental and sales operations.

The contribution to consolidated total revenue and consolidated earnings (loss) from continuing operations before income taxes is shown in Exhibit 36.5. In this computation, the operating expenses of the company have been allocated to its subsidiaries as management fees, calculated to approximate the administrative expense attributable to the subsidiary.

Clymstrone leased furniture at prices that generally permitted recovery of the purchase price after 10 months of rental. Rental inventory was depreciated on a straight-line basis at an average rate of 12.5 percent per year and was accounted for on a first-in, first-out basis. When furniture was transferred from rental inventory for sale as rental furniture, the average age was 18 to 24 months. The company attempted to sell rental return furniture at prices equal to the depreciated book value of the furniture, and this, coupled with extensive advertising of rental return furniture, attracted customers to the company's retail stores.

The increased number of customers generated by the sale of rental return furniture provided Clymstrone with another source of revenue, the sale of new furniture. Combining sales of new furniture with sales of rental return furniture at a given location led to more rapid inventory turnover and better utilization of personnel and facilities. These factors allowed the company to pursue pricing levels below those of most competitors. Clymstrone implemented this policy by periodic surveys of the prices of other furniture stores. Exhibit 36.5 shows the contribution to consolidated total revenue of furniture rental and sales.

Clymstrone rented furniture primarily to apartment residents such as students, young singles, newly marrieds, divorced people, single parents, military personnel, and persons requiring relocation for temporary periods. For these groups, the company offered a month-to-month rental agreement and a three-month rental agreement at a reduced monthly rate. A delivery time of 24 hours was offered by the company as well as permission to exchange rental furniture for a small service charge. As a further incentive to rent furniture, Clymstrone offered a purchase option that allowed the customer to apply 100 percent of rental payments toward the purchase of the rented furniture.

The company rented furniture to individual apartment residents through showrooms that attractively grouped rental furniture for display. These displays consisted primarily of living room, dining area, and bedroom furniture as well as accessories such as lamps and pictures. The average showroom contained 2,700 square feet, was open seven days a week, and had adjacent parking facilities. To allow for high visibility, the showrooms were usually located on streets with a high traffic count and near malls and shopping centers.

Clymstrone also sold its furniture rental services through apartment managers. The company employed a sales force that called on these managers to seek assistance in referring prospective customers.

Clymstrone sold new and rental return furniture through its retail stores. These facilities were staffed by sales personnel on commission, were open seven days a week, and had adjacent parking. The company's retail stores contained an average of 13,500 square feet, ranging between 5,400 and 27,000 square feet.

The company purchased furniture from a number of manufacturers and was, therefore, not dependent on any one source of supply. Although Clymstrone utilized single suppliers for some items, alternate sources of supply were readily available. The company's business had not experienced interruptions due to delays in acquiring furniture.

Clymstrone also leased industrial and commercial equipment to firms located on the East Coast. Equipment was purchased at the request and according to the specifications of the customer. The leases were of the full-payout type, noncancelable during the initial term, generally for a period of three to six years. They usually contained an option, exercisable at the end of the initial term, that permitted the lessee to renew the lease for a specific term at a reduced rental and a provision requiring that the lessee guarantee that the company would realize the residual value of the equipment stated in the lease. The lessee was required to pay license fees and insurance, to maintain and repair the leased equipment, and to pay taxes.

The company required credit applications from prospective customers and performed credit checks before approving such applications. Company policy required the return of rental furniture from customers who missed two consecutive monthly rental payments. In its furniture sales operations, Clymstrone honored a number of bank credit cards. Some furniture was sold by time sale contracts, which were then sold to consumer finance companies. In its equipment leasing business, the company conducted credit investigations of prospective lessees, which included review of financial statements, credit reports, and credit references.

The nature of Clymstrone's competition depended on which operation was involved. In its furniture rental operations, principal competition came from the large number of apartment owners who purchased furniture for rental to tenants. The company also competed with other furniture rental companies. Management believed that price, condition of the furniture, size of selection, lease terms, speed of delivery, exchange privilege, purchase option, and the absence of deposit requirements were the principal factors that influenced apartment residents in selecting a company. In retail sales of furniture, the company competed with numerous furniture dealers. Here, management felt that price was the principal competitive factor. In the equipment leasing business, the company competed with leasing companies, sales finance companies, equipment manufacturers, commercial banks, and other financial institutions. Many of these competitors were able to borrow at lower costs.

As of December 31, 1987, the company employed 675 persons, of whom 650 were employed in the furniture rental and sales business, 20 were engaged in corporate administration, and 5 were employed in the equipment leasing business. Most employees were compensated on a base salary plus a commission on sales. Management believed this method improved employee morale and productivity. Unlike some competitors, the employees did not belong to a collective bargaining unit. Benefit programs included a profit-sharing plan; sick leave; paid vacations; and group life, disability, and hospitalization insurance.

The growth of the furniture rental and sales business since 1985 had resulted primarily from increased business in existing market areas. The company expected to continue to emphasize this expansion by increasing sales personnel and investment in inventory and service equipment.

The company had developed a plan for entering new market areas that called for opening both rental showrooms and retail stores at or about the same time. Management expected that the combined operating profits would shorten the period that would otherwise be required to achieve operating profits from furniture rental operations alone. According to this plan, rental return furniture would be provided to new retail stores either through the shipment of furniture from existing stores or the purchase of furniture from other furniture rental companies.

In 1987, Clymstrone broadened its rental furniture product line by offering office furniture for rent in four test market areas. Encouraged by the results, the company intended to begin renting office furniture in the other areas served by the company. If the office furniture rental business were to expand, the company would enlarge its rental showrooms and hire additional sales personnel. Initially, the company planned to offer returned office furniture for sale in its present retail stores, but ultimately these goods would be merchandised in separate stores.

Mr. Richardson had determined that $4,000,000 would be needed to finance the proposed expansion. The current market price of the common stock was $11.00. To sell a new issue of common stock, the underwriting firm of Wilner and Freeman determined that the stock would have to be priced at $10.25 per share. The underwriting discount of $.75 would leave $9.50 per share as proceeds to the company. To raise the required funds, approximately 421,053 shares needed to be sold. An alternative would be to issue 30-year, 9 percent face-value convertible bonds. The conversion price would be set at $12.50 per share, and the bond could be sold at par. After underwriting discounts, the proceeds from each bond would be 98.825 percent. After the expansion, the earnings before interest on long-term debt for fiscal 1988 was estimated at $3,000,000. Interest on current long-term debt was forecasted at $340,000 for fiscal 1988. Mr. Richardson also determined that the coupon rate on bonds of similar risk with no convertible feature was 11 percent. Mr. Richardson decided to use a marginal tax rate of 40 percent in all his calculations.

Selected ratios for the furniture industry and the furniture leasing industry are presented as Exhibit 36.6 and Exhibit 36.7.

EXHIBIT 36.1

Clymstrone Corporation

Balance Sheet for the Year Ending December 31, 1987

Assets:	
Cash	$ 828
Accounts and Notes Receivable	2,984
Inventory	3,670
Prepaids	232
Total Current Assets	$ 7,714
Property, Plant, and Equipment, Net	7,009
Other Assets	893
Total Assets	$15,616
Liabilities and Stockholders' Equity:	
Accounts Payable	$ 993
Accrued Expenses	301
Notes Payable, Short-Term	4,527
Current Maturities of Long-Term Debt	466
Total Current Liabilities	$ 6,287
Long-Term Debt	3,362
Stockholders' Equity	
Common Stock, $0.10 Par	153
Paid-in Capital	3,543
Retained Earnings	2,753
	$ 6,449
Treasury Stock at Cost,	
124,000 shares	482
Total Stockholders' Equity	$ 5,967
Total Liabilities and	
Stockholders' Equity	$15,616

EXHIBIT 36.2

Clymstrone Corporation

Income Statement for the Year Ending December 31, 1987
(In Thousands)

	Rental of Furniture	Sale of Furniture	Total
Net Revenue	$11,797	$13,189	$24,986
Cost of Sales	0	7,929	7,929
Gross Profit	$11,797	$ 5,260	$17,057
Operating Expenses	10,022	3,865	$13,887
Operating Profit	$ 1,775	$ 1,395	$ 3,170
Other Expenses, Including Interest	*	*	1,156
Net Profit Before Taxes	*	*	$ 2,014
Federal and State Income Taxes	*	*	804
Net Income After Taxes	*	*	$ 1,210

* No allocation made on these items.

EXHIBIT 36.3

Clymstrone Corporation

Types of Apartments Utilizing Rental Furniture

	1984	1985	1986	1987
Number	18,765	16,265	16,470	24,025
Percent Residents	60%	64%	70%	72%
Percent Apartment Owners	40%	36%	30%	28%

EXHIBIT 36.4

Clymstrone Corporation

Contribution to Furniture Rental and Sales (In Thousands)

	1984	1985	1986	1987
Rental Revenue	$6,797	$6,841	$ 7,106	$ 9,850
Sales, Revenue, Rental				
Return Furniture	2,166	1,958	2,683	4,424
Sales Revenue, New Furniture	0	518	2,384	8,765
Total Revenue	$8,963	$9,317	$12,173	$23,039

EXHIBIT 36.5

Clymstrone Corporation

*Contribution to Consolidated Total Revenue and Earnings
Before Taxes (In Thousands)*

	1984	1985	1986	1987
Total Revenue				
Furniture Rental and Sales	$ 8,963	$ 9,317	$12,173	$23,039
Equipment Leasing	1,123	1,339	1,695	1,914
Other	540	503	407	33
Consolidated Total Revenue	$10,626	$11,159	$14,275	$24,986
Earnings Before Income Taxes				
Furniture Rental and Sales	$ 305	$ (244)	$ 359	$ 1,665
Equipment Leasing	139	(76)	211	301
Other	97	235	11	48
Consolidated Earnings	$ 541	$ (85)	$ 581	$ 2,014

EXHIBIT 36.6

Clymstrone Corporation

Selected Ratios for the Furniture Industry for the Following Calendar Periods

	1984	1985	1986	1987
Liquidity:				
1. Current Ratio	1.9	2.0	1.9	1.8
2. Acid Test	0.7	0.6	0.5	0.5
3. Current Assets/Total Assets (%)	80.8	79.9	78.9	79.7
Activity:				
4. Receivables Turnover	11.7	13.4	13.5	15.6
5. Cost of Goods Sold/Inventory	2.6	2.5	2.5	2.5
6. Net Sales/Net Working Capital	5.5	5.6	6.1	6.1
7. Net Sales/Total Assets	2.1	2.1	2.0	2.1
Leverage:				
8. Total Debt/Total Assets (%)	58.1	59.5	62.0	63.0
9. Debt/Net Worth	1.5	1.6	1.7	1.8
10. EBIT/Interest	3.4	2.2	1.8	1.6
Profitability:				
11. COGS/Net Sales (%)	60.1	59.8	60.8	60.5
12. Operating Profit/Net Sales (%)	4.1	3.3	2.8	1.9
13. Profit Before Taxes/Net Sales (%)	4.0	2.7	1.6	1.2
14. Profit Before Taxes/Total Assets (%)	6.7	4.3	3.4	2.5
15. Profit Before Taxes/Net Worth (%)	17.1	11.6	9.5	7.0

EXHIBIT 36.7

Clymstrone Corporation

*Selected Ratios for the Furniture Leasing Industry for the
Following Calendar Periods*

	1984	*1985*	*1986*	*1987*
Liquidity:				
1. Current Ratio	0.9	0.9	0.9	0.8
2. Acid Test	0.7	0.6	0.6	0.5
3. Current Assets/Total Assets (%)	29.2	27.9	29.1	27.5
Activity:				
4. Receivables Turnover	9.5	9.8	8.8	10.3
5. Cost of Goods Sold/Inventory	—	—	—	—
6. Net Sales/Net Working Capital	9.9	15.7	11.7	15.1
7. Net Sales/Total Assets	1.1	1.1	1.1	1.1
Leverage:				
8. Total Debt/Total Assets (%)	63.1	65.7	67.7	66.0
9. Debt/Net Worth	1.9	2.3	2.4	2.1
10. EBIT/Interest	2.7	2.8	2.4	1.9
Profitability:				
11. COGS/Net Sales	—	—	—	—
12. Operating Profit/Net Sales (%)	15.9	15.4	15.1	13.4
13. Profit Before Taxes/Net Sales (%)	11.6	8.9	6.9	6.6
14. Profit Before Taxes/Total Assets (%)	8.5	6.9	5.6	4.9
15. Profit Before Taxes/Net Worth (%)	24.4	22.0	23.0	17.0

QUESTIONS

1. Calculate the number of shares of common stock outstanding and the earnings per share under the common stock financing alternative. (Use the earnings estimate before interest on long-term debt for fiscal 1988.)

2. Calculate the number of shares of common stock outstanding and the earnings per share associated with the bond issue prior to conversion of the bond. (Use the earnings estimate before interest on long-term debt for fiscal 1988.)

3. Calculate the number of shares outstanding and the earnings per share associated with the bond, assuming all the bonds have been converted. (Use the earnings estimate before interest on long-term debt for fiscal 1988.)

4. Calculate the straight value of the bond.

5. Calculate the conversion value of the bond when the market price of the common stock is $8, $10, $12, and $16 per share.

6. What would you recommend to Mr. Presley and the Board of Directors?

PART VI

SELECTED TOPICS IN FINANCIAL MANAGEMENT

Modern Cleaning Methods, Inc.
MULTINATIONAL FINANCE

Modern Cleaning Methods, Inc., headquartered in Pittsburgh, Pennsylvania, was a leading manufacturer and marketer of chemical products and systems for cleaning and sanitation. The company was organized into three divisions: Institutional, Industrial, and Consumer. A balance sheet and an income statement are included as Exhibit 37.1 and Exhibit 37.2.

The Institutional Division's major customers were schools, hospitals, prisons, franchise restaurants, and the armed forces. Sales included detergents and sanitizers, systems for general housekeeping and for cleaning laundry, as well as cleaning management services.

The Consumer Division sold primarily to supermarkets. Sixty-five percent of its products were used in automatic dishwashers.

The Industrial Division sold 60 percent of its output to the metalworking industry and 40 percent to the paper industry. Products included detergents, lubricants, solvents, and coatings.

Modern Cleaning Methods sold both in the United States and in foreign countries. Sales for the last three years, divided into foreign and domestic, are shown in Exhibit 37.3.

The vice-president for finance of MCM was Doris Burstein. She had been with the company for nearly 15 years after graduating from the University of Pittsburgh with a BBA. During that time, she had also met the qualifications to be a CPA. In August 1987, Ms. Burstein, in response to a directive from the president of the firm, Irwin Hale, began gathering information as to the feasibility of investing in plant and equipment in foreign countries. To accomplish that task, she needed a list of possible capital projects. She assigned the duty to her assistant, Creighton Johnson, and informed him that a report was needed by the first of September.

She knew the issue of foreign investment had been a hot topic among company executives for a number of years. The most vocal advocate of investing was Elywn Roberts, the head of the Consumer Division. He had pointed out that foreign sales accounted for more than 41 percent of his division's sales, up from about 30 percent in 1980. He stressed that a production facility located overseas would have numerous benefits. First, labor costs would be lower.

Second, transportation costs would be reduced. Third, and especially important to the Consumer Division, sales would be increased. This last benefit could be achieved because a local plant would be able to respond much faster to local conditions and could design products tailored to that particular locale.

Ms. Burstein discovered in her research that most firms become multinational by degree. Their first experience with foreign activity is usually with exports, as was the case with MCM. The next step is usually to set up a foreign subsidiary and licensing agreement. The final step often involves the actual location of physical assets in a foreign country.

Normally, firms only contemplate investment in capital projects when they are forced to do so. That may occur, for example, when there are export or import barriers.

In conversations with Mr. Roberts, Ms. Burstein was left with the impression that growth in the sales of the Consumer Division could not be maintained by exports alone. Mr. Roberts agreed that the competitive advantages enjoyed by foreign competitors would limit future expansion at home.

Ms. Burstein understood that the firm would be taking political risks if it continued to sell abroad without investing in the host country. She knew that whenever an American company achieved a certain sales volume, the government would suggest that unless capital expenditures were made, restrictions on imports would be necessary. In the extreme case, the authorities might choose to nationalize the assets of MCM. Exactly what they would do depended on the political environment.

Another fundamental issue involved the manner in which the new segment should be organized: a branch or a subsidiary. In studying the issue, she found that the decision involved a comparison of tax rates. If U.S. tax rates were less than foreign tax rates and if the excess tax credits could not be utilized, then a branch would be favored. Of course, the reverse would be true if rates in the United States exceeded foreign rates.

To perform his part of the assignment, Mr. Johnson began gathering information on a plant designed to manufacture products for the Consumer Division. The fixed asset possibilities were in country A, a European location, or in country B, a North African location. In country A, the cost of the asset would range from $5,600,000 to $6,400,000. This uncertainty in construction costs was due to the difficulty of forecasting direct labor costs. In country B, construction costs were estimated to be between $4,000,000 and $7,000,000. This greater variance in costs was due to the greater variability in the time required to secure and transport construction materials. Even so, average construction costs would be lower in country B due to lower wage rates. Mr. Johnson estimated the expected cost for country A to be $6,000,000 and for country B to be $5,500,000.

Estimated yearly earnings on the investment in country A was 12,000,000 Ados during the period from 1990 to 1999 and 10,000,000 Ados from 2000 to 2009. Mr. Johnson knew the exchange rate between Ados and dollars could vary from year to year, but he decided that since the currency had been fairly stable over the last few years, he would use the prevailing rate of five Ados to the dollar in his calculations. He was also aware that even though country A levied a 42 percent tax on earnings before taxes, the amount paid could be applied as a credit against U.S. taxes.

In both country A and country B, plants would have a life of 20 years and a terminal value equal to 15 percent of average construction costs. Mr. Johnson assumed further that these construction costs would occur in fiscal 1989 and that the benefits would begin in the next fiscal year.

Estimated yearly earnings on the investment in country B was 25,000,000 Bdos during the period from 1990 to 1999 and 21,000,000 Bdos from 2000 to 2009. Mr. Johnson was convinced, based on his research, that the exchange rate for Bdos would decline markedly due to high inflation in country B. He therefore decided, in contrast to the prevailing rate of 8 Bdos to the dollar, that he would use 10 Bdos for the first 10 years of the project and 12 Bdos for the last 10 years in his calculations. Country B levied a 35 percent tax on earnings before taxes, but, as in country A, the amount paid could be applied as a credit against U.S. taxes.

Selected ratios for specialty cleaning and sanitation preparations and manufacturers are presented in Exhibit 37.4.

EXHIBIT 37.1

Modern Cleaning Methods, Inc.

Condensed Balance Sheets as of July 31 (In Thousands)

	1986	1987	1988
Assets:			
Cash and Equivalents	$ 55,910	$ 70,223	$ 53,251
Accounts Receivable, Net	89,060	95,523	118,995
Inventory	72,836	81,140	111,766
Prepaids	4,930	3,118	2,783
Total Current Assets	$222,736	$250,004	$286,785
Other Assets	7,546	9,204	61,881
Fixed Assets, Gross	166,832	198,364	253,277
Accumulated Depreciation	(52,610)	(60,818)	(78,091)
Net Fixed Assets	$114,222	$137,546	$175,186
Total Assets	$344,504	$396,754	$523,852
Liabilities and Stockholders' Equity:			
Notes Payable	$ 11,646	$ 12,933	$ 14,691
Accounts Payable, Trade	34,390	38,915	44,667
Accruals	36,501	42,759	48,104
Total Current Liabilities	$ 82,537	$ 94,607	$107,462
Long-Term Debt Obligations	64,000	75,500	163,124
Stockholders' Equity	197,967	226,647	253,266
Total Liabilities and Stockholders' Equity	$344,504	$396,754	$523,852

EXHIBIT 37.2

Modern Cleaning Methods, Inc.

Condensed Statement of Net Income for the Fiscal Years Ending July 31 (In Thousands)

	1986	1987	1988
Net Sales	$517,790	$603,720	$711,974
Cost of Sales	243,962	278,721	333,525
Gross Profit	$273,828	$324,999	$378,449
Operating Expenses	220,087	255,947	304,992
EBIT	$ 53,741	$ 69,052	$ 73,457
Net Interest Expense (Income)	2,304	(3,291)	3,541
Net Income Before Taxes	$ 51,437	$ 72,343	$ 69,916
Federal and State Income Taxes	20,134	28,305	27,427
Net Income	$ 31,303	$ 44,038	$ 42,489

EXHIBIT 37.3

Modern Cleaning Methods, Inc.

Sales by Division and by Location (In Thousands)

	1986	1987	1988
Institutional			
Domestic	$241,447	$287,425	$320,622
Foreign	63,655	74,209	94,315
Total	$305,102	$361,634	$414,937
Industrial			
Domestic	41,405	48,279	56,110
Foreign	21,395	24,733	28,066
Total	$ 62,800	$ 73,012	$ 84,176
Consumer			
Domestic	89,851	99,083	124,242
Foreign	60,037	69,991	88,619
Total	$149,888	$169,074	$212,861
Total Domestic	$372,703	$434,787	$500,974
Total Foreign	145,087	168,933	211,000
Total Sales	$517,790	$603,720	$711,974

EXHIBIT 37.4

Modern Cleaning Methods, Inc.

*Selected Ratios for Specialty Cleaning and Sanitation
Preparations Manufacturers for the Following
Calendar Periods*

	1985	*1986*	*1987*	*1988*
Liquidity:				
1. Current Ratio	1.8	1.8	1.6	1.7
2. Acid Test	1.1	1.0	1.1	1.1
3. Current Assets/Total Assets (%)	66.0	64.7	65.9	66.0
Activity:				
4. Receivables Turnover	9.0	7.7	8.5	8.7
5. Cost of Goods Sold/Inventory	6.6	7.0	6.3	6.5
6. Net Sales/Net Working Capital	9.2	8.8	10.7	10.3
7. Net Sales/Total Assets	2.7	2.4	2.6	2.5
Leverage:				
8. Total Debt/Total Assets (%)	58.2	61.0	57.1	57.5
9. Debt/Net Worth	1.4	1.6	1.0	1.0
10. EBIT/Interest	3.5	3.4	4.4	4.5
Profitability:				
11. COGS/Net Sales (%)	62.6	62.6	56.6	60.5
12. Operating Profit/Net Sales (%)	3.7	5.2	5.5	5.8
13. Profit Before Taxes/Net Sales (%)	2.9	4.0	4.4	4.8
14. Profit Before Taxes/Total Assets (%)	7.9	9.6	9.5	9.6
15. Profit Before Taxes/Net Worth (%)	20.3	22.2	25.4	25.7

QUESTIONS

1. Compute the net present value of the plant investment in Country A. (Assume that the plant is established as a wholly owned subsidiary and that country A's income is consolidated with the income of the parent firm. In addition, make the following assumptions: (a) The full U.S. tax rate of 45 percent is applied to the earnings of the subsidiary before the taxes of country A. (b) Repatriated earnings are 85 percent of the net profit after the taxes of country A. (c) Modern Cleaning Methods is given a credit against U.S. taxes. (d) The discount rate is 16 percent, the average rate on projects of a similar nature in the United States.)

2. Compute the net present value of the plant investment in country B. (Assume that the plant is established as a wholly owned subsidiary and that country B's income is consolidated with the income of the parent firm. In addition, make the following assumptions: (a) The full U.S. tax rate of 45 percent is applied to the earnings of

the subsidiary before the taxes of country B. (b) Repatriated earnings are 80 percent of the net profit after the taxes of country B. (c) Modern Cleaning Methods is given a credit against U.S. taxes. (d) The discount rate is 16 percent, the average rate on projects of a similar nature in the United States.)

3. Discuss the use of the average discount rate for projects in both country A and country B. (In the discussion, consider reasons for using a different discount rate for each country. Without making new calculations, indicate the effect on net present values of changes in the discount rate.)

4. Compare organization of the foreign activity by joint venture versus a wholly owned subsidiary.

5. Discuss what general economic factors influence exchange rates between countries. (In the discussion, consider the reasonableness of Mr. Johnson's assumptions concerning exchange rates between each of the two countries and the United States.)

6. Which project, if any, should Modern Cleaning Methods choose?

7. Compute the net present values of the plant investment in country A and in country B.

Alderson, Inc.
TAKEOVERS

In January 1989, Ms. Roberta Hardencourt, president of Alderson, Inc., a firm headquartered in Louisville, Kentucky, was studying an information packet concerning Lastor, Inc., a prime acquisition candidate of the company.

Alderson, Inc. was founded in 1937 for the purpose of manufacturing glass for the automotive industry. Until 1965, this had been the only product produced by the firm. In that year, management decided that the risk of being tied solely to the fortunes of the automobile industry was too great to continue to bear. As a result they acquired Parkin Company, a supplier of flat and tinted glass for the residential, industrial, and commercial construction glass markets. This part of the business experienced a faster growth rate than did automobile glass and by the end of 1988 accounted for 55 percent of the firm's total sales and approximately 60 percent of its profits. Balance sheets and income statements are included as Exhibit 38.1 and Exhibit 38.2.

In late 1988, President Hardencourt met with the vice-presidents of finance, manufacturing, marketing, and human resources to debate the wisdom of acquiring Lastor, Inc., a major supplier of decorative laminates and custom-engineered molded plastic products for the automotive, building construction, and furniture industries. At this meeting the consensus agreement was that an attempt should be made to acquire Lastor, although some objections to the acquisition were voiced. Balance sheets and income statements are provided for Lastor, Inc. as Exhibit 38.3 and Exhibit 38.4. Average 1988 market prices for both Alderson and Lastor are given by Exhibit 38.5.

Doris Pandrika, vice-president for manufacturing, reminded the group the company had never dealt with any other material than glass. Ms. Pandrika, who had been with the firm for 28 years, stated that it had taken her at least 20 years to feel confident in handling glass. She said it was a long, slow process to become knowledgeable about a material, and she pointed out she was still learning. There was apprehension on her part that Alderson manufacturing executives would be totally dependent on Lastor executives for their knowledge of plastics. But Ms. Alderson knew this expertise was one of the factors that made Lastor an attractive takeover candidate. She was also aware that the top five executives, who averaged only 45 years in age, viewed the takeover in a favorable light and were likely to remain with Alderson.

Zane Wegand, vice-president for marketing, said that Lastor provided a fine fit from a marketing standpoint. He pointed out that both firms sold a significant portion of their output to the construction and building industries, and he felt some cost savings could be obtained by combining sales forces. Mr. Wegand further believed that Lastor sold an excessive number of products, thereby reducing manufacturing efficiency and causing inventories to be higher than necessary.

Ms. Hardencourt reminded the group of rumors circulating throughout the financial community that A. L. Spantos Company also might be interested in purchasing Lastor. Although she knew of no formal offer, she believed the rumors had some validity. Spantos was a competitor in the commercial and industrial glass field, but not in the automotive glass sector. She was worried that if Spantos were successful in acquiring Lastor, it would gain a dominant position in the commercial and industrial glass market. She knew, however, that she did not want to offer a price for Lastor that would impair the financial integrity of her firm. Also she did not want to become involved in a bidding war with Spantos.

Ms. Hardencourt wanted to have a decision on Lastor by February 1989. She knew that waiting any longer would be detrimental to Alderson.

Selected ratios for the glass and plastics industries are presented as Exhibit 38.6 and Exhibit 38.7.

EXHIBIT 38.1

Alderson, Inc.

Balance Sheets as of December 31 (In Thousands)

	1987	1988
Assets:		
Cash and Marketable Securities	$ 8,428	$ 6,897
Accounts Receivable, Net	83,376	106,605
Inventories	114,623	148,258
Other Current Assets	4,009	5,604
Total Current Assets	$210,436	$267,364
Plant and Equipment, Gross	320,083	351,978
Accumulated Depreciation	(158,839)	(172,976)
Net Plant and Equipment	161,244	179,002
Other Assets	18,871	14,008
Total Assets	$390,551	$460,374

EXHIBIT 38.1 (Continued)

Alderson, Inc.

Balance Sheets as of December 31 (In Thousands)

	1987	1988
Liabilities and Stockholders' Equity:		
Accounts Payable	$ 29,113	$ 43,856
Notes Payable	28,600	36,774
Accrued Expenses	7,462	18,253
Current Maturities of Long-Term Debt	5,140	5,200
Other Current Liabilities	0	4,313
Total Current Liabilities	$ 70,315	$108,396
Long-Term Debt	70,215	80,914
Deferred Income Taxes	4,560	6,237
Stockholders' Equity		
Common Stock, $10 Par	50,860	51,510
Paid-in Capital	24,625	25,991
Retained Earnings	169,976	187,326
Total Stockholders' Equity	$245,461	$264,827
Total Liabilities and Stockholders' Equity	$390,551	$460,374

EXHIBIT 38.2

Alderson, Inc.

Income Statements as of December 31 (In Thousands)

	1987	1988
Net Sales	$466,808	$662,355
Cost of Goods Sold	365,792	500,223
Gross Profit	$101,016	$162,132
Selling and General Administrative Expenses	53,704	86,666
Engineering, Research and Development	10,627	20,413
Operating Profit	$ 36,685	$ 55,053
Other Expenses, Including Interest	7,533	8,098
Other Income (Loss)	(1,874)	(4,000)
Net Profit Before Taxes	$ 31,026	$ 50,955
Federal and State Income Taxes	12,398	20,112
Net Income After Taxes	$ 18,628	$ 30,843
Dividends per Share	$2.00	$2.60

EXHIBIT 38.3

Alderson, Inc.

Balance Sheets for Lastor, Inc., as of December 31
(In Thousands)

	1987	1988
Assets:		
Cash and Marketable Securities	$ 7,387	$ 6,926
Accounts Receivable, Net	26,072	24,756
Inventories	26,389	30,783
Other Current Assets	4,389	3,606
Total Current Assets	$64,237	$66,071
Plant and Equipment, Gross	50,783	54,730
Accumulated Depreciation	(20,325)	(22,520)
Net Plant and Equipment	$30,458	$32,210
Other Assets	1,983	1,046
Total Assets	$96,678	$99,327
Liabilities and Stockholders' Equity:		
Accounts Payable	$ 9,892	$ 9,369
Notes Payable	8,000	0
Accrued Expenses	7,021	7,565
Current Maturities of Long-Term Debt	4,350	4,465
Other Current Liabilities	3,076	2,913
Total Current Liabilities	$32,339	$24,312
Long-Term Debt	21,465	26,545
Deferred Income Taxes	1,662	3,047
Stockholders' Equity		
Common Stock, $10 Par	7,850	8,010
Paid-in Capital	6,430	6,525
Retained Earnings	26,932	30,888
Total Stockholders' Equity	$41,212	$45,423
Total Liabilities and Stockholders' Equity	$96,678	$99,327

EXHIBIT 38.4

Alderson, Inc.

Income Statements for Lastor, Inc., as of December 31
(In Thousands)

	1987	1988
Net Sales	$180,064	$186,748
Cost of Goods Sold	139,634	139,127
Gross Profit	$ 40,430	$ 47,621
Selling and General Administrative Expenses	28,089	29,011
Engineering, Research, and Development	7,222	7,685
Operating Profit	$ 5,119	$ 10,925
Other Expenses, Including Interest	2,364	2,619
Other Income (Loss)	(419)	(204)
Net Profit Before Taxes	$ 3,174	$ 8,510
Federal and State Income Taxes	1,212	3,400
Net Income After Taxes	$ 1,962	$ 5,110
Dividends per Share	$1.40	$1.40

EXHIBIT 38.5

Alderson, Inc.

Average 1988 Market Prices on Stocks for the Months Listed

	Alderson	Lastor
January	49½	40½
February	50	40⅞
March	52	40¾
April	51	39⅛
May	53¼	38⅞
June	56⅛	40¼
July	60½	43¾
August	58⅞	46
September	56½	45½
October	55¾	47
November	54⅞	46
December	55½	44⅞

EXHIBIT 38.6

Alderson, Inc.

Selected Ratios for the Glass Industry for the Following
Calendar Periods (Pertinent to Alderson)

	1985	1986	1987	1988
Liquidity:				
1. Current Ratio	1.9	1.5	2.2	2.0
2. Acid Test	1.0	1.1	1.0	1.0
3. Current Assets/Total Assets (%)	60.3	60.7	58.4	59.6
Activity:				
4. Receivables Turnover	8.4	8.0	7.8	8.1
5. Cost of Goods Sold/Inventory	6.2	6.4	6.6	6.6
6. Net Sales/Net Working Capital	7.0	8.0	7.9	7.6
7. Net Sales/Total Assets	2.0	2.1	2.1	2.2
Leverage:				
8. Total Debt/Total Assets (%)	60.6	60.8	64.3	62.9
9. Debt/Net Worth	1.5	1.5	1.7	1.6
10. EBIT/Interest	3.0	2.7	2.3	2.4
Profitability:				
11. COGS/Net Sales (%)	71.9	71.4	72.6	73.3
12. Operating Profit/Net Sales (%)	4.1	4.0	3.9	4.3
13. Profit Before Taxes/Net Sales (%)	2.3	2.2	2.1	2.4
14. Profit Before Taxes/Total Assets (%)	4.4	4.3	3.8	4.2
15. Profit Before Taxes/Net Worth (%)	8.6	9.0	7.1	8.2

EXHIBIT 38.7

Alderson, Inc.

Selected Ratios for the Plastics Products Industry for the
Following Calendar Periods (Pertinent to Lastor)

	1985	1986	1987	1988
Liquidity:				
1. Current Ratio	1.4	1.6	1.5	1.5
2. Acid Test	0.8	0.9	0.8	0.9
3. Current Assets/Total Assets (%)	59.0	57.3	57.4	57.3
Activity:				
4. Receivables Turnover	7.8	8.2	8.0	7.8
5. Cost of Goods Sold/Inventory	7.2	7.5	7.4	7.6
6. Net Sales/Net Working Capital	11.8	11.1	12.1	12.0
7. Net Sales/Total Assets	2.1	2.1	2.1	2.0
Leverage:				
8. Total Debt/Total Assets (%)	61.5	61.0	61.8	61.6
9. Debt/Net Worth	1.7	1.6	1.6	1.7
10. EBIT/Interest	3.7	2.4	2.4	2.1
Profitability:				
11. COGS/Net Sales (%)	74.2	74.5	74.5	74.0
12. Operating Profit/Net Sales (%)	6.1	5.0	5.4	4.4
13. Profit Before Taxes/Net Sales (%)	4.6	3.5	3.7	2.8
14. Profit Before Taxes/Total Assets (%)	9.5	6.7	7.2	5.4
15. Profit Before Taxes/Net Worth (%)	26.4	19.4	21.0	16.5

QUESTIONS

1. Discuss the pros and cons of acquiring Lastor, Inc., using the material in Exhibit 38.3, Exhibit 38.4, and Exhibit 38.5.
2. What additional information would be useful to Ms. Hardencourt in determining the value of Lastor to Alderson?
3. What is the maximum price per share that Ms. Hardencourt can pay for Lastor, Inc., and still keep the takeover advantageous to Alderson? (Explain how you arrived at that value.)
4. What is the minimum price that Lastor, Inc. is likely to accept for its shares? (Explain how you arrived at that value.)
5. What is the likely price and terms of the buyout, assuming that a deal is struck between Alderson and Lastor?

Advanced Power Systems
MERGERS

In January 1989, Randy Pate, president of Advanced Power Systems of Grand Rapids, Michigan, was reviewing acquisition candidates for a possible merger. The leading candidate appeared to be Henderson Hydraulics, Inc. (HHI) of Augusta, Georgia, a manufacturer of high-pressure pumps, motors, and related valves. Mr. Pate had become familiar with HHI while attending the Masters Tournament in Augusta the previous April.

Advanced Power Systems was a leading manufacturer of fluid power systems and related components. Fluid power involved the transfer and control of power through the medium of liquid, gas, or air. Simple fluid power systems included a pump for pressure generation, valves for fluid flow control, a cylinder for translating fluid pressure into mechanical energy, a filter to remove contaminants, and numerous hoses, couplings, fittings, clamps, and seals. A balance sheet and historical operating results are included as Exhibit 39.1 and Exhibit 39.2.

Company products were classified into three categories: industrial, aerospace, and automotive. Industrial products included cylinders, valves, controls, tube fittings, filters, power systems, hose fittings, connectors, sealing devices, and clamps. Aerospace products included components and systems for ground fueling of aircraft, marine fueling operations, and highway vehicle loading of bulk liquids. Automotive products consisted of worm-drive hose clamps, tire valves, gauges, automotive radio antennas, thermostats, and brake-fluid pumps.

APS's more than 30,000 customers were involved in virtually every major manufacturing, transportation, and processing industry. The major markets for industrial products were agricultural machinery, food production, industrial machinery, instrumentation, machine tools, mining, mobile equipment, petrochemical, textile, transportation, and all major production and processing industries. Aerospace sales were primarily related to military and commercial aircraft. The majority of automotive products were sold to replacement markets through warehouse distributors and mass merchandisers.

Henderson Hydraulics, Inc. manufactured hydraulic pumps, motors, and related valves in a wide range of sizes, pressure ratings, and rates of flow. In recent years, the company had concentrated on high-pressure, large-flow pumps and motors that were utilized as the central element of the hydraulic power system of heavy mobile earth-moving and materials-handling machines. The total product line consisted of three basic pump designs and four basic valve designs that could be adapted into approximately 925 different models. A balance sheet and historical operating results are included as Exhibit 39.3 and Exhibit 39.4.

Approximately 80 percent of HHI's sales in 1988 were of products used in the basic types of heavy mobile earth-moving and materials-handling machines. The remainder of sales were primarily to manufacturers of dump trucks and solid waste refuse compactors, for use in hydraulic systems.

Advanced Power System's foreign operations were conducted primarily in Western Europe, although subsidiaries were located in Argentina, Australia, Brazil, Canada, Denmark, Finland, France, Germany, Great Britain, Italy, Mexico, Norway, Singapore, South Africa, Spain, and Venezuela. Henderson Hydraulics, Inc., in contrast, depended on eight major heavy mobile machine manufacturers in the United States for most of its business.

APS maintained research and development laboratories in 25 of its 45 manufacturing locations. The research and development staff included chemists and physicists as well as mechanical and electrical engineers. The company spent $16,893,000 in the year ending December 31, 1988 on research activities relating to the development of new products or services and to the improvement of existing ones. HHI, on the other hand, employed 5 engineers and 15 technicians specializing in hydraulic pump, motor, and valve design and development. During 1988, HHI spent $826,000 on its research and development activities.

Three of HHI's eight major customers had required variable pumps on at least one model of their excavators. At the end of 1988, HHI had no plans to manufacture that kind of pump. The company's two principal competitors, with substantially greater financial resources, were planning to introduce the variable-volume pumps in 1989.

Advanced Power Systems and Henderson Hydraulics, Inc. differed in the market price of their common stock. As of December 31, 1988, APS sold for $58.50 per share, and HHI sold for $25.00 per share.

Selected ratios for industrial controls manufacturers are presented in Exhibit 39.5.

EXHIBIT 39.1

Advanced Power Systems

Balance Sheet as of December 31, 1988 (In Thousands)

Assets:	
Cash	$ 11,214
Accounts Receivable	
Customers	94,720
Other Receivables	5,426
	$100,146
Inventories	
Finished Products	76,308
Work-in-Process	87,564
Raw Materials	29,314
	$193,186
Prepaid Expenses	7,124
Total Current Assets	$311,670
Other Assets	2,988
Plant and Equipment	
Land and Land Improvements	14,914
Buildings and Building Equipment	93,096
Machinery and Equipment	187,286
Construction in Progress	8,494
	$303,790
Accumulated Depreciation	(138,116)
	$165,674
Patents and Licenses	1,620
Excess of Cost of Investments in Consolidated	
Subsidiaries over Equities in Net Assets	1,898
Total Assets	$483,850
Liabilities and Stockholders' Equity:	
Notes Payable, Banks	$ 17,766
Notes Payable, Commercial Paper	18,000
Accounts Payable, Trade	28,906
Accrued Payrolls, Commissions	
and Other Compensations	14,464
Accrued Taxes, Other than Income Taxes	9,392
Accrued Taxes, Federal, State, and Foreign	19,060
Other Accounts Payable and Accrued Expenses	19,604
Total Current Liabilities	$127,192
Deferred Federal Income Tax	7,318
Long-Term Liabilities	126,134
Total Liabilities	$260,644
Stockholders' Equity	
Commn Stock	2,612
Additional Capital	29,682
Retained Earnings	190,912
Total Stockholders' Equity	$223,206
Total Liabilities and	
Stockholders' Equity	$483,850

EXHIBIT 39.2

Advanced Power Systems

Condensed Income and Stockholder Information for Years
Ending December 31 (In Thousands)

	1985	1986	1987	1988
Net Sales	$469,486	$582,576	$715,556	$740,072
Cost of Sales	352,872	444,098	551,942	559,064
Gross Profit	$116,614	$138,478	$163,614	$181,008
Selling, General, and				
Administrative Expenses	69,444	75,736	98,308	107,170
Income, Operations	$ 47,170	$ 62,742	$ 65,306	$ 73,838
Other Deductions				
Debenture Interest	6,472	7,784	12,890	14,482
Other Interest	720	226	538	1,708
Interest Income	(184)	(368)	(460)	(484)
Miscellaneous Expense	(736)	128	(2,682)	(12)
Income Before Taxes	$ 40,898	$ 54,972	$ 55,020	$ 58,144
Federal and State				
Income Taxes	20,138	27,990	21,832	23,324
Net Income	$ 20,760	$ 26,982	$ 33,188	$ 34,820
Earnings per Share	$3.58	$4.64	$5.68	$5.96
Dividends per Share	$1.84	$1.88	$1.92	$1.98

EXHIBIT 39.3

Advanced Power Systems

HHI Balance Sheet as of December 31, 1988 (In Thousands)

Assets:	
Cash	$ 336
Accounts Receivable	5,888
Inventories	
Finished Parts	5,894
Work-in-Process	2,890
Raw Material	3,180
Total Inventories	$11,964
Prepaid Expense	330
Total Current Assets	$18,518
Property, Plant, and Equipment	
Land	14
Building and Improvements	2,660
Machinery and Equipment	14,230
Construction in Progress	232
	$17,136
Accumulated Depreciation	(5,176)
	$11,960
Other Assets	78
Total Assets	$30,556
Liabilities and Stockholders' Equity:	
Notes Payable	$ 432
Accounts Payable	1,534
Accrued Expenses	
Salaries, Wages, Commissions	422
Reserve for Warranty	404
Interest	166
Other	74
Income Taxes	80
Current Maturities, Long-Term Debt	104
Total Current Liabilities	$ 3,216
Long-Term Debt	8,734
Deferred Income Taxes	1,132
Total Liabilities	$13,082
Stockholders' Equity	
Common Shares, $1 Par	3,130
Additional Capital	290
Retained Earnings	14,054
Total Stockholders' Equity	$17,474
Total Liabilities and	
Stockholders' Equity	$30,556

EXHIBIT 39.4

Advanced Power Systems

*HHI Condensed Operating and Stockholder Information for
Years Ending December 31 (In Thousands)*

	1985	1986	1987	1988
Revenues				
Net Sales	$18,094	$25,768	$39,596	$40,910
Other	106	76	92	178
	$18,200	$25,844	$39,688	$41,088
Costs and Expenses				
Cost of Goods Sold	$11,364	$17,408	$28,278	$30,180
Selling, General, and Administrative	1,990	2,594	3,386	3,050
Engineering and Development	1,426	1,038	1,198	1,124
Interest				
Long-Term Debt	200	448	1,102	980
Other	8	64	76	80
	$14,988	$21,552	$34,040	$35,414
Earnings Before Income Taxes	3,212	4,292	5,648	5,674
Income Taxes	1,450	1,868	2,664	2,566
Net Earnings	$ 1,762	$ 2,424	$ 2,984	$ 3,108
Earnings per Share	$1.14	$1.54	$1.90	$1.98
Dividends per Share	$0.14	$0.16	$0.20	$0.22

EXHIBIT 39.5

Advanced Power Systems

Selected Ratios for Industrial Controls Manufacturers for the Following Calendar Periods

	1985	*1986*	*1987*	*1988*
Liquidity:				
1. Current Ratio	1.9	2.0	2.0	1.8
2. Acid Test	1.1	1.0	1.0	0.9
3. Current Assets/Total Assets (%)	40.9	39.2	43.5	42.8
Activity:				
4. Receivables Turnover	6.0	6.6	6.0	6.1
5. Cost of Goods Sold/Inventory	3.0	3.7	3.8	3.1
6. Net Sales/Net Working Capital	6.3	5.1	5.4	5.8
7. Net Sales/Total Assets	2.0	1.8	1.8	1.7
Leverage:				
8. Total Debt/Total Assets (%)	48.8	51.5	56.8	56.8
9. Debt/Net Worth	0.9	1.0	1.4	1.3
10. EBIT/Interest	8.2	3.2	3.5	3.0
Profitability:				
11. COGS/Net Sales (%)	59.0	62.2	62.5	59.6
12. Operating Profit/Net Sales (%)	10.5	4.4	4.6	5.8
13. Profit Before Taxes/Net Sales (%)	9.2	2.6	3.7	5.2
14. Profit Before Taxes/Total Assets (%)	16.1	8.5	6.9	8.7
15. Profit Before Taxes/Net Worth (%)	32.9	18.2	22.2	22.2

QUESTIONS

1. Why would Mr. Pate of Advanced Power Systems try to gain control of Henderson Hydraulics?

2. What price should Advanced Power Systems offer for Henderson Hydraulics?

3. What would be the long-run effect on earnings per share for Advanced Power Systems?

Carter Communications, Inc.
REORGANIZATION

Carter Communications, Inc. was engaged in providing cable television (CATV) and FM radio broadcasting service to over 100,000 subscribers in 10 western states. The CATV industry began in the late 1940s in rural and mountainous areas where the quality of television reception was poor due to the distance to the nearest transmitter or due to the intervening terrain. When the company was formed in 1970, viewers were still interested in better reception and in having a larger number of stations. In recent years, however, the emphasis of the company had moved toward pay services, which included not only a straight monthly fee for options such as HBO, but also pay-for-play events such as championship fights. The balance sheet as of December 31, 1988 is shown as Exhibit 40.1. Condensed income statements are presented in Exhibit 40.2.

A CATV system receives television and radio signals by means of high-antenna, microwave, or satellite transmissions to earth stations. These signals are then amplified and distributed by coaxial cable to subscribers. The system's hardware consists of two connecting sections: the head-end and the distribution facilities. The towers, antennas, microwave receivers, and earth stations necessary to receive, convert, and amplify the signals prior to distribution are located at the head-end. The distribution facilities consist of trunk lines that originate at the head-end, amplifiers, smaller distribution cables to carry the signal to the general vicinity of the subscribers, and drop cables to reach the individual homes.

Carter's CATV systems offered a wide variety of programming. During the early 1970s, choices were limited to the three major networks, educational stations, and a few independents. But by the end of 1988, Carter had added TBS, CNN, ESPN, USA, CBN, ARTS, and Nickelodeon as well as pay services such as HBO and Cinemax. The company wanted to import a few more distant stations by microwave, but Federal Communications Commission (FCC) regulations limited the carriage of such signals.

Carter systems, depending on equipment capacity, carried Associated Press, stock market reports, weather information, and a local origination channel. The original equipment for all the systems had a capacity of only 12 channels.

By the end of 1988, about half the systems had been converted to multichannel capability.

A CATV system is normally operated under a franchise granted by the local governing body of the area served. Franchise terms specify rate-making procedures, sale of the system, and the scope of operations, including free public services. Franchise fees, ranging from 3 to 5 percent, are generally nonexclusive. Even though contracts expire at varying dates, termination can occur for failure to comply with terms or conditions. During the previous three years, Carter had lost two franchises in that manner. The operation of CATV systems is a capital-intensive business requiring large outlays for installation of distribution facilities before service can be provided. Loss of the two franchises resulted in significant losses to Carter.

The company charged a base rate of $9.95 per month for subscribers with only one outlet, increasing the bill $1.00 for each additional set. Pay services, such as HBO or Cinemax, were $9.00. The installation fee was set at $25.00, but for some jobs, the cost to the company exceeded that figure. From time to time, Carter would even offer free installation to attract new customers. With increases in the rates subject to approval by local authorities, the company's experience in obtaining increases was not favorable.

Carter had planned to expand its activities in the area of pay-for-play events. These programs were to be supplied by two companies. One of the companies with whom Carter had placed a large deposit was facing bankruptcy proceedings. Management conceded that the deposit had been lost.

CATV distribution equipment was usually installed on telephone poles, but Carter had to use buried cable in locations where utilities were underground. In recent years, an increasing number of communities had moved in that direction. Although the initial installation cost was higher, advocates had sold their idea based on reduced maintenance. But Carter had experienced higher costs and a higher percentage of service interruptions with underground facilities.

The company used promotional campaigns to develop new systems and to increase the density of the present systems. The campaigns were conducted either by Carter personnel or by independent marketing organizations. Marketing techniques included television commercials, direct mailings, door-to-door sales, and telephone solicitation.

The FCC had jurisdiction over and had adopted a regulatory program governing the cable television industry under authority derived from the Communications Act of 1934. The regulations limited the television signals carried on cable systems and governed program origination, commercial sponsorship, engineering standards, and other matters. Many FCC regulations varied with the size of the television market the system served.

A market was defined by a circle with a 35-mile radius drawn from a specified point in the community in which a commercial television station was licensed. From this, the FCC had established a list of the top 100 markets. The signals of all local stations, more distant stations regularly viewed in the cable area, and all educational stations within the broadcast range had to be carried by the system.

By June 21, 1986, FCC regulations required all existing CATV systems serving more than 3,500 subscribers to have a minimum of 20-channel potential capacity, to have nonvoice two-way communication between the subscriber and others, and to dedicate four channels to provide access to public, educational, and local government users. The foregoing channel capacity and access requirements had already increased capital requirements for Carter and would create additional operating expenses in the future.

In December 1988, a subsidiary of Carter Communications received a deficiency notice from the Internal Revenue Service relating to an examination of income tax returns for the years 1980 through 1985. The IRS had asserted that a portion of the purchase price paid by the subsidiary for certain facilities in 1975 should be allocated to intangible assets that would not be depreciable for tax purposes. If the IRS were to prevail, the charge against income through June 30, 1991 (the end of the depreciable life), arising from the resulting federal tax increase, amounted to $1,540,800, of which $572,000 would accrue through December 31, 1988.

Mr. Paul Carter, president of the firm, believed that reorganization of the firm was a strong possibility if the IRS judgment was affirmed. Even without the judgment, he believed that reorganization was a likelihood with which he should be prepared to deal.

Selected ratios for the CATV industry are presented in Exhibit 40.3.

EXHIBIT 40.1

Carter Communications, Inc.

Balance Sheet as of December 31, 1988

Assets:	
Cash	$ 538,000
Accounts Receivable	1,033,600
Prepaid Expenses and Supplies	329,600
Total Current Assets	$ 1,901,200
Property and Equipment	
Land, Buildings, and Leasehold Improvements	2,923,200
Equipment	34,720,000
Reserve for Depreciation	(19,395,200)
Total Property and Equipment	$18,248,000
Franchises, Net of Amortization	12,260,800
Deferred Financing, Net of Amortization	817,600
Other Assets	289,600
Total Assets	$33,517,200

EXHBIT 40.1 (Continued)

Carter Communications, Inc.

Balance Sheet as of December 31, 1988

Liabilities and Stockholders' Equity:	
Current Portion of Long-Term Debt	$ 1,723,200
Accounts Payable	1,422,400
Accrued Interest Payable	856,000
Employee Compensation and Related Taxes	139,200
Other Accrued Expenses	337,600
CATV Advance Billings and Payments	604,800
Current Income Taxes	1,091,200
Total Current Liabilities	$ 6,174,400
Long-Term Debt	
Principal Amount	22,592,000
Unamortized Discount	(2,188,800)
Net Long-Term Debt	$20,403,200
Deferred Income Taxes	1,201,600
Stockholders' Equity	
Common Stock	1,008,000
Paid-in Capital	2,207,200
Retained Earnings	2,522,800
Total Stockholders' Equity	$ 5,738,000
Total Liabilities and Stockholders' Equity	$33,517,200

EXHIBIT 40.2

Carter Communications, Inc.

Condensed Income Statements for the Years Ending December 31

	1987	1988
Net Sales	$19,461,000	$20,072,300
Operating Expenses	17,767,000	18,070,900
Operating Profit	$ 1,694,000	$ 2,001,400
Other Expenses, Including Interest	1,988,000	2,260,400
Profit Before Taxes (Loss)	$ (294,000)	$ (259,000)
Federal and State Income Taxes	(116,000)	(103,000)
Net Profit After Taxes	$ (178,000)	$ (156,000)

EXHIBIT 40.3

Carter Communications, Inc.

*Selected Ratios for the CATV Industry for the Following
Calendar Periods*

	1985	1986	1987	1988
Liquidity:				
1. Current Ratio	0.6	0.5	0.6	0.6
2. Acid Test	0.4	0.4	0.3	0.3
3. Current Assets/Total Assets (%)	16.9	18.4	25.3	20.7
Activity:				
4. Receivables Turnover	24.3	25.3	27.5	20.3
5. Cost of Goods Sold/Inventory	—	—	—	—
6. Net Sales/Net Working Capital	(8.3)	(8.0)	(6.0)	(7.6)
7. Net Sales/Total Assets	0.6	0.6	0.7	0.8
Leverage:				
8. Total Debt/Total Assets (%)	84.4	76.8	77.6	74.9
9. Debt/Net Worth	14.7	4.7	4.1	2.9
10. EBIT/Interest	1.8	2.5	2.0	2.4
Profitability:				
11. COGS/Net Sales (%)	—	—	—	—
12. Operating Profit/Net Sales (%)	4.9	3.9	3.4	3.0
13. Profit Before Taxes/Net Sales (%)	4.4	4.7	4.5	5.4
14. Profit Before Taxes/Total Assets (%)	4.4	4.7	4.5	5.4
15. Profit Before Taxes/Net Worth (%)	32.4	26.3	31.6	24.2

QUESTIONS

1. Discuss factors that may lead to the failure of Carter Communications.
2. Is the firm facing technical insolvency or bankruptcy?
3. What would be the effect of a voluntary settlement?
4. What would happen if Carter and its creditors could not agree on a voluntary settlement?
5. What procedures would be involved in the reorganization of Carter?
6. Determine whether or not the trustee should recommend reorganization assuming a liquidation value of $25,400,000, expected future after-tax cash flows of $3,400,000 per year, and a capitalization rate of 12 percent.

PART VII

APPENDICES

APPENDIX A—PRESENT VALUE AND FUTURE VALUE TABLES

TABLE A–1. Compound-value interest factors for one dollar, CVIF

Periods	1%	2%	3%	4%	5%	6%	7%	8%	9%	10%
1	1.010	1.020	1.030	1.040	1.050	1.060	1.070	1.080	1.090	1.100
2	1.020	1.040	1.061	1.082	1.102	1.124	1.145	1.166	1.188	1.200
3	1.030	1.061	1.093	1.125	1.158	1.191	1.225	1.260	1.295	1.331
4	1.041	1.082	1.126	1.170	1.216	1.262	1.311	1.360	1.412	1.464
5	1.051	1.104	1.159	1.217	1.276	1.338	1.403	1.469	1.539	1.611
6	1.062	1.126	1.194	1.265	1.340	1.419	1.501	1.587	1.677	1.772
7	1.072	1.149	1.230	1.316	1.407	1.504	1.606	1.714	1.828	1.949
8	1.083	1.172	1.267	1.369	1.477	1.594	1.718	1.851	1.993	2.144
9	1.094	1.195	1.305	1.423	1.551	1.689	1.838	1.999	2.172	2.358
10	1.105	1.219	1.344	1.480	1.629	1.791	1.967	2.159	2.367	2.594
11	1.116	1.243	1.384	1.539	1.710	1.898	2.105	2.332	2.580	2.853
12	1.127	1.268	1.426	1.601	1.796	2.012	2.252	2.518	2.813	3.138
13	1.138	1.294	1.469	1.665	1.886	2.133	2.410	2.720	3.066	3.452
14	1.149	1.319	1.513	1.732	1.980	2.261	2.579	2.937	3.342	3.797
15	1.161	1.346	1.558	1.801	2.079	2.397	2.759	3.172	3.642	4.177
16	1.173	1.373	1.605	1.873	2.183	2.540	2.952	3.426	3.970	4.595
17	1.184	1.400	1.653	1.948	2.292	2.693	3.159	3.700	4.328	5.054
18	1.196	1.428	1.702	2.026	2.407	2.854	3.380	3.996	4.717	5.560
19	1.208	1.457	1.754	2.107	2.527	3.026	3.617	4.316	5.142	6.116
20	1.220	1.486	1.806	2.191	2.653	3.207	3.870	4.661	5.604	6.727
21	1.232	1.516	1.860	2.279	2.786	3.400	4.141	5.034	6.109	7.400
22	1.245	1.546	1.916	2.370	2.925	3.604	4.430	5.437	6.659	8.140
23	1.257	1.577	1.974	2.465	3.072	3.820	4.741	5.871	7.258	8.954
24	1.270	1.608	2.033	2.563	3.225	4.049	5.072	6.341	7.911	9.850
25	1.282	1.641	2.094	2.666	3.386	4.292	5.427	6.848	8.623	10.835

TABLE A–1. Compound-value interest factors for one dollar, CVIF (Continued)

Periods	11%	12%	13%	14%	15%	16%	17%	18%	19%	20%
1	1.110	1.120	1.130	1.140	1.150	1.160	1.170	1.180	1.190	1.200
2	1.232	1.254	1.277	1.300	1.322	1.346	1.369	1.392	1.416	1.440
3	1.368	1.405	1.443	1.482	1.521	1.561	1.602	1.643	1.685	1.728
4	1.518	1.574	1.630	1.689	1.749	1.811	1.874	1.939	2.005	2.074
5	1.685	1.762	1.842	1.925	2.011	2.100	2.192	2.228	2.386	2.488
6	1.870	1.974	2.082	2.195	2.313	2.436	2.565	2.700	2.840	2.986
7	2.076	2.211	2.353	2.502	2.660	2.826	3.001	3.185	3.379	3.583
8	2.305	2.476	2.658	2.853	3.059	3.278	3.511	3.759	4.021	4.300
9	2.558	2.773	3.004	3.252	3.518	3.803	4.108	4.435	4.785	5.160
10	2.839	3.106	3.395	3.707	4.046	4.411	4.807	5.234	5.695	6.192
11	3.152	3.479	3.836	4.226	4.652	5.117	5.624	6.176	6.777	7.430
12	3.493	3.896	4.335	4.818	5.350	5.936	6.580	7.288	8.064	8.916
13	3.883	4.363	4.898	5.492	6.153	6.886	7.699	8.599	9.596	10.699
14	4.310	4.887	5.535	6.261	7.076	7.988	9.007	10.147	11.420	12.839
15	4.785	5.474	6.254	7.138	8.137	9.266	10.539	11.974	13.590	15.407
16	5.311	6.130	7.067	8.137	9.358	10.748	12.330	14.129	16.172	18.488
17	5.895	6.866	7.986	9.276	10.761	12.468	14.426	16.672	19.244	22.186
18	6.544	7.690	9.024	10.575	12.375	14.463	16.879	19.673	22.901	26.623
19	7.263	8.613	10.197	12.056	14.232	16.777	19.748	23.214	27.252	31.948
20	8.062	9.646	11.523	13.743	16.367	19.461	23.106	27.393	32.429	38.338
21	8.949	10.804	13.021	15.668	18.822	22.574	27.034	32.324	38.591	46.005
22	9.934	12.100	14.714	17.861	21.645	26.186	31.629	38.142	45.923	55.206
23	11.026	13.552	16.627	20.362	24.891	30.376	37.006	45.008	54.649	66.247
24	12.239	15.179	18.788	23.212	28.625	35.236	43.297	53.109	65.032	79.497
25	13.585	17.000	21.231	26.462	32.919	40.874	50.658	62.669	77.388	95.396

TABLE A–1. Compound-value interest factors for one dollar, CVIF (Continued)

Periods	21%	22%	23%	24%	25%	26%	27%	28%	29%	30%
1	1.210	1.220	1.230	1.240	1.250	1.260	1.270	1.280	1.290	1.300
2	1.464	1.488	1.513	1.538	1.563	1.588	1.613	1.638	1.664	1.690
3	1.772	1.816	1.861	1.907	1.953	2.000	2.048	2.097	2.147	2.197
4	2.144	2.215	2.289	2.364	2.441	2.520	2.601	2.684	2.769	2.856
5	2.594	2.703	2.815	2.932	3.052	3.176	3.304	3.436	3.572	3.713
6	3.138	3.297	3.463	3.635	3.815	4.002	4.196	4.398	4.608	4.827
7	3.797	4.023	4.259	4.508	4.768	5.042	5.329	5.629	5.945	6.275
8	4.595	4.908	5.239	5.590	5.960	6.353	6.768	7.206	7.669	8.157
9	5.560	5.987	6.444	6.931	7.451	8.005	8.595	9.223	9.893	10.604
10	6.727	7.305	7.926	8.594	9.313	10.086	10.915	11.806	12.761	13.786
11	8.140	8.912	9.749	10.657	11.642	12.708	13.862	15.112	16.462	17.922
12	9.850	10.872	11.991	13.215	14.552	16.012	17.605	19.343	21.236	23.298
13	11.918	13.264	14.749	16.386	18.190	20.175	22.359	24.759	27.395	30.288
14	14.421	16.182	18.141	20.319	22.737	25.421	28.396	31.691	35.339	39.374
15	17.449	19.742	22.314	25.196	28.422	32.030	36.062	40.565	45.587	51.186
16	21.114	24.086	27.446	31.243	35.527	40.358	45.799	51.923	58.808	66.542
17	25.548	29.384	33.759	38.741	44.409	50.851	58.165	66.461	75.862	86.504
18	30.913	35.849	41.523	48.039	55.511	64.072	73.870	85.071	97.862	112.455
19	37.404	43.736	51.074	59.568	69.389	80.731	93.815	108.890	126.242	146.192
20	45.259	53.358	62.821	73.864	86.736	101.721	119.145	139.380	162.852	190.050
21	54.764	65.096	77.269	91.592	108.420	128.169	151.314	178.406	210.080	247.065
22	66.264	79.418	95.041	113.574	135.525	161.492	192.168	228.360	271.003	321.184
23	80.180	96.889	116.901	140.831	169.407	203.480	244.054	292.300	349.593	417.539
24	97.017	118.205	143.788	174.631	211.758	256.385	309.948	374.144	450.976	542.801
25	117.391	144.210	176.859	216.542	264.698	323.045	393.634	478.905	581.759	705.641

TABLE A–1. Compound-value interest factors for one dollar, CVIF (Continued)

Periods	31%	32%	33%	34%	35%	36%	37%	38%	39%	40%
1	1.310	1.320	1.330	1.340	1.350	1.360	1.370	1.380	1.390	1.400
2	1.716	1.742	1.769	1.796	1.822	1.850	1.877	1.904	1.932	1.960
3	2.248	2.300	2.353	2.406	2.460	2.515	2.571	2.628	2.686	2.744
4	2.945	3.036	3.129	3.224	3.322	3.421	3.523	3.627	3.733	3.842
5	3.858	4.007	4.162	4.320	4.484	4.653	4.826	5.005	5.189	5.378
6	5.054	5.290	5.535	5.789	6.053	6.328	6.612	6.907	7.213	7.530
7	6.621	6.983	7.361	7.758	8.172	8.605	9.058	9.531	10.025	10.541
8	8.673	9.217	9.791	10.395	11.032	11.703	12.410	13.153	13.935	14.758
9	11.362	12.166	13.022	13.930	14.894	15.917	17.001	18.151	19.370	20.661
10	14.884	16.060	17.319	18.666	20.107	21.647	23.292	25.049	26.925	28.925
11	19.498	21.199	23.034	25.012	27.144	29.439	31.910	34.568	37.425	40.496
12	25.542	27.983	30.635	33.516	36.644	40.037	43.717	47.703	52.021	56.694
13	33.460	36.937	40.745	44.912	49.470	54.451	59.892	65.831	72.309	79.371
14	43.833	48.757	54.190	60.182	66.784	74.053	82.052	90.846	100.510	111.120
15	57.421	64.359	72.073	80.644	90.158	100.713	112.411	125.368	139.708	155.568
16	75.221	84.954	95.858	108.063	121.714	136.969	154.003	173.008	194.194	217.795
17	98.540	112.139	127.491	144.804	164.314	186.278	210.984	238.751	269.930	304.913
18	129.087	148.024	169.562	194.038	221.824	253.338	289.048	329.476	375.203	426.879
19	169.104	195.391	225.518	260.011	299.462	344.540	395.996	454.677	521.532	597.630
20	221.527	257.916	299.939	348.414	404.274	468.574	542.514	627.454	724.930	836.683
21	290.200	340.449	398.919	466.875	545.769	637.261	743.245	865.886	1007.653	1171.356
22	380.162	449.393	530.562	625.613	736.789	866.674	1018.245	1194.923	1400.637	1639.898
23	498.012	593.199	705.647	838.321	994.665	1178.677	1394.996	1648.994	1946.885	2295.857
24	652.396	783.023	938.511	1123.350	1342.797	1603.001	1911.145	2275.611	2706.171	3214.200
25	854.638	1033.590	1248.220	1505.289	1812.776	2180.081	2618.268	3140.344	3761.577	4499.880

TABLE A–2. Compound-value interest factors for a one-dollar annuity, CVIFA

n	1%	2%	3%	4%	5%	6%	7%	8%	9%	10%
1	1.000	1.000	1.000	1.000	1.000	1.000	1.000	1.000	1.000	1.000
2	2.010	2.020	2.030	2.040	2.050	2.060	2.070	2.080	2.090	2.100
3	3.030	3.060	3.091	3.122	3.152	3.184	3.215	3.246	3.278	3.310
4	4.060	4.122	4.184	4.246	4.310	4.375	4.440	4.506	4.573	4.641
5	5.101	5.204	5.309	5.416	5.526	5.637	5.751	5.867	5.985	6.105
6	6.152	6.308	6.468	6.633	6.802	6.975	7.153	7.336	7.523	7.716
7	7.214	7.434	7.662	7.898	8.142	8.394	8.654	8.923	9.200	9.487
8	8.286	8.583	8.892	9.214	9.549	9.897	10.260	10.637	11.028	11.436
9	9.368	9.755	10.159	10.583	11.027	11.491	11.978	12.488	13.021	13.579
10	10.462	10.950	11.464	12.006	12.578	13.181	13.816	14.487	15.193	15.937
11	11.567	12.169	12.808	13.486	14.207	14.972	15.784	16.645	17.560	18.531
12	12.682	13.412	14.192	15.026	15.917	16.870	17.888	18.977	20.141	21.384
13	13.809	14.680	15.618	16.627	17.713	18.882	20.141	21.495	22.953	24.523
14	14.947	15.974	17.086	18.292	19.598	21.015	22.550	24.215	26.019	27.975
15	16.097	17.923	18.599	20.023	21.578	23.276	25.129	27.152	29.361	31.772
16	17.258	18.639	20.157	21.824	23.657	25.672	27.888	30.324	33.003	35.949
17	18.430	20.012	21.761	23.697	25.840	28.213	30.840	33.750	36.973	40.544
18	19.614	21.412	23.414	25.645	28.132	30.905	33.999	37.450	41.301	45.599
19	20.811	22.840	25.117	27.671	30.539	33.760	37.379	41.446	46.018	51.158
20	22.019	24.297	26.870	29.778	33.066	36.785	40.995	45.762	51.159	57.274
21	23.239	25.783	28.676	31.969	35.719	39.992	44.865	50.422	56.764	64.002
22	24.471	27.299	30.536	34.248	38.505	43.392	49.005	55.456	62.872	71.402
23	25.716	28.845	32.452	36.618	41.430	46.995	53.435	60.893	69.531	79.542
24	26.973	30.421	34.426	39.082	44.501	50.815	58.176	66.764	76.789	88.496
25	28.243	32.030	36.459	41.645	47.726	54.864	63.248	73.105	84.699	98.346
30	34.784	40.567	47.575	56.084	66.438	79.057	94.459	113.282	136.305	164.491
40	48.885	60.401	75.400	95.024	120.797	154.758	199.630	259.052	337.872	442.580
50	64.461	84.577	112.794	152.664	209.341	290.325	406.516	573.756	815.051	1163.865

TABLE A–2. Compound-value interest factors for a one-dollar annuity, CVIFA (Continued)

n	11%	12%	13%	14%	15%	16%	17%	18%	19%	20%
1	1.000	1.000	1.000	1.000	1.000	1.000	1.000	1.000	1.000	1.000
2	2.110	2.120	2.130	2.140	2.150	2.160	2.170	2.180	2.190	2.200
3	3.342	3.374	3.407	3.440	3.472	3.506	3.539	3.572	3.606	3.640
4	4.710	4.779	4.850	4.921	4.993	5.066	5.141	5.215	5.291	5.368
5	6.228	6.353	6.480	6.610	6.742	6.877	7.014	7.154	7.297	7.442
6	7.913	8.115	8.323	8.535	8.754	8.977	9.207	9.442	9.683	9.930
7	9.783	10.089	10.405	10.730	11.067	11.414	11.772	12.141	12.523	12.916
8	11.859	12.300	12.757	13.233	13.727	14.240	14.773	15.327	15.902	16.499
9	14.164	14.776	15.416	16.085	16.786	17.518	18.285	19.086	19.923	20.799
10	16.722	17.549	18.420	19.337	20.304	21.321	22.393	23.521	24.709	25.959
11	19.561	20.655	21.814	23.044	24.349	25.733	27.200	28.755	30.403	32.150
12	22.713	24.133	25.650	27.271	29.001	30.850	32.824	34.931	37.180	39.580
13	26.211	28.029	29.984	32.088	34.352	36.786	39.404	42.218	45.244	48.496
14	30.095	32.392	34.882	37.581	40.504	43.672	47.102	50.818	54.841	59.196
15	34.405	37.280	40.417	43.842	47.580	51.659	56.109	60.965	66.260	72.035
16	39.190	42.753	46.671	50.980	55.717	60.925	66.648	72.938	79.850	87.442
17	44.500	48.883	53.738	59.117	65.075	71.673	78.978	87.067	96.021	105.930
18	50.396	55.749	61.724	68.393	75.836	84.140	93.404	103.739	115.265	128.116
19	56.939	63.439	70.748	78.968	88.211	98.603	110.283	123.412	138.165	154.739
20	64.202	72.052	80.946	91.024	102.443	115.379	130.031	146.626	165.417	186.687
21	72.264	81.698	92.468	104.767	118.809	134.840	153.136	174.019	197.846	225.024
22	81.213	92.502	105.489	120.434	137.630	157.414	180.169	206.342	236.436	271.028
23	91.147	104.602	120.203	138.295	159.274	183.600	211.798	244.483	282.359	326.234
24	102.173	118.154	136.829	158.656	184.166	213.976	248.803	289.490	337.007	392.480
25	114.412	133.333	155.616	181.867	212.790	249.212	292.099	342.598	402.038	471.976
30	199.018	241.330	293.192	356.778	434.738	530.306	647.423	790.932	966.698	1181.865
40	581.812	767.080	1013.667	1341.979	1779.048	2360.724	3134.412	4163.094	5529.711	7343.715
50	1668.723	2399.975	3459.344	4994.301	7217.488	10435.449	15088.805	21812.273	31514.492	45496.094

TABLE A–2. Compound-value interest factors for a one-dollar annuity, CVIFA (Continued)

n	21%	22%	23%	24%	25%	26%	27%	28%	29%	30%
1	1.000	1.000	1.000	1.000	1.000	1.000	1.000	1.000	1.000	1.000
2	2.210	2.220	2.230	2.240	2.250	2.260	2.270	2.280	2.290	2.300
3	3.674	3.708	3.743	3.778	3.813	3.848	3.883	3.918	3.954	3.990
4	5.446	5.524	5.604	5.684	5.766	5.848	5.931	6.016	6.101	6.187
5	7.589	7.740	7.893	8.048	8.207	8.368	8.533	8.700	8.870	9.043
6	10.183	10.442	10.708	10.980	11.259	11.544	11.837	12.136	12.442	12.756
7	13.321	13.740	14.171	14.615	15.073	15.546	16.032	16.534	17.051	17.583
8	17.119	17.762	18.430	19.123	19.842	20.588	21.361	22.163	22.995	23.858
9	21.714	22.670	23.669	24.712	25.802	26.940	28.129	29.369	30.664	32.015
10	27.274	28.657	30.113	31.643	33.253	34.945	36.723	38.592	40.556	42.619
11	34.001	35.962	38.039	40.238	42.566	45.030	47.639	50.398	53.318	56.405
12	42.141	44.873	47.787	50.895	54.208	57.738	61.501	65.510	69.780	74.326
13	51.991	55.745	59.778	64.109	68.760	73.750	79.106	84.853	91.016	97.624
14	63.909	69.009	74.528	80.496	86.949	93.925	101.465	109.611	118.411	127.912
15	78.330	85.191	92.669	100.815	109.687	119.346	129.860	141.302	153.750	167.285
16	95.779	104.933	114.983	126.010	138.109	151.375	165.922	181.867	199.337	218.470
17	116.892	129.019	142.428	157.252	173.636	191.733	211.721	233.790	258.145	285.011
18	142.439	158.403	176.187	195.993	218.045	242.583	269.885	300.250	334.006	371.514
19	173.351	194.251	217.710	244.031	273.556	306.654	343.754	385.321	431.868	483.968
20	210.755	237.986	268.783	303.598	342.945	387.384	437.568	494.210	558.110	630.157
21	256.013	291.343	331.603	377.461	429.681	489.104	556.710	633.589	720.962	820.204
22	310.775	356.438	408.871	469.052	538.101	617.270	708.022	811.993	931.040	1067.265
23	377.038	435.854	503.911	582.624	673.626	778.760	900.187	1040.351	1202.042	1388.443
24	457.215	532.741	620.810	723.453	843.032	982.237	1144.237	1332.649	1551.634	1805.975
25	554.230	650.944	764.596	898.082	1054.791	1238.617	1454.180	1706.790	2002.608	2348.765
30	1445.111	1767.044	2160.459	2460.881	3227.172	3941.953	4812.891	5873.172	7162.785	8729.805
40	9749.141	12936.141	17153.691	22728.367	30088.621	39791.957	52570.707	69376.562	91447.375	120389.375
45	25294.223	34970.230	48300.660	66638.937	91831.312	126378.937	173692.875	238384.312	326686.375	447005.062

TABLE A-2. Compound-value interest factors for a one-dollar annuity, CVIFA (Continued)

n	31%	32%	33%	34%	35%	36%	37%	38%	39%	40%
1	1.000	1.000	1.000	1.000	1.000	1.000	1.000	1.000	1.000	1.000
2	2.310	2.320	2.330	2.340	2.350	2.360	2.370	2.380	2.390	2.400
3	4.026	4.062	4.099	4.136	4.172	4.210	4.247	4.284	4.322	4.360
4	6.274	6.362	6.452	6.542	6.633	6.725	6.818	6.912	7.008	7.104
5	9.219	9.398	9.581	9.766	9.954	10.146	10.341	10.539	10.741	10.946
6	13.077	13.406	13.742	14.086	14.438	14.799	15.167	15.544	15.930	16.324
7	18.131	18.696	19.277	19.876	20.492	21.126	21.779	22.451	23.142	23.853
8	24.752	25.678	26.638	27.633	28.664	29.732	30.837	31.982	33.167	34.395
9	33.425	34.895	36.429	38.028	39.696	41.435	43.247	45.135	47.103	49.152
10	44.786	47.062	49.451	51.958	54.590	57.351	60.248	63.287	66.473	69.813
11	59.670	63.121	66.769	70.624	74.696	78.998	83.540	88.335	93.397	98.739
12	79.167	84.320	89.803	95.636	101.840	108.437	115.450	122.903	130.822	139.234
13	104.709	112.302	120.438	129.152	138.484	148.474	159.166	170.606	182.842	195.928
14	138.169	149.239	161.183	174.063	187.953	202.925	219.058	236.435	255.151	275.299
15	182.001	197.996	215.373	234.245	254.737	276.978	301.109	327.281	355.659	386.418
16	239.421	262.354	287.446	314.888	344.895	377.690	413.520	452.647	495.366	541.985
17	314.642	347.307	383.303	422.949	466.608	514.658	567.521	625.652	689.558	759.778
18	413.180	459.445	510.792	567.751	630.920	700.935	778.504	864.399	959.485	1064.689
19	542.266	607.467	680.354	761.786	852.741	954.271	1067.551	1193.870	1334.683	1491.563
20	711.368	802.856	905.870	1021.792	1152.200	1298.809	1463.544	1648.539	1856.208	2089.188
21	932.891	1060.769	1205.807	1370.201	1556.470	1767.380	2006.055	2275.982	2581.128	2925.862
22	1223.087	1401.215	1604.724	1837.068	2102.234	2404.636	2749.294	3141.852	3588.765	4097.203
23	1603.243	1850.603	2135.282	2462.669	2839.014	3271.304	3767.532	4336.750	4989.379	5737.078
24	2101.247	2443.795	2840.924	3300.974	3833.667	4449.969	5162.516	5985.711	6936.230	8032.906
25	2753.631	3226.808	3779.428	4424.301	5176.445	6052.957	7073.645	8261.273	9642.352	11247.062
30	10632.543	12940.672	15737.945	19124.434	23221.258	28172.016	34148.906	41357.227	50043.625	60500.207
35	41028.887	51868.563	65504.199	82634.625	104134.500	131082.625	164818.438	206998.375	259680.313	325394.688

258

TABLE A–3. Present-value interest factors for one dollar, PVIF

Periods	1%	2%	3%	4%	5%	6%	7%	8%	9%	10%
1	0.990	0.980	0.971	0.962	0.952	0.943	0.935	0.926	0.917	0.909
2	0.980	0.961	0.943	0.925	0.907	0.890	0.873	0.857	0.842	0.826
3	0.971	0.942	0.915	0.889	0.864	0.840	0.816	0.794	0.772	0.751
4	0.961	0.924	0.888	0.855	0.823	0.792	0.763	0.735	0.708	0.683
5	0.951	0.906	0.863	0.822	0.784	0.747	0.713	0.681	0.650	0.621
6	0.942	0.888	0.837	0.790	0.746	0.705	0.666	0.630	0.596	0.564
7	0.933	0.871	0.813	0.760	0.711	0.665	0.623	0.583	0.547	0.513
8	0.923	0.853	0.789	0.731	0.677	0.627	0.582	0.540	0.502	0.467
9	0.914	0.837	0.766	0.703	0.645	0.592	0.544	0.500	0.460	0.424
10	0.905	0.820	0.744	0.676	0.614	0.558	0.508	0.463	0.422	0.386
11	0.896	0.804	0.722	0.650	0.585	0.527	0.475	0.429	0.388	0.350
12	0.887	0.788	0.701	0.625	0.557	0.497	0.444	0.397	0.356	0.319
13	0.879	0.773	0.681	0.601	0.530	0.469	0.415	0.368	0.326	0.290
14	0.870	0.758	0.661	0.577	0.505	0.442	0.388	0.340	0.299	0.263
15	0.861	0.743	0.642	0.555	0.481	0.417	0.362	0.315	0.275	0.239
16	0.853	0.728	0.623	0.534	0.458	0.394	0.339	0.292	0.252	0.218
17	0.844	0.714	0.605	0.513	0.436	0.371	0.317	0.270	0.231	0.198
18	0.836	0.700	0.587	0.494	0.416	0.350	0.296	0.250	0.212	0.180
19	0.828	0.686	0.570	0.475	0.396	0.331	0.277	0.232	0.194	0.164
20	0.820	0.673	0.554	0.456	0.377	0.312	0.258	0.215	0.178	0.149
21	0.811	0.660	0.538	0.439	0.359	0.294	0.242	0.199	0.164	0.135
22	0.803	0.647	0.522	0.422	0.342	0.278	0.226	0.184	0.150	0.123
23	0.795	0.634	0.507	0.406	0.326	0.262	0.211	0.170	0.138	0.112
24	0.788	0.622	0.492	0.390	0.310	0.247	0.197	0.158	0.126	0.102
25	0.780	0.610	0.478	0.375	0.295	0.233	0.184	0.146	0.116	0.092
26	0.772	0.598	0.464	0.361	0.281	0.220	0.172	0.135	0.106	0.084
27	0.764	0.586	0.450	0.347	0.268	0.207	0.161	0.125	0.098	0.076
28	0.757	0.574	0.437	0.333	0.255	0.196	0.150	0.116	0.090	0.069
29	0.749	0.563	0.424	0.321	0.243	0.185	0.141	0.107	0.082	0.063
30	0.742	0.552	0.412	0.308	0.231	0.174	0.131	0.099	0.075	0.057
40	0.672	0.453	0.307	0.208	0.142	0.097	0.067	0.046	0.032	0.022
50	0.608	0.372	0.228	0.141	0.087	0.054	0.034	0.021	0.013	0.009

TABLE A–3. Present-value interest factors for one dollar, PVIF (Continued)

Periods	11%	12%	13%	14%	15%	16%	17%	18%	19%	20%
1	0.901	0.893	0.885	0.877	0.870	0.862	0.855	0.847	0.840	0.833
2	0.812	0.797	0.783	0.769	0.756	0.743	0.731	0.718	0.706	0.694
3	0.731	0.712	0.693	0.675	0.658	0.641	0.624	0.609	0.593	0.579
4	0.659	0.636	0.613	0.592	0.572	0.552	0.534	0.516	0.499	0.482
5	0.593	0.567	0.543	0.519	0.497	0.476	0.456	0.437	0.419	0.402
6	0.535	0.507	0.480	0.456	0.432	0.410	0.390	0.370	0.352	0.335
7	0.482	0.452	0.425	0.400	0.376	0.354	0.333	0.314	0.296	0.279
8	0.434	0.404	0.376	0.351	0.327	0.305	0.285	0.266	0.249	0.233
9	0.391	0.361	0.333	0.308	0.284	0.263	0.243	0.225	0.209	0.194
10	0.352	0.322	0.295	0.270	0.247	0.227	0.208	0.191	0.176	0.162
11	0.317	0.287	0.261	0.237	0.215	0.195	0.178	0.162	0.148	0.135
12	0.286	0.257	0.231	0.208	0.187	0.168	0.152	0.137	0.124	0.112
13	0.258	0.229	0.204	0.182	0.163	0.145	0.130	0.116	0.104	0.093
14	0.232	0.205	0.181	0.160	0.141	0.125	0.111	0.099	0.088	0.078
15	0.209	0.183	0.160	0.140	0.123	0.108	0.095	0.084	0.074	0.065
16	0.188	0.163	0.141	0.123	0.107	0.093	0.081	0.071	0.062	0.054
17	0.170	0.146	0.125	0.108	0.093	0.080	0.069	0.060	0.052	0.045
18	0.153	0.130	0.111	0.095	0.081	0.069	0.059	0.051	0.044	0.038
19	0.138	0.116	0.098	0.083	0.070	0.060	0.051	0.043	0.037	0.031
20	0.124	0.104	0.087	0.073	0.061	0.051	0.043	0.037	0.031	0.026
21	0.112	0.093	0.077	0.064	0.053	0.044	0.037	0.031	0.026	0.022
22	0.101	0.083	0.068	0.056	0.046	0.038	0.032	0.026	0.022	0.018
23	0.091	0.074	0.060	0.049	0.040	0.033	0.027	0.022	0.018	0.015
24	0.082	0.066	0.053	0.043	0.035	0.028	0.023	0.019	0.015	0.013
25	0.074	0.059	0.047	0.038	0.030	0.024	0.020	0.016	0.013	0.010
26	0.066	0.053	0.042	0.033	0.026	0.021	0.017	0.014	0.011	0.009
27	0.060	0.047	0.037	0.029	0.023	0.018	0.014	0.011	0.009	0.007
28	0.054	0.042	0.033	0.026	0.020	0.016	0.012	0.010	0.008	0.006
29	0.048	0.037	0.029	0.022	0.017	0.014	0.011	0.008	0.006	0.005
30	0.044	0.033	0.026	0.020	0.015	0.012	0.009	0.007	0.005	0.004
40	0.015	0.011	0.008	0.005	0.004	0.003	0.002	0.001	0.001	0.001
50	0.005	0.003	0.002	0.001	0.001	0.001	0.000	0.000	0.000	0.000

TABLE A–3. Present-value interest factors for one dollar, PVIF (Continued)

Periods	21%	22%	23%	24%	25%	26%	27%	28%	29%	30%
1	0.826	0.820	0.813	0.806	0.800	0.794	0.787	0.781	0.775	0.769
2	0.683	0.672	0.661	0.650	0.640	0.630	0.620	0.610	0.601	0.592
3	0.564	0.551	0.537	0.524	0.512	0.500	0.488	0.477	0.466	0.455
4	0.467	0.451	0.437	0.423	0.410	0.397	0.384	0.373	0.361	0.350
5	0.386	0.370	0.355	0.341	0.328	0.315	0.303	0.291	0.280	0.269
6	0.319	0.303	0.289	0.275	0.262	0.250	0.238	0.227	0.217	0.207
7	0.263	0.249	0.235	0.222	0.210	0.198	0.188	0.178	0.168	0.159
8	0.218	0.204	0.191	0.179	0.168	0.157	0.148	0.139	0.130	0.123
9	0.180	0.167	0.155	0.144	0.134	0.125	0.116	0.108	0.101	0.094
10	0.149	0.137	0.126	0.116	0.107	0.099	0.092	0.085	0.078	0.073
11	0.123	0.122	0.103	0.094	0.086	0.079	0.072	0.066	0.061	0.056
12	0.102	0.092	0.083	0.076	0.069	0.062	0.057	0.052	0.047	0.043
13	0.084	0.075	0.068	0.061	0.055	0.050	0.045	0.040	0.037	0.033
14	0.069	0.062	0.055	0.049	0.044	0.039	0.035	0.032	0.028	0.025
15	0.057	0.051	0.045	0.040	0.035	0.031	0.028	0.025	0.022	0.020
16	0.047	0.042	0.036	0.032	0.028	0.025	0.022	0.019	0.017	0.015
17	0.039	0.034	0.030	0.026	0.023	0.020	0.017	0.015	0.013	0.012
18	0.032	0.028	0.024	0.021	0.018	0.016	0.014	0.012	0.010	0.009
19	0.027	0.023	0.020	0.017	0.014	0.012	0.011	0.009	0.008	0.007
20	0.022	0.019	0.016	0.014	0.012	0.010	0.008	0.007	0.006	0.005
21	0.018	0.015	0.013	0.011	0.009	0.008	0.007	0.006	0.005	0.004
22	0.015	0.013	0.011	0.009	0.007	0.006	0.005	0.004	0.004	0.003
23	0.012	0.010	0.009	0.007	0.006	0.005	0.004	0.003	0.003	0.002
24	0.010	0.008	0.007	0.006	0.005	0.004	0.003	0.003	0.002	0.002
25	0.009	0.007	0.006	0.005	0.004	0.003	0.003	0.002	0.002	0.001
26	0.007	0.006	0.005	0.004	0.003	0.002	0.002	0.002	0.001	0.001
27	0.006	0.005	0.004	0.003	0.002	0.002	0.002	0.001	0.001	0.001
28	0.005	0.004	0.003	0.002	0.002	0.002	0.001	0.001	0.001	0.001
29	0.004	0.003	0.002	0.002	0.002	0.001	0.001	0.001	0.001	0.000
30	0.003	0.003	0.002	0.002	0.001	0.001	0.001	0.001	0.000	0.000
40	0.000	0.000	0.000	0.000	0.000	0.000	0.000	0.000	0.000	0.000
50	0.000	0.000	0.000	0.000	0.000	0.000	0.000	0.000	0.000	0.000

TABLE A–3. Present-value interest factors for one dollar, PVIF (Continued)

Periods	31%	32%	33%	34%	35%	36%	37%	38%	39%	40%
1	0.763	0.758	0.752	0.746	0.741	0.735	0.730	0.725	0.719	0.714
2	0.583	0.574	0.565	0.557	0.549	0.541	0.533	0.525	0.518	0.510
3	0.445	0.435	0.425	0.416	0.406	0.398	0.389	0.381	0.372	0.364
4	0.340	0.329	0.320	0.310	0.301	0.292	0.284	0.276	0.268	0.260
5	0.259	0.250	0.240	0.231	0.223	0.215	0.207	0.200	0.193	0.186
6	0.198	0.189	0.181	0.173	0.165	0.158	0.151	0.145	0.139	0.133
7	0.151	0.143	0.136	0.129	0.122	0.116	0.110	0.105	0.100	0.095
8	0.115	0.108	0.102	0.096	0.091	0.085	0.081	0.076	0.072	0.068
9	0.088	0.082	0.077	0.072	0.067	0.063	0.059	0.055	0.052	0.048
10	0.067	0.062	0.058	0.054	0.050	0.046	0.043	0.040	0.037	0.035
11	0.051	0.047	0.043	0.040	0.037	0.034	0.031	0.029	0.027	0.025
12	0.039	0.036	0.033	0.030	0.027	0.025	0.023	0.021	0.019	0.018
13	0.030	0.027	0.025	0.022	0.020	0.018	0.017	0.015	0.014	0.013
14	0.023	0.021	0.018	0.017	0.015	0.014	0.012	0.011	0.010	0.009
15	0.017	0.016	0.014	0.012	0.011	0.010	0.009	0.008	0.007	0.006
16	0.013	0.012	0.010	0.009	0.008	0.007	0.006	0.006	0.005	0.005
17	0.010	0.009	0.008	0.007	0.006	0.005	0.005	0.004	0.004	0.003
18	0.008	0.007	0.006	0.005	0.005	0.004	0.003	0.003	0.003	0.002
19	0.006	0.005	0.004	0.004	0.003	0.003	0.003	0.002	0.002	0.002
20	0.005	0.004	0.003	0.003	0.002	0.002	0.002	0.002	0.001	0.001
21	0.003	0.003	0.003	0.002	0.002	0.002	0.001	0.001	0.001	0.001
22	0.003	0.002	0.002	0.002	0.001	0.001	0.001	0.001	0.001	0.001
23	0.002	0.002	0.001	0.001	0.001	0.001	0.001	0.001	0.001	0.000
24	0.002	0.001	0.001	0.001	0.001	0.001	0.000	0.000	0.000	0.000
25	0.001	0.001	0.001	0.001	0.001	0.000	0.000	0.000	0.000	0.000
26	0.001	0.001	0.001	0.000	0.000	0.000	0.000	0.000	0.000	0.000
27	0.001	0.001	0.000	0.000	0.000	0.000	0.000	0.000	0.000	0.000
28	0.001	0.000	0.000	0.000	0.000	0.000	0.000	0.000	0.000	0.000
29	0.000	0.000	0.000	0.000	0.000	0.000	0.000	0.000	0.000	0.000
30	0.000	0.000	0.000	0.000	0.000	0.000	0.000	0.000	0.000	0.000
40	0.000	0.000	0.000	0.000	0.000	0.000	0.000	0.000	0.000	0.000
50	0.000	0.000	0.000	0.000	0.000	0.000	0.000	0.000	0.000	0.000

TABLE A-4. Present-value interest factors for a one-dollar annuity, PVIFA

Periods	1%	2%	3%	4%	5%	6%	7%	8%	9%	10%
1	0.990	0.980	0.971	0.962	0.952	0.943	0.935	0.926	0.917	0.909
2	1.970	1.942	1.913	1.886	1.859	1.833	1.808	1.783	1.759	1.736
3	2.941	2.884	2.829	2.775	2.723	2.673	2.624	2.577	2.531	2.487
4	3.902	3.808	3.717	3.630	3.546	3.465	3.387	3.312	3.240	3.170
5	4.853	4.713	4.580	4.452	4.329	4.212	4.100	3.993	3.890	3.791
6	5.795	5.601	5.417	5.242	5.076	4.917	4.767	4.623	4.486	4.355
7	6.728	6.472	6.230	6.002	5.786	5.582	5.389	5.206	5.033	4.868
8	7.652	7.325	7.020	6.733	6.463	6.210	5.971	5.747	5.535	5.335
9	8.566	8.162	7.786	7.435	7.108	6.802	6.515	6.247	5.995	5.759
10	9.471	8.983	8.530	8.111	7.722	7.360	7.024	6.710	6.418	6.145
11	10.368	9.787	9.253	8.760	8.306	7.887	7.499	7.139	6.805	6.495
12	11.255	10.575	9.954	9.385	8.863	8.384	7.943	7.536	7.161	6.814
13	12.134	11.348	10.635	9.986	9.394	8.853	8.358	7.904	7.487	7.103
14	13.004	12.106	11.296	10.563	9.899	9.295	8.745	8.244	7.786	7.367
15	13.865	12.849	11.938	11.118	10.380	9.712	9.108	8.559	8.061	7.606
16	14.718	13.578	12.561	11.652	10.838	10.106	9.447	8.851	8.313	7.825
17	15.562	14.292	13.166	12.166	11.274	10.477	9.763	9.122	8.544	8.024
18	16.398	14.992	13.754	12.659	11.690	10.828	10.059	9.372	8.756	8.204
19	17.226	15.678	14.324	13.134	12.085	11.158	10.336	9.604	8.950	8.362
20	18.046	16.351	14.877	13.590	12.462	11.470	10.594	9.818	9.129	8.511
21	18.857	17.011	15.415	14.029	12.821	11.764	10.836	10.017	9.292	8.649
22	19.660	17.658	15.837	14.451	13.163	12.042	11.061	10.201	9.442	8.772
23	20.456	18.292	16.444	14.857	13.489	12.303	11.272	10.371	9.580	8.883
24	21.243	18.914	16.936	15.247	13.799	12.550	11.469	10.529	9.707	8.985
25	22.023	19.523	17.413	15.622	14.094	12.783	11.654	10.675	9.823	9.077
26	22.795	20.121	17.877	15.983	14.375	13.003	11.826	10.810	9.929	9.161
27	23.560	20.707	18.327	16.330	14.643	13.211	11.987	10.935	10.027	9.237
28	24.316	21.281	18.764	16.663	14.898	13.406	12.137	11.051	10.116	9.307
29	25.066	21.844	19.188	16.984	15.141	13.591	12.278	11.158	10.198	9.370
30	25.808	22.396	19.600	17.292	15.372	13.765	12.409	11.258	10.274	9.427
40	32.835	27.355	23.115	19.793	17.159	15.046	13.332	11.925	10.757	9.779
50	39.196	31.424	25.730	21.482	18.256	15.762	13.801	12.233	10.962	9.915

TABLE A–4. Present-value interest factors for a one-dollar annuity, PVIFA (Continued)

Periods	11%	12%	13%	14%	15%	16%	17%	18%	19%	20%
1	0.901	0.893	0.885	0.877	0.870	0.862	0.855	0.847	0.840	0.833
2	1.713	1.690	1.668	1.647	1.626	1.605	1.585	1.566	1.547	1.528
3	2.444	2.402	2.361	2.322	2.283	2.246	2.210	2.174	2.140	2.106
4	3.102	3.037	2.974	2.914	2.855	2.798	2.743	2.690	2.639	2.589
5	3.696	3.605	3.517	3.433	3.352	3.274	3.199	3.127	3.058	2.991
6	4.231	4.111	3.998	3.889	3.784	3.685	3.589	3.498	3.410	3.326
7	4.712	4.564	4.423	4.288	4.160	4.039	3.922	3.812	3.706	3.605
8	5.146	4.968	4.799	4.639	4.487	4.344	4.207	4.078	3.954	3.837
9	5.537	5.328	5.132	4.946	4.772	4.607	4.451	4.303	4.163	4.031
10	5.889	5.650	5.426	5.216	5.019	4.833	4.659	4.494	4.339	4.192
11	6.207	5.938	5.687	5.453	5.234	5.029	4.836	4.656	4.486	4.327
12	6.492	6.194	5.918	5.660	5.421	5.197	4.988	4.793	4.611	4.439
13	6.750	6.424	6.122	5.842	5.583	5.342	5.118	4.910	4.715	4.533
14	6.982	6.628	6.302	6.002	5.724	5.468	5.229	5.008	4.802	4.611
15	7.191	6.811	6.462	6.142	5.847	5.575	5.324	5.092	4.876	4.675
16	7.379	6.974	6.604	6.265	5.954	5.668	5.405	5.162	4.938	4.730
17	7.549	7.120	6.729	6.373	6.047	5.749	5.475	5.222	4.990	4.775
18	7.702	7.250	6.840	6.467	6.128	5.818	5.534	5.273	5.033	4.812
19	7.839	7.366	6.938	6.550	6.198	5.877	5.584	5.316	5.070	4.843
20	7.963	7.469	7.025	6.623	6.259	5.929	5.628	5.353	5.101	4.870
21	8.075	7.562	7.102	6.687	6.312	5.973	5.665	5.384	5.127	4.891
22	8.176	7.645	7.170	6.743	6.359	6.011	5.696	5.410	5.149	4.909
23	8.266	7.718	7.230	6.792	6.399	6.044	5.723	5.432	5.167	4.925
24	8.348	7.784	7.283	6.835	6.434	6.073	5.746	5.451	5.182	4.937
25	8.422	7.843	7.330	6.873	6.464	6.097	5.766	5.467	5.195	4.948
26	8.488	7.896	7.372	6.906	6.491	6.118	5.783	5.480	5.206	4.956
27	8.548	7.943	7.409	6.935	6.514	6.136	5.798	5.492	5.215	4.964
28	8.602	7.984	7.441	6.961	6.534	6.152	5.810	5.502	5.223	4.970
29	8.650	8.022	7.470	6.983	6.551	6.166	5.820	5.510	5.229	4.975
30	8.694	8.055	7.496	7.003	6.566	6.177	5.829	5.517	5.235	4.979
40	8.951	8.244	7.634	7.105	6.642	6.233	5.871	5.548	5.258	4.997
50	9.042	8.304	7.675	7.133	6.661	6.246	5.880	5.554	5.262	4.999

TABLE A–4. Present-value interest factors for a one-dollar annuity, PVIFA (Continued)

Periods	21%	22%	23%	24%	25%	26%	27%	28%	29%	30%
1	0.826	0.820	0.813	0.806	0.800	0.794	0.787	0.781	0.775	0.769
2	1.509	1.492	1.474	1.457	1.440	1.424	1.407	1.392	1.376	1.361
3	2.074	2.042	2.011	1.981	1.952	1.923	1.896	1.868	1.842	1.816
4	2.540	2.494	2.448	2.404	2.362	2.320	2.280	2.241	2.203	2.166
5	2.926	2.864	2.803	2.745	2.689	2.635	2.583	2.532	2.483	2.436
6	3.245	3.167	3.092	3.020	2.951	2.885	2.821	2.759	2.700	2.643
7	3.508	3.416	3.327	3.242	3.161	3.083	3.009	2.937	2.868	2.802
8	3.726	3.619	3.518	3.421	3.329	3.241	3.156	3.076	2.999	2.925
9	3.905	3.786	3.673	3.566	3.463	3.366	3.273	3.184	3.100	3.019
10	4.054	3.923	3.799	3.682	3.571	3.465	3.364	3.269	3.178	3.092
11	4.177	4.035	3.902	3.776	3.656	3.543	3.437	3.335	3.239	3.147
12	4.278	4.127	3.985	3.851	3.725	3.606	3.493	3.387	3.286	3.190
13	4.362	4.203	4.053	3.912	3.780	3.656	3.538	3.427	3.322	3.223
14	4.432	4.265	4.108	3.962	3.824	3.695	3.573	3.459	3.351	3.249
15	4.489	4.315	4.153	4.001	3.859	3.726	3.601	3.483	3.373	3.268
16	4.536	4.357	4.189	4.033	3.887	3.751	3.623	3.503	3.390	3.283
17	4.576	4.391	4.219	4.059	3.910	3.771	3.640	3.518	3.403	3.295
18	4.608	4.419	4.243	4.080	3.928	3.786	3.654	3.529	3.413	3.304
19	4.635	4.442	4.263	4.097	3.942	3.799	3.664	3.539	3.421	3.311
20	4.657	4.460	4.279	4.110	9.954	3.808	3.673	3.546	3.427	3.316
21	4.675	4.476	4.292	4.121	3.963	3.816	3.679	3.551	3.432	3.320
22	4.690	4.488	4.302	4.130	3.970	3.822	3.684	3.556	3.436	3.323
23	4.703	4.499	4.311	4.137	3.976	3.827	3.689	3.559	3.438	3.325
24	4.713	4.507	4.318	4.143	3.981	3.831	3.692	3.562	3.441	3.327
25	4.721	4.514	4.323	1.147	3.985	3.834	3.694	3.564	3.442	3.329
26	4.728	4.520	4.328	4.151	3.988	3.837	3.696	3.566	3.444	3.330
27	4.734	4.524	4.332	4.154	3.990	3.839	3.698	3.567	3.445	3.330
28	4.739	4.528	4.335	4.157	3.992	3.840	3.699	3.568	3.446	3.331
29	4.743	4.531	4.337	4.158	3.994	3.841	3.700	3.569	3.446	3.332
30	4.746	4.534	4.339	4.160	3.995	3.842	3.701	3.570	3.447	3.332
40	4.760	4.544	4.347	4.166	3.910	3.846	3.703	3.571	3.448	3.333
50	4.762	4.545	4.348	4.167	3.910	3.846	3.703	3.571	3.448	3.333

TABLE A–4. Present-value interest factors for a one-dollar annuity, PVIFA (Continued)

Periods	31%	32%	33%	34%	35%	36%	37%	38%	39%	40%
1	0.763	0.758	0.752	0.746	0.741	0.735	0.730	0.725	0.719	0.714
2	1.346	1.331	1.317	1.303	1.289	1.276	1.263	1.250	1.237	1.224
3	1.791	1.766	1.742	1.719	1.696	1.673	1.652	1.630	1.609	1.589
4	2.130	2.096	2.062	2.029	1.997	1.966	1.935	1.906	1.877	1.849
5	2.390	2.345	2.302	2.260	2.220	2.181	2.143	2.106	2.070	2.035
6	2.588	2.534	2.483	2.433	2.385	2.339	2.294	2.251	2.209	2.168
7	2.739	2.677	2.619	2.562	2.508	2.455	2.404	2.355	2.308	2.263
8	2.854	2.786	2.721	2.658	2.598	2.540	2.485	2.432	2.380	2.331
9	2.942	2.868	2.798	2.730	2.665	2.603	2.544	2.487	2.432	2.379
10	3.009	2.930	2.855	2.784	2.715	2.649	2.587	2.527	2.469	2.414
11	3.060	2.978	2.899	2.824	2.752	2.683	2.618	2.555	2.496	2.438
12	3.100	3.013	2.931	2.853	2.779	2.708	2.641	2.576	2.515	2.456
13	3.129	3.040	2.956	2.876	2.799	2.727	2.658	2.592	2.529	2.469
14	3.152	3.061	2.974	2.892	2.814	2.740	2.670	2.603	2.539	2.478
15	3.170	3.076	2.988	2.905	2.825	2.750	2.679	2.611	2.546	2.484
16	3.183	3.088	2.999	2.914	2.834	2.757	2.685	2.616	2.551	2.489
17	3.193	3.097	3.007	2.921	2.840	2.763	2.690	2.621	2.555	2.492
18	3.201	3.104	3.012	2.926	2.844	2.767	2.693	2.624	2.557	2.494
19	3.207	3.109	3.017	2.930	2.848	2.770	2.696	2.626	2.559	2.496
20	3.211	3.113	3.020	2.933	2.850	2.772	2.698	2.627	2.561	2.497
21	3.215	3.116	3.023	2.935	2.852	2.773	2.699	2.629	2.562	2.498
22	3.217	3.118	3.025	2.936	2.853	2.775	2.700	2.629	2.562	2.498
23	3.219	3.120	3.026	2.938	2.854	2.775	2.701	2.630	2.563	2.499
24	3.221	3.121	3.027	2.939	2.855	2.776	2.701	2.630	2.563	2.499
25	3.222	3.122	3.028	2.939	2.856	2.777	2.702	2.631	2.563	2.499
26	3.223	3.123	3.028	2.940	2.856	2.777	2.702	2.631	2.564	2.500
27	3.224	3.123	3.029	2.940	2.856	2.777	2.702	2.631	2.564	2.500
28	3.224	3.124	3.029	2.940	2.857	2.777	2.702	2.631	2.564	2.500
29	3.225	3.124	3.030	2.941	2.857	2.777	2.702	2.631	2.564	2.500
30	3.225	3.124	3.030	2.941	2.857	2.778	2.702	2.631	2.564	2.500
40	3.226	3.125	3.030	2.941	2.857	2.778	2.703	2.632	2.564	2.500
50	3.226	3.125	3.030	2.941	2.857	2.778	2.703	2.632	2.564	2.500

APPENDIX B—STANDARDIZED NORMAL DISTRIBUTION

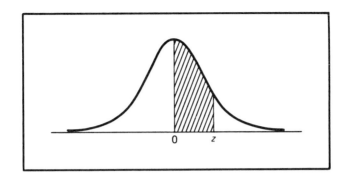

z	.00	.01	.02	.03	.04	.05	.06	.07	.08	.09
0.0	.0000	.0040	.0080	.0120	.0160	.0199	.0239	.0279	.0319	.0359
0.1	.0398	.0438	.0478	.0517	.0557	.0596	.0636	.0675	.0714	.0753
0.2	.0793	.0832	.0871	.0910	.0948	.0987	.1026	.1064	.1103	.1141
0.3	.1179	.1217	.1255	.1293	.1331	.1368	.1406	.1443	.1480	.1517
0.4	.1554	.1591	.1628	.1664	.1700	.1736	.1772	.1808	.1844	.1879
0.5	.1915	.1950	.1985	.2019	.2054	.2088	.2123	.2157	.2190	.2224
0.6	.2257	.2291	.2324	.2357	.2389	.2422	.2454	.2486	.2517	.2549
0.7	.2580	.2611	.2642	.2673	.2704	.2734	.2764	.2794	.2823	.2852
0.8	.2881	.2910	.2939	.2967	.2995	.3023	.3051	.3078	.3106	.3133
0.9	.3159	.3186	.3212	.3238	.3264	.3289	.3315	.3340	.3365	.3389
1.0	.3413	.3438	.3461	.3485	.3508	.3531	.3554	.3577	.3599	.3621
1.1	.3643	.3665	.3686	.3708	.3729	.3749	.3770	.3790	.3810	.3830
1.2	.3849	.3869	.3888	.3907	.3925	.3944	.3962	.3980	.3997	.4015
1.3	.4032	.4049	.4066	.4082	.4099	.4115	.4131	.4147	.4162	.4177
1.4	.4192	.4207	.4222	.4236	.4251	.4265	.4279	.4292	.4306	.4319
1.5	.4332	.4345	.4357	.4370	.4382	.4394	.4406	.4418	.4429	.4441
1.6	.4452	.4463	.4474	.4484	.4495	.4505	.4515	.4525	.4535	.4545
1.7	.4554	.4564	.4573	.4582	.4591	.4599	.4608	.4616	.4625	.4633
1.8	.4641	.4649	.4656	.4664	.4671	.4678	.4686	.4693	.4699	.4706
1.9	.4713	.4719	.4726	.4732	.4738	.4744	.4750	.4756	.4761	.4767
2.0	.4772	.4778	.4783	.4788	.4793	.4798	.4803	.4808	.4812	.4817
2.1	.4821	.4826	.4830	.4834	.4838	.4842	.4846	.4850	.4854	.4857
2.2	.4861	.4864	.4868	.4871	.4875	.4878	.4881	.4884	.4887	.4890
2.3	.4893	.4896	.4898	.4901	.4904	.4906	.4909	.4911	.4913	.4916
2.4	.4918	.4920	.4922	.4925	.4927	.4929	.4931	.4932	.4934	.4936
2.5	.4938	.4940	.4941	.4943	.4945	.4946	.4948	.4949	.4951	.4952
2.6	.4953	.4955	.4956	.4957	.4959	.4960	.4961	.4962	.4963	.4964
2.7	.4965	.4966	.4967	.4968	.4969	.4970	.4971	.4972	.4973	.4974
2.8	.4974	.4975	.4976	.4977	.4977	.4978	.4979	.4979	.4980	.4981
2.9	.4981	.4982	.4982	.4983	.4984	.4984	.4985	.4985	.4986	.4986
3.0	.4987	.4987	.4987	.4988	.4988	.4989	.4989	.4989	.4990	.4990